# Narrative Management in Corporate Japan

T0359074

Scandals and failures in some of the best-known international Japanese-owned companies have shown that there is sometimes a considerable difference between the public and internal narratives of Japanese firms. This book explores the extent to which Japanese firms' public claims reflect wider reality.

Exploring how and why corporate narrative management is accepted or rejected by external and internal audiences in Japan, the book clarifies what narrative management means for Japanese organizations. It argues that the role of narrative management has become much more prevalent in Japan in recent years, but that it does not serve quite the same role as it does in the Western environments in which the theory and practice first emerged. The author presents interview-based case studies of four very different large Japanese organizations, all of which have deployed and loudly proclaimed new restructuring plans based largely on Western models of corporate 'best practice'. The book aims to describe and account for these Japanese corporate narratives, and asks what they are, why they are deployed and who believes in them.

As the first narrative-related work in the Japanese context, this volume provides an insight into the development of Japanese narrative management. It will appeal to students and scholars of Japanese Business, International Business and Organizational Studies.

**Chie Yorozu** is an Assistant Professor at Nagoya University, Graduate School of Economics in Japan.

# Sheffield Centre for Japanese Studies/Routledge Series

Celebrating 50 Years of Japanese Studies at The University of Sheffield, 1963–2013

Series Editor: Glenn D. Hook

*Professor of Japanese Studies, University of Sheffield*

This series, published by Routledge in association with the Centre for Japanese Studies at the University of Sheffield, both makes available original research on a wide range of subjects dealing with Japan and provides introductory overviews of key topics in Japanese Studies.

1. **The Internationalization of Japan**
   *Edited by Glenn D. Hook and Michael Weiner*

2. **Race and Migration in Imperial Japan**
   *Michael Weiner*

3. **Japan and the Pacific Free Trade Area**
   *Pekka Korhonen*

4. **Greater China and Japan**
   Prospects for an economic partnership?
   *Robert Taylor*

5. **The Steel Industry in Japan**
   A comparison with the UK
   *Hasegawa Harukiyo*

6. **Race, Resistance and the Ainu of Japan**
   *Richard Siddle*

7. **Japan's Minorities**
   The illusion of homogeneity
   *Edited by Michael Weiner*

8. **Japanese Business Management**
   Restructuring for low growth and globalization
   *Edited by Hasegawa Harukiyo and Glenn D. Hook*

9. **Japan and Asia Pacific Integration**
   Pacific romances 1968–1996
   *Pekka Korhonen*

10. **Japan's Economic Power and Security**
    Japan and North Korea
    *Christopher W. Hughes*

11. **Japan's Contested Constitution**
    Documents and analysis
    *Glenn D. Hook and Gavan McCormack*

12. **Japan's International Relations**
    Politics, economics and security
    *Glenn D. Hook, Julie Gilson, Christopher W. Hughes and Hugo Dobson*

13. **Japanese Education Reform**
Nakasone's legacy
*Christopher P. Hood*

14. **The Political Economy of
Japanese Globalisation**
*Glenn D. Hook and
Hasegawa Harukiyo*

15. **Japan and Okinawa**
Structure and subjectivity
*Edited by Glenn D. Hook and
Richard Siddle*

16. **Japan and Britain in the
Contemporary World**
Responses to common issues
*Edited by Hugo Dobson and
Glenn D. Hook*

17. **Japan and United Nations
Peacekeeping**
New pressures, new responses
*Hugo Dobson*

18. **Japanese Capitalism and
Modernity in a Global Era**
Re-fabricating lifetime
employment relations
*Peter C. D. Matanle*

19. **Nikkeiren and Japanese
Capitalism**
*John Crump*

20. **Production Networks in Asia
and Europe**
Skill formation and technology
transfer in the automobile
industry
*Edited by Rogier Busser and
Yuri Sadoi*

21. **Japan and the G7/8**
1975–2002
*Hugo Dobson*

22. **The Political Economy of
Reproduction in Japan**
Between nation-state and
everyday life
*Takeda Hiroko*

23. **Grassroots Pacifism in
Post-War Japan**
The rebirth of a nation
*Mari Yamamoto*

24. **Interfirm Networks in the
Japanese Electronics Industry**
*Ralph Paprzycki*

25. **Globalisation and Women in the
Japanese Workforce**
*Beverley Bishop*

26. **Contested Governance in Japan**
Sites and issues
*Edited by Glenn D. Hook*

27. **Japan's International Relations**
Politics, economics and security
Second edition
*Glenn D. Hook, Julie Gilson,
Christopher W. Hughes and
Hugo Dobson*

28. **Japan's Changing Role in
Humanitarian Crises**
*Yukiko Nishikawa*

29. **Japan's Subnational Governments
in International Affairs**
*Purnendra Jain*

30. **Japan and East Asian Monetary Regionalism**
Towards a proactive leadership role?
*Shigeko Hayashi*

31. **Japan's Relations with China**
Facing a rising power
*Lam Peng-Er*

32. **Representing the Other in Modern Japanese Literature**
A critical approach
*Edited by Rachael Hutchinson and Mark Williams*

33. **Myth, Protest and Struggle in Okinawa**
*Miyume Tanji*

34. **Nationalisms in Japan**
*Edited by Naoko Shimazu*

35. **Japan's Security Policy and the ASEAN Regional Forum**
The search for multilateral security in the Asia-Pacific
*Takeshi Yuzawa*

36. **Global Governance and Japan**
The institutional architecture
*Edited by Glenn D. Hook and Hugo Dobson*

37. **Japan's Middle East Security Policy**
Theory and cases
*Yukiko Miyagi*

38. **Japan's Minorities**
The illusion of homogeneity
Second edition
*Edited by Michael Weiner*

39. **Japan and Britain at War and Peace**
*Edited by Nobuko Kosuge and Hugo Dobson*

40. **Japan's National Identity and Foreign Policy**
Russia as Japan's 'other'
*Alexander Bukh*

41. **Japanese Cinema and Otherness**
Nationalism, multiculturalism and the problem of Japanesenesss
*Mika Ko*

42. **Asian Regionalism and Japan**
The politics of membership in regional diplomatic, financial and trade groups
*Shintaro Hamanaka*

43. **Decoding Boundaries in Contemporary Japan**
The Koizumi administration and beyond
*Edited by Glenn D. Hook*

44. **Japan's International Relations**
Politics, economy and security
Third edition
*Glenn D. Hook, Julie Gilson, Christopher W. Hughes and Hugo Dobson*

45. **Japan's Security Identity**
From a peace-state to an international-state
*Bhubhindar Singh*

46. **Nationalism and Power Politics in Japan's Relations with China**
A neoclassical realist interpretation
*Lai Yew Meng*

47. **Risk and Securitization in Japan**
1945–60
*Piers Williamson*

48. **Japan's Relations with North Korea and the Recalibration of Risk**
*Ra Mason*

49. **The Politics of War Memory in Japan**
Progressive civil society groups and contestation of memory of the Asia-Pacific War
*Kamila Szczepanska*

50. **Governing Insecurity in Japan**
The domestic discourse and policy response
*Edited by Wilhelm Vosse, Reinhard Drifte and Verena Blechinger-Talcott*

51. **Regional Risk and Security in Japan**
Whither the everyday
*Glenn D. Hook, Ra Mason and Paul O'Shea*

52. **Narrative Management in Corporate Japan**
Investor relations as pseudo-reform
*Chie Yorozu*

# Narrative Management in Corporate Japan

Investor relations as pseudo-reform

**Chie Yorozu**

Routledge
Taylor & Francis Group

LONDON AND NEW YORK

First published 2016
by Routledge

2 Park Square, Milton Park, Abingdon, Oxfordshire OX14 4RN
52 Vanderbilt Avenue, New York, NY 10017

*Routledge is an imprint of the Taylor & Francis Group, an informa business*

First issued in paperback 2020

*British Library Cataloguing in Publication Data*
A catalogue record for this book is available from the British Library

*Library of Congress Cataloging in Publication Data*
Yorozu, Chie.
    Narrative management in corporate Japan : investor relations as pseudo-
reform / Chie Yorozu. – 1 Edition.
        pages cm. – (Sheffield Centre for Japanese studies / Routledge series ; 52)
    Includes bibliographical references and index.
    1. Management–Japan. 2. Corporate culture–Japan. I. Title.
    HD70.J3Y5723 2016
    658.4'50952–dc23
                        2015016541

ISBN: 978-1-138-88762-6 (hbk)
ISBN: 978-0-367-59761-0 (pbk)

Typeset in Times New Roman
by Taylor & Francis Books

# Contents

*List of illustrations*                                                         xii
*Acknowledgments*                                                               xiii

1   Introduction: Why don't we question the myths about corporate
    narratives?                                                                 1

    *1.1 Understanding the Japanese business model 1*
    *1.2 The aim of the book 5*
    *1.3 Case studies 5*
    *1.4 Definitions and terminology 7*
    *1.5 Organization of the book 8*

2   Narrative management and the crisis of change                               10

    *2.1 The Japanese model of capitalism and Japanese*
        *organizations: making comparisons with stock market*
        *capitalism 10*
    *2.2 Two types of restructuring in large Japanese organizations 13*
    *2.3 Research questions 19*
    *2.4 What is narrative management? 20*
    *2.5 Debate on 'continuity and change' in the Japanese*
        *economy 28*

3   Nissan Motor: An ongoing and sophisticated narrative
    management strategy                                                         37

    *3.1 Introduction 37*
    *3.2 Nissan's new reform plans 38*
    *3.3 External and internal acceptance of Nissan's new reform*
        *plans 41*
    *3.4 Nissan's narrative management 46*

*3.5 Lessons from Nissan Motor: on-going and sophisticated narrative management 55*

4 Bank of Tokyo-Mitsubishi UFJ: Brand-led narrative management   60

*4.1 Introduction 60*
*4.2 BTMU's US-style reform plans 60*
*4.3 External and internal acceptance of BTMU's reform plans 66*
*4.4 BTMU's narrative management 71*
*4.5 A lesson from BTMU 79*

5 Shinsei Bank: A financialized, Anglo-Saxon style of narrative management   84

*5.1 Introduction 84*
*5.2 Shinsei Bank's new reform plans 84*
*5.3 External and internal scepticism about SVA management 88*
*5.4 Shinsei's narrative management: SVA management 95*
*5.5 A lesson from Shinsei Bank 103*

6 Yokohama City Council: Temporary and political form of narrative management with new public management   109

*6.1 Introduction 109*
*6.2 Yokohama City Council's new reform plans: New Public Management 109*
*6.3 External acceptance and internal distrust of the Yokohama Revival Plan 114*
*6.4 Yokohama City Council's narrative management 120*
*6.5 A lesson from Yokohama City Council 128*

7 Explaining narrative management in Japan   133

*7.1 Introduction 133*
*7.2 'Continuity and change' in the Japanese economy and organizations 133*
*7.3 'Continuity and change' revisited 136*
*7.4 Narrative management in Japan 140*

8   Conclusion: Lessons for the future                    144

   *8.1 Introduction  144*
   *8.2 Summary of the findings and research questions  144*
   *8.3 Implications, recommendations and further research  147*
   *8.4 Conclusion  149*

   *Appendix*                                             150
   *Bibliography*                                         156
   *Index*                                                170

# List of illustrations

**Figures**

1.1 Nikkei Stock Index 1980–2011                                            2
3.1 Nissan's net income (1997–2010)                                        44

**Tables**

1.1 The four Japanese organizations                                          6
3.1 Nissan restructuring plans since 2000                                   40
3.2 Interbrand brand performance                                            43
3.3 Nissan's workforce (1999–2008)                                          49
4.1 Consolidated assets of domestic large financial groups in Japan
    (as of December 2008)                                                   61
4.2 History of BTMU                                                         62
4.3 BTMU's financial performance (2000–10)                                  69
4.4 Number of employees at BTMU (2002–10)                                   72
4.5 Mitsubishi committee                                                    75
4.6 Net incomes of Bank of Tokyo-Mitsubishi and UFJ Bank                    78
5.1 Number of employees at Shinsei Bank (taken from Toyokeizai
    2008–11)                                                                96
5.2 Executive earnings in relation to employee earnings                     98
5.3 Total balance of corporate customer account and asset-building
    savings (1999–2009)                                                    100
5.4 Shinsei Bank and BTMU's dividends                                      102
6.1 Total staff headcount: Yokohama City Council (2003–10)                 122
6.2 Total amount of debts                                                  127
7.1 Comparative organizational restructuring by the four
    organizations: continuity and change                                   135

# Acknowledgments

Many steps were needed to achieve the publication of this book. They were all valuable steps, which interestingly were taken in different places: Manchester, Sheffield and London in the UK, and Tokyo and Nagoya in Japan.

This book is based on my PhD thesis, written at the Manchester Business School, University of Manchester, UK. I remember each trial and error step, but the most impressive step was the last, which was taken when I visited the UK in August 2014 to meet my PhD supervisor, Professor Leo McCann. He helped me to finalize my book draft as well as giving me encouragement and confidence. I completed and submitted my draft to the publisher in the UK. After returning to Nagoya in September, I received great news from the publisher that my book proposal and sample had been accepted for publication. The publication process then started in earnest. My deepest appreciation goes to Professor McCann for all his support during this time. He gave me many valuable insights and provided expert supervision. He was always willing to listen to my views, devoted hours to reading my many drafts and offered me continuous feedback on them.

I also wish to acknowledge the following people who helped and guided me during the process of completing this book.

Professor Damian Hodgson of Manchester Business School, Professor Daniel Muzio of Newcastle University Business School and Dr Peter Matanle of the University of Sheffield were very supportive of my research theme, thus paving the way for me to shape and develop my papers in the future. Professor Muzio and Dr Matanle suggested that I should publish my thesis in book form after completing my PhD. Their encouragement gave me the confidence to try.

I was very fortunate to hold many interviews at several large Japanese organizations. My fieldwork benefited from the help of many interviewees. Numerous people made a big effort to understand and participate in this research. I would like to thank all the people who gave me so much precious time to take part in the interviews and their practical insights. My gratitude goes to all the staff at Routledge, who were instrumental in helping me to complete this project. Finally, I would like to thank my parents who gave me immense support and encouragement on my academic journey. That is why I was able to work hard to make each moment special. I will always remember this time with gratitude.

The author and publishers wish to thank the following publishers who have kindly granted permission to reproduce previously published material:

- SAGE for the reproduction of an updated version of an article by Yorozu, C. (2015) 'An American Hedge Fund in Japan: Exploring the Role of Investor Relations as a Form of False Signalling', *Competition & Change: The Journal of Global Business and Political Economy*, 19(1): 56–69. The article can be found here: http://cch.sagepub.com/.
- Electronic Journal of Contemporary Japanese Studies for the reproduction of the article by Yorozu, C. (2014) 'The Diffusion of New Public Management Strategy in Japan: To what extent does a Japanese local government organisation change?', *Electronic Journal of Contemporary Japanese Studies*, 14(3) (Article 10 in 2014). The article can be found here: http://www.japanesestudies.org.uk/.
- Taylor and Francis for the reproduction of an updated version of an article by Yorozu, C., McCann, L., Hassard, J. and Morris, J. (2013) 'Japan, Corporate Organisational Reform and the Global Financial Crisis: The case of Shinsei Bank', *Asia Pacific Business Review*, 19(2): 200–216. The original article can be found here: http://www.tandfonline.com/.

# 1 Introduction

## Why don't we question the myths about corporate narratives?

### 1.1 Understanding the Japanese business model

The distinctive Japanese corporate business system has been widely praised for its massive contribution to Japan's strong economic growth. Following the Second World War there was little money for investment and the product distribution system in Japan was weak. In addition, goods were scarce, which led to high consumer demand. Individual consumption doubled in the seven years from 1957 to 1964, according to an Economic White Paper (1965), so Japanese firms were forced to cooperate with each other in order to achieve efficiency and to meet the needs of this situation. In order to aid effective interaction between companies, most firms adopted the Japanese-style business model. Three main characteristics are integral to this model: life-time employment with a seniority-based pay system; cross-shareholdings; and a *keiretsu* business group.[1] Expectations of life-time employment and the seniority system led to the salaryman culture and meant that employees tended to be incredibly loyal to their employers. Cross-shareholdings between firms are regarded as a way of maintaining long-term relationships with other firms and banks, in order to cement business deals and to seek help in the event of crises. The *keiretsu* system allows companies to do business together both vertically and horizontally. It sees lending, investment and distribution as part of a long-term business cycle.

*Keiretsu* organizations were eager to increase cross-shareholdings in order to forge stronger relationships for sharing risks and profits. This Japanese model became a major form of cooperation and efficiency among Japanese firms, and not unsurprisingly became embedded in the Japanese corporate business system. It contributed to high economic growth, boosted Japan's position to that of the second largest economy[2] in the world, and won the Japanese people's confidence. The Japanese business model was also reflected in Japan's stock prices. These increased almost exponentially between 1980 and 1989 (see Figure 1.1), and the benchmark Nikkei 225 index (Japan's equivalent of the Dow Jones Industrial) reached a maximum of 38,915 on 29 December 1989. These impressive results meant that in the 1980s US firms widely imitated the Japanese model, especially in the automobile and electronic industries.[3]

However, the Japanese business model ran into unexpected difficulties in the late 1980s. The index decreased sharply to 14,485 in 1995, less than half the price it had reached ten years previously. Things were about to get worse. The so-called bubble economy burst in 1991, and caused a prolonged economic slump in Japan from which the country has yet to recover. In 2009 the Nikkei reached a record low of 7,054.98. The Japanese business system became the target of reformers in the Japanese government after this recession, and was stripped of its 'model' status.[5]

As a result of this calamity, the Japanese government has increasingly encouraged large Japanese organizations to follow a US pattern of reform in order to enhance their micro-economic performance. The government judged that the Japanese business framework had developed problems and expected the US business model to rescue the depressed Japanese economy. (See Chapter 2 for a broader explanation of the Japanese model based on the new institutional economics, and the 'Varieties of Capitalism' perspective.) The government maintains that the system has reached a turning point and that an overhaul is in order now that the Japanese economy has experienced over ten years of post-bubble recession. In addition, the effects of globalization have become more and more pronounced. A large number of Japanese firms, and even local governments such as that in Yubari City in Hokkaido prefecture, went bankrupt in the late 1990s. In the financial services sector, 19 banks and securities companies went bankrupt between 1995 and 2003. This included large firms such as Yamaichi Securities, Sanyo Securities, Hokkaido Takushoku Bank, Nippon Credit Bank, and Long-Term Credit Bank (now

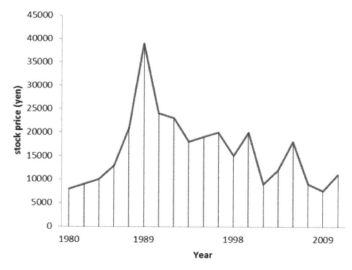

*Figure 1.1* Nikkei Stock Index 1980–2011
Source: Tokyo Stock Exchange[4]

Shinsei Bank). These successive bankruptcies led to severe anxiety for the future[6] and prompted the government to learn and absorb the lessons of success from the US framework of corporate systems. Indeed, when the government nationalized Long-Term Credit Bank in 1998, it chose to import the US business model by selling the bank to Ripplewood, a US private equity and venture capital firm, at the very low price of ¥121 billion. This takeover by a US fund manager, the first in Japanese history, was highly symbolic, marking the first significant attempted adoption of the US business model into the heart of the Japanese system.

Since then, there has been significant pressure on Japanese businesses to undergo organizational change. The government accelerated deregulation and imposed new regulations through the introduction of the Japanese version of the 'Big Bang' financial reforms of 1998. Successive US-style business management ideologies were brought in by foreign-affiliated firms such as Merrill Lynch (which took over Yamaichi Securities); the car manufacturer Renault, following the Nissan-Renault alliance; and the US hedge fund, Cerberus Capital Management, which took over Nippon Credit Bank (now Aozora Bank) following its bankruptcy. In keeping with the government's actions, the Japanese media (as well as financial and security analysts, government bureaucrats and university professors) shifted its focus on to the US model of capitalism. The media began to report on more US-influenced restructuring by Japanese organizations. Meanwhile, business magazines and newspapers coined a new term, *Risutora*, (meaning restructuring) and increasingly made positive public comments about restructuring in Japanese organizations. Thus the external pressure on firms to abandon traditional Japanese modes of organization and to shift towards US practice rose significantly. Japanese banks in particular have been forced to adopt the US model, because since 1998 they have all been recipients of public funds, and are therefore heavily influenced by the government.

However, the external environment, including the build-up of pressure for change, does not cause organizations to immediately instigate genuine change. Existing research on Japan has concluded that since the recession little real change has taken place in most Japanese firms.[7] Recently the behaviour of Japanese organizations has been subtly but rapidly changing in response to significant external pressure. Japanese firms have increasingly started to use public relations (PR) activities and to announce US-style reform programs. A wide plethora of Japanese organizations have publicly acknowledged the need to change and have announced dramatic reform plans. These include both foreign-owned firms and Japanese pre-war *zaibatsu* firms[8] (the Mitsubishi *keiretsu* group, Bank of Tokyo-Mitsubishi UFJ), and even public sector employers such as local government organizations (e.g. Yokohama City Council).

One of the best examples of 'continuity and change' is Toyota, which is often regarded as a paradigmatic example of a successful giant Japanese firm. Toyota has maintained a traditional Japanese business strategy since 1951, but the US credit ratings company, Moody's Investors Service, downgraded it in 1998 because the company maintained the life-time employment system, and according to US financial analysts this can cause a lack of efficiency and weaken a firm's competitiveness.[9] Recently, however, Toyota has adopted US-generated knowledge in its public communications. Toyota's President, Akio Toyoda, quoted from US author Jim Collins' book, *How the Mighty Fall*, when discussing the Toyota 'sticky' pedals scandal in October 2009. Collins argues that there are five stages involved in a great firm's decline. Toyoda applied Collins's concept to Toyota, explaining that Toyota had already gone through the first three stages[10] and had now arrived at the fourth stage: 'We are grasping for salvation', he said, using Collins's description of the fourth stage. 'Toyota has become too big and distant from its customers'.[11] Thus, in response to external pressures over recent years, significant change seems to be occurring with regard to Japanese organizations' readiness to announce reform proposals and engage in sophisticated forms of corporate communication.

However, to what extent do firms' public claims reflect wider reality? Why is the US model so often said to be the only realistic option for Japanese firms to emulate? Restructuring cannot by itself effectively create the desired corporate structure if such restructuring is the sole method used when attempting to generate value.

These US-style corporate strategies clearly go against a long history of business practice in Japan. Japanese firms have a reputation for being risk- and change-averse; most of them still maintain traditional modi operandi despite exposure to global pressure, and most experts on Japan do not expect the US-style business approach to work in Japanese firms.[12] However, if this is true, why do Japanese firms publicly pledge to enforce change within their organizations?

It could be argued that there is a gap between the consensus and recent actual events in Japan. This gap has led us to question whether public messages issued by Japanese organizations are part of a broader attempt at public image restructuring, i.e. corporate narrative management. However, the concept of narrative management[13] has not been discussed in Japan. In light of the major growth in the spinning of official messages from firms in Japan this is a shortcoming. Investor Relations (IR) has become a major activity within Japanese organizations. Do we assume that narratives are unnecessary for Japanese firms? If so, how can we explain the increase in the number of public announcements issued by Japanese firms?

When organizations gather externally positive reactions through narrative making, a 'legitimacy gap' can open up with employees. It is very important to understand the differences between public and internal narratives. No previous research has included interviews with internal stakeholders in diverse Japanese firms concerning the myths that surround company narratives. This book highlights internal legitimacy perceptions as one determinant of long-term effective narrative management, alongside the more short-term focus of external announcements. Staff are not only recipients of narratives; over time they can become narrative makers. This book clarifies and accounts for these narratives, and explains the complex ways in which these narratives are effectively smokescreens that serve to obscure the internal workings of Japanese organizations from public view, while pretending to do just the opposite.

## 1.2 The aim of the book

This book explains how Japanese firms make narratives, and what purpose they serve in Japan where 'investor capitalism' has still not really emerged. There have been no previous narrative-related texts in the Japanese context, as mentioned earlier, and this book aims to provide an initial insight into the development of Japanese narrative management. Also, as the majority of research defines narrative management from an external perspective (such as focusing on the impact of narrative management on outsiders and especially investors) few insights are available to allow us to understand narrative management from the perspective of internal interpretations: how does narrative management affect employees' daily behaviour? Therefore, this book will clarify the concept of narrative management from the employee's perspective, as well as highlighting the role of internal perceptions.

For academics and students this book provides a progressive guide and new knowledge about what Japanese firms are doing, encouraging a reflexive approach, which helps to develop critical thinking on international contexts and sources – 'thinking without borders'. This research examines diverse fields of study and organizations, and also provides some pertinent suggestions for managers, especially the importance of harnessing external and internal support for the organization.

The book also responds to today's highly information-oriented society, in which more and more information is made available to the public, while at the same time it is getting harder for outsiders to understand what public claims issued by firms actually mean. It will decode corporate narratives which can be said to be integral to sociology studies.

## 1.3 Case studies

This book is based on qualitative data derived from research interviews conducted in four Japanese organizations, using a comparative case study design based on the methodology of in-depth interviewing. The four major Japanese organizations are Nissan Motor, Bank of Tokyo-Mitsubishi UFJ, Shinsei Bank and Yokohama City Council (see Table 1.1).

All four organizations have embarked on restructuring plans for different reasons, developing and iterating complex and multi-layered aims. Nissan Motor and Shinsei Bank, originally traditional Japanese firms with long histories, are now controlled by foreign owners, while Bank of Tokyo-Mitsubishi

*Table 1.1* The four Japanese organizations

| | Head of organization | Foreign ownership (%) | Number of employees (non-consolidated basis) | Net income (fiscal year 2006–10) | Major restructuring plans |
|---|---|---|---|---|---|
| Nissan Motor Co., Ltd (Renault) | Foreign CEO, Carlos Ghosn | 67.4 | 30,718 | 2006: ¥ 460 billion<br>2007: ¥ 482 billion<br>2008: ¥ −233 billion<br>2009: ¥ 42.4 billion<br>2010: ¥ 319 billion | • Progressive restructuring plans<br>• Nissan Revival Plan (1999–2001),<br>• Nissan 180 (2002–04),<br>• Nissan Value Up (2005–07),<br>• GT2012 (2008–12)<br>• Value-based management |
| Bank of Tokyo-Mitsubishi UFJ, Ltd | Japanese president, Miki Shigemitsu (now has Katsunori Nagayasu) | 4.64% | 33,827 | 2006: ¥ 494 billion<br>2007: ¥ 669 billion<br>2008: ¥ 550 billion<br>2009: ¥ −366 billion<br>2010: ¥ 342 billion | • US-style reforms<br>• shareholder-value creation<br>• employment downsizing |
| Shinsei Bank (J.C. Flowers & Co. LLC) | Foreign president and CEO, Thierry Porté (bank now has Japanese CEO, Shigeki Toma) | 62.4 | 6,116 (consolidated) | 2006: ¥ −60.9 billion<br>2007: ¥ 60.1 billion<br>2008: ¥ −143 billion<br>2009: ¥ −140 billion<br>2010: ¥ 42.6 billion | • Shareholder value-added management<br>• Restructuring under the US-style hedge fund model |
| Yokohama City Council | Japanese mayor, Hiroshi Nakada (new mayor, Fumiko Hayashi August 2009) | n/a | 15,000 | Tax revenue<br>2005: ¥ 1.32 trillion<br>2006: ¥ 1.34 trillion<br>2007: ¥ 1.36 trillion<br>2008: ¥ 1.45 trillion<br>2009: ¥ 1.57 trillion | • Yokohama City Revival Plan<br>• Named after Nissan Revival Plan<br>• Administer downsizing/reorganizing the internal system for municipal workers |

Source: The four organizations' annual reports 2006–10 and corporate websites as of August 2011

UFJ and Yokohama City Council remain under the control of Japanese owners. Bank of Tokyo-Mitsubishi UFJ in particular is a pre-war *zaibatsu* firm and is now the biggest Mitsubishi *keiretsu* firm.

While the four case studies show different processes of restructuring, they have all confronted similar external pressures, and each of the organizations has clearly used versions of US-style restructuring in their public announcements. In particular, Japanese local governments provide us with very useful data, in that public sector organizations are very rarely scrutinized in the literature on Japanese organizational change. To see US-style restructuring penetrating into this kind of ultra-conservative field may be particularly insightful.

These four organizations were selected not only to show the details of individual cases, but also to allow some discussion about change in Japanese industry at a fairly general level. As tertiary industry has been expanding in Japan (according to the Cabinet Office, Government of Japan 2011), and its contribution to gross domestic product in Japan has reached 68 per cent (compared to 77 per cent in the USA, 73 per cent in the UK and 70 per cent in Germany, according to the World Investment Report 2006[14]), with secondary industry contributing 27.8 per cent in 2004, Three organizations from the services industry and one from the manufacturing industry were therefore chosen.

## 1.4 Definitions and terminology

It is important that key terms and concepts used in this book are defined here to establish the positions that are taken in this book.

### *1.4.1 Narrative management*

Drawing on Froud *et al.*'s (2000) concept of corporate narrative management in business contexts, corporate narrative management is defined as visual, verbal and imaginary contexts created by organizations under their planned aims and accompanied by a gap between 'saying and doing'. Froud *et al.*'s concept focuses on external stakeholders, as befits its usage in the investor-driven, shareholder value-driven context of Anglo-Saxon economies. This research expands the use of the concept of narrative management, suggesting that it can be applied not only to external audiences, such as shareholders and investors, but also to the audience of the firm's employees.

### *1.4.2 US business model, US-style restructuring measures*

The US brand of capitalism has been referred to as 'stock market capitalism',[15] whereby share prices are the chief measure of a firm's success, while the Japanese style of capitalism has been called 'alliance capitalism'.[16] The two types of capitalism reflect quite different styles of economic activity. This research broadly follows the varieties of capitalism (VoC) concept,[17] which explains the diversified characteristics of Japanese and US models of capitalism. This book defines the US business model as more liberal, arm's-length and with contractual relations based on short-term thinking, whereas the Japanese business model is based on coordinated and cooperative long-term relationships. Also drawing on the VoC concept, this research examines the US-style restructuring measures and find that in comparison to those employed in Japan they offer lower employment protection, are radical in laying off white-collar staff, and place much greater priority on maximizing shareholder profits.

### 1.4.3 Investor Relations

IR is a strategic management responsibility; firms provide investors with financial information on their own initiative. IR is not only communication with investors, but also with the press, who play a mediating role between firms and the financial community.[18] This research draws on the widely used definition of IR in Japan: 'public relations activity towards the population'. The Japan Investor Relations Association defines IR as follows:[19] (1) IR provides fair and reliable information that will enable investors to make correct decisions; (2) the disclosure of information is undertaken spontaneously and pro-actively; (3) information is disclosed in an open manner to market intermediaries, such as analysts and rating agencies, and disseminated widely to both individuals and corporations.

### 1.4.4 Shareholder value and financialization

After the end of Fordism, the financial market, or financialization, has developed as a new form of economy – a neo-liberal, post-industrial, investor-driven economy.[20] However, financialization does not yet have a specific definition.[21] Debates on financialization have grown in recent years, mostly based around political economy and cultural economy theories. Drawing on the existing articles, this research defines financialization as the growing dominance of the authority of shareholder value logic. The term 'shareholder value' is ambiguous[22] but previous debate has assumed that under shareholder value logic, the stock price is the measure of success for a firm.[23]

This research analyzes the collected data and develops the argument based on the above definitions.

## 1.5 Organization of the book

This book is organized into eight chapters. Chapter 2 begins with a historical overview of the Japanese model of capitalism and Japanese organizational restructuring. It then presents the concepts of narrative management and 'continuity and change' debates, which are useful in examining Japanese organizations' narrative management.

Chapters 3–6 are case studies based on interview data from Nissan Motor, Bank of Tokyo-Mitsubishi UFJ, Shinsei Bank and Yokohama City Council. These chapters advance the central argument of the book, that the four Japanese organizations have proposed US-style reform plans and developed complex and advanced forms of IR activities. This research demonstrates that they have chosen to use narrative management to respond to external pressure to follow the US business model, but this narrative management, rather than being a genuine indicator of fundamental change towards US-style business systems, actually operates more as an external smokescreen that masks the ways in which internally Japanese firms remain somewhat conservative and unreformed.

Chapter 7 revisits narrative management in Japan, as well as Japanese organizational reforms. Finally, in Chapter 8 a summary is provided, conclusions are reached, and lessons for readers (academics, managers, investors, regulators and so on) are addressed.

## Notes

1  See, for example, Abegglen (1958); Dore (2000).
2  The third largest economy since 2011.
3  See, for example, Womack *et al.* (1990).
4  Available at http://www.tse.or.jp/
5  See, for example, Dore (2000).
6  See, for example, Omori (2000).
7  See, for example, Dore (2000); Morgan and Takahashi (2002).
8  Conglomorates.
9  See Katayama (2002).
10  According to Collins the first three stages are (1) hubris born of success; (2) undisciplined pursuit of further success; and (3) denial of risk and peril.
11  http://www.gminsidenews.com/forums/f37/toyota-head-toyota-brink-capitulation-irr elevance-death-84691/http://www.economist.com/node/15065913 and http://www. businessweek.com/blogs/eyeonasia/archives/2009/10/toyoda_on_toyot.html
12  See Amable (2003) and Whitley (1999).
13  See Froud *et al.* (2000).
14  http://www.meti.go.jp/report/tsuhaku2007/2007honbun/html/i3120000.html
15  See Dore (2000).
16  See Gerlach (1992).
17  See Amable (2003) and Hall and Soskice (2001).
18  See Olcott (2009a: 202).
19  https://www.jira.or.jp/
20  See, for example, Dore (2000).
21  See, for example, Stockhammer (2004).
22  See, for example, Froud *et al.* (2000).
23  See Dore (2000).

# 2 Narrative management and the crisis of change

This chapter begins with a historical overview of Japanese capitalism and organization, and describes the emergence of the more recent forms of narrative management in Japan. The first section introduces the Japanese business model and the Japanese view of capitalism, and comparisons are made with the more liberal market-based business model of Anglo-Saxon capitalism. This section describes how the traditional Japanese corporate model has fallen into disrepute in recent decades, so that even as the Anglo-Saxon economies face economic retrenchment and corporate governance scandals, there is renewed pressure on Japanese firms to reform themselves in Anglo-Saxon directions.

The next section looks at restructuring in large Japanese organizations. At a micro level it explores Japanese organizational reforms over the past twenty years, and offers several reasons why Japanese companies, whatever they might say in public, are very reluctant reformers.

The last section introduces the concept of narrative management, as previously used in the literature about Anglo-Saxon firms, and shows why this concept has so far had little traction in the literature about Japan, and also justifies its use in this book.

## 2.1 The Japanese model of capitalism and Japanese organizations: making comparisons with stock market capitalism

Despite the often excited claims made by globalization and convergence theorists, it appears that a great diversity of styles of economic activities continues to exist in the world. The Japanese model of capitalism exhibits some fairly clear characteristics. Institutional theory has been widely used to describe the differences between world business models, and focuses on institutional relationships. It suggests that different national environments have different institutional contexts.[1] This means that complex methods are adopted by different countries in the makeup and behaviour of firms and markets – the so-called varieties of capitalism (VoC) concept. VoC theory rests on the idea of embeddedness (economic performance is embedded into social structure), path-dependence (the role of history), and complementarity (the interlocking but mutually strengthening effects of institutions). Of these, many theorists highlight 'institutional complementarity', which explains well the characteristics of the Japanese model of capitalism.

They identify that the Japanese model of capitalism is fundamentally different from the US business model – the Japanese model is coordinated while the US model is liberal.[2] The Japanese model is basically a credit-based system which largely depends on indirect financing, unlike the direct financing found in the US model. It has been suggested that typically Japanese firms have not cared about shareholders' interests because the Japanese financial system has depended on indirect finance since 1940.[3] Greater priority is given to the protection of internal stakeholders rather than external shareholders,[4] which makes it possible for firms to enhance their prosperity by looking to the long term. Under the lifetime employment system, the Japanese model has long-term internal promotion systems which are important for internal staff under a strong managerial hierarchy. Market share, rather than share price, is the chief measure of a firm's success.[5] Internal staff try to increase sales through cooperation, as teamwork is typically rewarded and encouraged by the firm's headquarters. Japanese firms are highly centralized, represented by large headquarters[6] and powerful human resource departments.[7] Some theorists have suggested that the Japanese business model is similar to so-called alliance capitalism,[8] as corporations are linked into 'group companies' and complex systems of friendly shareholding. Japanese firms are thus slower to reform and much more cautious about any actions that may break up these relationships.

On the other hand, the Anglo-American business model is characterized as being more flexible, quicker to instigate to reform and more fast-moving than the Japanese model.[9] Following the end of Fordism, the rapid development of the financial markets has played an important role in recent US capitalism. Corporate profit is generated largely through financial transactions rather than through outputs and trade of products. Even non-financial firms rely on their revenues from the financial markets.[10] One theorist suggests that non-financial firms' dependence on the financial markets is due to a general economic slowdown.[11] This market-based capitalism is correlated with the long-term maturation and slowdown of advanced capitalism that has occurred since the 1970s. Following the growth of shareholder activism since the 1980s, share price has become the main measure of the performance of US firms[12]. Their behaviours are required to take into account quick returns on investments, so that the main goal of corporate management is the maximizing of shareholder value.[13] Accounting and financial departments have strong powers in US firms[14] and a focus on 'core competencies', individualized pay systems and career progression are the main incentives for staff. Employment protection is low, because the priority is achieving profits for shareholders.[15] Management tends to be more ruthless in laying off white- and blue-collar workers and more radical in the de-layering of a firm, especially after the 1980s slowdown. In comparison to the long-term and cooperative relations found in the Japanese model, the US model is all about arm's-length and contractual relations based on shorter-term goals.[16] The US firms 'downsize and distribute' while the Japanese firms 'retain and reinvest'.[17] Given these characteristics, Dore calls the US model 'stock market capitalism' and the Japanese model 'welfare capitalism'.[18] Drawing on Dore's work, this book defines the US model of capitalism as 'stock market capitalism'.

One of the biggest differences between alliance capitalism and stock market capitalism is the role of the government. There is considerable state intervention in Japanese capitalism, whereas there is limited intervention or protection provided by the government in US capitalism.[19] In the case of Japan, the '1940 system' that was developed in the Second World War with strong support from the government helped to bring about the rapid growth of the Japanese economy in the post-war years and still has a powerful influence on areas such as the economy, finance, education and corporate behaviour.[20] The *keiretsu* business system is one of the most remarkable and enduring examples.[21]

Following the Second World War, *keiretsu* groups, which succeeded the *zaibatsu*, big Japanese monopolistic enterprisers run by prominent families (the six largest being Mitsui, Mitsubishi, Sumitomo, Fuyo, Sanwa and Dai-Ichi Kangyo) joined forces with the government to rebuild ties between companies in the form of *keiretsu* networks. For example, in the Mitsubishi *keiretsu* network strong ties among Tokyo-Mitsubishi UFJ Bank, Tokyo Marine & Fire Insurance, Mitsubishi Motor, Mitsubishi Heavy Industries, and Mitsubishi Trust Bank have been developed around a core bank, Bank of Tokyo-Mitsubishi UFJ.[22] Usually *keiretsu* are comprised of a production system (supplier system) and a system that restricts distribution and price both vertically, within *keiretsu* groups, and horizontally, across groups. A key function of horizontal *keiretsu* is their organization around a main bank which finances product manufacturers as well as *sogoshosha* – general trading companies which distribute these goods. In addition, operating within the *keiretsu* vertical structure, subsidiaries and affiliated companies built up long-term relationships with their parent companies. This type of organization allowed them consistently to make products efficiently (one of the best examples is Toyota's 'just-in-time' lean production system).[23] These vertical and horizontal *keiretsu* systems shaped the Japanese business model. In particular, the *keiretsu* system distinctively articulates many dimensions to diverging business strategies in terms of labor systems, financial systems, innovation systems and the role of government.[24]

The employment system is closely connected to the vertical *keiretsu* system. Although the age of retirement is officially 60 years, all employees except board executives are forced to move to a subsidiary within the same *keiretsu* at the age of 45–50 years, and they work there until they reach 60 years of age.[25] Thus the lifetime employment system can be maintained in *keiretsu* networks. With regard to financial and investment systems, cross-shareholdings, one characteristic of a horizontal *keiretsu* network, also works in favour of *keiretsu* firms. Most companies increase the ratio of cross-shareholdings in order to strengthen the relationship in the triangle formed by the banks, *sogoshosha* and manufacturers.[26] There are four advantages to cross-share-holdings. First, they prevent takeovers, resulting in stable corporate management.[27] Second, sharing stocks allows individual companies to maintain the lowest possible dividend, although stock sharing within *keiretsu* networks and using an in-house bank is extremely different from the way stocks are traded in the USA, since this system does not make stock available to stockholders outside an organization's own *keiretsu*. Moreover, when companies increase their capital and issue convertible and warrant bonds, the high stock prices obtained through sharing stocks are favourable to those companies.[28] In other words, sharing stocks keeps those companies' stock prices high for equity finance. As a result, Japanese firms can increase their capital at a high stock price as well as issue the above bonds with low interest rates. Raising large sums of money at low interest rates is greatly advantageous to companies joining *keiretsu* networks. Finally, the same group members share not only risks but also profits. The purpose of cross-shareholding is to stabilize the management of companies, one of the goals of the controlled economy. During the post-Second World War years the *keiretsu* functioned as a substitute for the government in the private sector. The horizontal *keiretsu* executed the government's plans according to the government's wishes, leading to stable economic outcomes across the nation.[29] Such institutional relationships characterize the Japanese business model.

However, this well-coordinated model of capitalism has been the target of much criticism since the bubble burst in the early 1990s and an acceleration in market-driven globalization and international competition ensued, although it has not yet been fully eroded.[30] The Japanese economy is still strongly controlled by the government, which is likely to maintain advantages to institutions while they adjust to economic changes.[31] Institutional complementarity makes it difficult for Japanese firms to reform, because institutions are critically dependent on one another,[32] which is why VoC theory suggests that diverging methods of operating economic activities are likely to persist indefinitely.[33] Given the wide influence of VoC theory, most of the existing literature on Japanese organizational reform suggests that the existing institutions in the Japanese model of capitalism form the structure through which any change in Japan will (or will not) take place. Unless every level of this complex system, which is embedded in laws, practices and norms, somehow effects very rapid change, earlier institutional forms will influence and probably restrict any transformation of the Japanese model.

## 2.2 Two types of restructuring in large Japanese organizations

Focusing on the Japanese traditional institutional relationship, past studies have converged towards the argument that most Japanese firms still maintain traditional ways of operating and restructuring (they are, therefore, not financialized).[34] Japanese firms have a reputation for being risk- and change-averse, but a few scholars refer to their movement towards more Westernized ways).[35] There have been two main arguments so far, namely 'slow change' and 'radical change'. The majority of academics agree that slow change applies in Japanese firms. In this section both arguments will be introduced in turn, and the research questions identified.

### 2.2.1 Slow change

Much of the existing literature agrees that change has been slow to take place in Japanese firms. One group has studied the effects of slow change on Japanese organizational restructuring, and has acknowledged the influence of globalization and that Japan is facing immense pressure to change.[36] This group tends to argue that in recent years firms have surely reached a turning point in light of the combined effects of serious recession, deflation and the central government's introduction of Big Bang reforms. These have shifted business in the direction of being more free, fair and global since the bubble burst in the 1990s.

However, this literature also forcefully argues that despite these obvious pressures, there has been little real change in the traditional ways of operating and restructuring in Japanese organizations.[37] Although Japanese firms are gradually adopting US methods, especially those that are under foreign control or have a greater proportion of foreign shareholders, they have not shown substantial signals of change.[38] The argument is that the '1940 system' remains largely in place and continues to causes inefficiency and friction in the economy.[39] Even though the financial system has undergone significant change since the bubble burst, through the introduction of the Big Bang liberalization of the financial sector in 1997 Japanese corporate systems have remained largely unaltered, and are very uncommunicative, opaque and somewhat dysfunctional. Firms do not much care for the interests of their shareholders and the whole system is underpinned by a strong internal employee promotion system.

Such studies typically analyze Japanese organizational change through the lens of Japan's powerful and enduring socio-institutional arrangements. Institutional restraints make it harder for Japanese firms to reform.[40] One author, who collected data in 1997, 1998 and 2004, suggests that there is limited institutional change and institutional adjustment because of the path-dependent effects of the highly coordinated business model.[41]

A good example of this is the human resources (HR) system in Japanese firms. HR in Japanese firms tends to be fairly static, which is commonly flagged up in the literature.[42] A large number of Japanese firms take HR for granted through maintaining lifetime employment, seniority-based pay systems and enterprise unions based on long-term thinking.[43] Noguchi[44] suggests that while lifetime employment and seniority-based pay systems have been partially modified, firms do not adopt outsourcing policies, but instead employ excessive numbers of staff. Although they modify some elements of the employment system, they basically continue to adhere to traditional styles of industrial relations. One of the reasons for this is the unique Japanese corporate environment, which is characterized by the absence of a functioning labor market, traditional pension systems, considerable levels of control exercised by central government,[45] and HR departments that wield substantial power over their organizations.[46] Jacoby[47] states that the corporate governance system depends on how strong the authority of the human resources department is. This is due to the large number of board members, who tend to be company 'lifers' who have worked their way up through the organization. Given these specific circumstances, so far the employment system has remained intact under virtually all circumstances. In other words, there are strong forms of institutional restraint that prevent Japanese firms from abandoning traditional employment systems. This institutional restraint, according to the VoC school and other institutional-type theories, means that the adoption of US-style management approaches is unlikely be attractive to Japanese firms, and, if implemented, are unlikely to work well.[48] Witt[49] also says that much greater levels of genuine belief in, and support for, change are needed among senior Japanese executives, if that change is ever really going to occur in Japan's complex and interlocked institutional arrangements.

Indeed, instead of retaining the current employment system, early retirement is the main way of employment downsizing in Japanese firms.[50] Some have introduced a voluntary early retirement system so that they can protect employees from unstable situations. Early retirement is temporarily adopted, just until the required number of employees has left. Such organizations also cut back on new graduate hiring, adopt work-sharing, transfer staff to affiliated firms and cut pay across the organization[51] in order to overcome long-term stagnation. Yet such Japanese-style downsizing is not regarded as being equivalent to the much harsher and more radical forms of downsizing employed in US companies.[52] Vogel[53] also discusses the 'overstatement' of layoffs by Japanese firms. Matanle[54] suggests that this is 'window-dressing' so that firms can reformat employees' mentalities under global competitive pressures and persuade employees of the need for deep reform. He states that these organizations have accepted the mood of inevitable change but fundamentally they try to postpone or avoid it.

In addition, by selling assets such as stocks, sanatoriums and company-owned houses purchased for employee use during the bubble years, Japanese organizations tend to adopt asset downsizing rather than employment downsizing.[55] When the Japanese economy was enjoying strong growth, Japanese firms were more interested in acquiring assets such as stock and land than in transferring their profits to their shareholders.[56] Stock prices kept increasing regardless; the Nikkei Dow Average reached a maximum of 38,915 in 1989. However, once it had started to decrease (down to 8,000 in 2003 which meant it had decreased by over three-quarters of its high); other asset prices reacted similarly to stock prices. The decrease in stock and land prices caused corporate assets to lose their value, while the capital strength of enterprises declined substantially. Japanese firms that had borrowed money to purchase assets before the start of the recession fell into debt once the value of those assets plummeted. Under these circumstances, they started asset downsizing. For example, Bank of Tokyo-Mitsubishi UFJ, Japan's leading bank in Japan, cashed out Union Bank of California (UBOC),[57] which it had acquired during the economic bubble. From 2003, when the Japanese economy started to pull out of the prolonged recession, Bank of Tokyo-Mitsubishi UFJ reacquired UBOC as a wholly owned subsidiary.[58] This is one of several examples of when employment downsizing was not prioritized.

Employment downsizing was adopted by Japanese firms during previous recessions (e.g. oil shocks or the appreciation of the yen)[59] and when they again came under similar pressure from the recession brought on by the subprime mortgage crisis. Shortly after Lehman Brothers collapsed in 2008, Toyota, Nissan and other leading automobile firms announced huge layoffs of non-regular employees.[60] Such restructuring is similar to what went on before. Large Japanese firms in particular tend to stick to the principle of lifetime employment as they consider anything else damaging for their long-term future.[61] They expect employees to show the loyalty which has been built up under the circumstance where employees are guaranteed a career for as long as they wish to work.[62] This is one of the reasons why the traditional employment system has never really changed.

While there has been agreement in the literature about slow change in Japanese firms under institutional restrictions, there is another argument that justifies maintaining institutional relationships because of their strong effect on firms' businesses. The literature about this point suggests that the Japanese way is economically rational. Japanese firms take benefit, cost and efficiency or effectiveness into account at all times. Gerlach[63] believes that in the future alliance capitalism will be built up beyond marketization and financialization, but that so far the rationality of the Japanese system has been underestimated. A significant example of institutional relationships is the *keiretsu*, an effective business group in terms of economic efficiency,[64] transaction costs[65] and risk sharing.[66] Some argue that the pressure of globalization is already having an effect on traditional institutional relationships in Japanese businesses. For instance, the number of in-out mergers and acquisitions (M&A) and in-in M&A between large firms has increased. Since the Big Bang, the ratio of in-in M&A reached an average of 73.7 per cent of all M&A during the early 2000s.[67] In-in M&A between large firms is mainly used to prevent takeovers by foreign-affiliated firms. Robinson and Shimizu[68] show that CEOs spend more time on M&A than they did in the past because they focus more on profit centres to find new business chances. Significant mergers to have taken place include one of the biggest *zaibatsu* or *keiretsu*, Bank of Tokyo-Mitsubishi (Mitsubishi *keiretsu*) and Bank of UFJ (Sanwa *keiretsu*),[69] Sakura bank (Mitsui *keiretsu*) and Sumitomo bank (Sumitomo *keiretsu*),[70] and between Isetan and Mitsukoshi, one of the biggest department stores in Japan.[71] Besides *zaibatsu* and *keiretsu* groups that had historically been competitors, fifteen major banks merged, leaving only three major banks in Japan.

Although it appears that Japanese firms are slowly reforming, it is clear that there are some very powerful continuities persisting. Interestingly, Japanese firms seemed temporarily to abandon the *keiretsu* relationship during the last recession, but recently this seems to have strengthened again.[72] Nissan, after making many announcements about the need to abandon *keiretsu* ties, seemed to have a change of heart and again expressed an interest in the *keiretsu* network.[73] In 2005 Nissan actually increased its stake in its supplier, Calsonic Kansei Corporation (which specializes in the production of modules assembled from multiple parts) from 27.6 per cent to 41.7 per cent.[74] It is possible that 'continuity and change' can occur in the *keiretsu* system, and the process of Japanese organizational restructuring is too complicated to be examined only by focusing on institutional norms .[75]

This implies that there are certain limitations to traditional institutional theory. Indeed, since it came under foreign control Nissan has achieved strong financial performance since 2001 (see Chapter 4 which explains and analyzes Nissan's stable financial performance in detail). More traditional VoC literature, which is largely based around 'old institutionalism' concepts, does not anticipate that the US-style management approach is likely to work in Japanese firms.[76] Furthermore, as shown in Chapter 1, the crafting of official messages from firms has been vastly increased. How can the slow change literature explain this phenomenon? Perhaps this social practice should not be regarded as one of slow change; rather, this new practice of narrative making by Japanese firms needs to be analysed through deeper and more internal perspectives that are typically neglected by the VoC school. Old institutional theory, which relies on concepts such as cognitive norms and deinstitutionalization, is limited in its vision of the detailed processes of organizational change. The more human aspects, the individual understanding about what is happening within organizations, are required in future research if we are to move beyond the rather static and technical approach associated with the literature that focuses on Japan's institutional structures.

### 2.2.2 Radical changes

In contrast to the discussion about slow change in Japanese firms, some scholars refer to the substantial movement towards more US ways of restructuring.[77] As time goes on, more literature on Japan seems to indicate significant changes.[78] The common aspect of this work and that focusing on slow change is that both develop their arguments about how much Japanese firms reform through the measurement of deinstitutionalization.

One group of scholars who insist that radical change is taking place in Japanese firms commonly state that globalization places huge pressure on these firms, thus encouraging them to make drastic reforms. Increased competition accelerated by globalization has acted as an incentive to reform the management style adopted by Japanese firms that are facing 'the end of the mass production system'.[79] It has also been indicated that Japanese firms under such global pressure face difficulties in maintaining the traditional employment system.[80] From the perspective of workplace ethnography, Graham,[81] who had worked for a Japanese firm, compiled data showing that one of the firms that she studied had cut out middle management, resulting in the ending of the lifetime employment system. She states that organizational structure, management ideology, organizational culture and norms have been rethought under the severe constraints of the poor economic outlook, while at the same time the Japanese employees, who are trained according to the traditional management system, struggle to adapt to new principles.[82] Other scholars also indicate that Japanese firms have started diversifying their employment systems. Seniority-based pay systems have already been replaced by ability-oriented management[83] and many organizations have recently introduced a new career course selection system in order to nuture 'independent individuals'.[84]

This group of scholars indicates major change to the Japanese employment system while the previously discussed group is in agreement about a largely unreformed HR system in Japanese firms. In addition, Ikeda[85] indicates changes in *keiretsu* systems and changes to large firms' subcontractors who can offer globally competitive advantages. Japanese firms take advantage of globalization which allows firms to extend their businesses into foreign countries and to use subcontractors from cheaper areas such as South Asia and the People's Republic of China.

This group also effectively uses the same measure in its analysis – changes to institutional arrangements are taken to equate to changes within Japanese firms. Recent studies that update this area are also based on an analysis of institutional arrangements. For example, Morgan and Kubo[86] explored the progress of the Japanese system across different specific economic sectors, and found that their empirical evidence shows significant transformations in the Japanese capital markets. Their interviews with Japanese company analysts demonstrate that an increasing number of analysts move between companies much more frequently than before, which is contrary to the Japanese lifetime employment system model. For analysts the external labor market has gradually begun to play an essential role, as the number of mid-career workers and temporary workers has increased since Japanese firms stopped recruiting new graduates and more foreign firms started recruiting Japanese staff.[87] Stock analysts have therefore had greater opportunities to change jobs. Having said that, it is important to note that for many years it ha been considered normal to change jobs for specific positions requiring technical knowledge and skill, such as those of security analysts, company analysts, hotel staff, or researchers in public and private institutions. Lifetime employment has only been applied to the general posts that most Japanese employees fill.[88] As explained in Chapter 1, the financial community in Japan has certainly been developing, but how Japanese firms react to this is not clear and much more sustained analysis is required if it is to be properly understood.

Although the focus so far has mostly been on institutional arrangements as a way of understanding the extent of Japanese firms' reforms, the new perspectives of neo-institutional theory show that both deinstitutionalization and institutionalization are driving organizational change. Using neo-institutional theory Ahmadjian and Robinson[89] indicate that more and more Japanese firms are carrying out employment downsizing, creating a spiral of layoffs. They suggest that there has been greater institutional pressure to drastically reform among Japanese firms. Other academics, including some who are adherents of slow change, also highlight changing ideologies within society and organizations. They suggest that Japanese firms and employees' consciousness have come to be more Americanized. Japanese society and employees have already realized that the traditional system does not suit the current era and needs to be changed. From a somewhat narrower point of view, Dore[90] suggests that Japanese companies have recognized the importance of shareholder value. Japanese firms have at last come to regard IR as important.[91]

If Japanese firms are already under shareholder value logic, as Dore's recent studies suggest, does the growth of public communication in Japanese firms aim to increase shareholder value, as it does in US firms? This remains unclear. Dore's work is derived from a macro-level perspective and does not substantially examine micro-level practices. We require more empirical data from firms themselves if we are fully to understand this area. Also, newer perspectives based on neo-institutional theory bring further information about restructuring in Japanese firms. Neo-institutional theory for Japanese organizational restructuring has not been widely used, except in a celebrated paper by Ahmadjian and Robinson,[92] who show a new aspect of change in more institutionalized practices and pressure among Japanese firms. Having said that, this work does not draw on any perspectives from within the firm, and indeed the VoC literature shares the same weak point.

The VoC literature that is based on embeddedness, path-dependence and complementarity has not really considered the role of agency. Mostly it takes a cognitive perspective,[93] which is insufficient to explain how and why organizations change or do not change. VoC theory depends strongly on ideal-typical models which do not pay attention to the various diversified actions of agency behind the model. Many researchers have reached agreement about slow change, and this has led to the stifling of the discussion about Japanese organizational change. The number of academics who debate the limitations of the VoC approach has gradually increased in recent years.[94] A greater focus on the role of agency and on internal perspectives is required in order to reveal the deeper aspects of organizational restructuring.

## 2.3 Research questions

As the above shows, the number of public announcements made by Japanese organizations has increased significantly. There has been a diffusion of US-style reform measures among large Japanese organizations, at least in the form of companies' public announcements of their intention to effect change. However, earlier studies reached consensus about slow change in many Japanese firms and little movement towards shareholder value logic. Previous literature that mostly rests on the VoC approach does not anticipate that US-style management is likely to work in Japanese organizations, but this literature does not seem to acknowledge the importance of the development whereby Japanese firms have increasingly used sophisticated policies of IR. This does represent a significant change. However, precisely what purpose these new forms of corporate communication actually serve in Japan is less well documented. This lack of information has led us to question whether public claims made by Japanese organizations are part of a broader attempt at image restructuring. A similar debate surrounds corporate narrative management that is accompanied by a gap between 'saying' and 'doing'.[95] One could argue that the increase in the number of public announcements issued by Japanese firms is therefore a form of narrative management.

In the meantime, the development of public claims made by Japanese organizations has provoked further questions. How and why have these organizations, which in the past have tended to choose a more conservative approach,[96] become more enthusiastic to develop new forms of public messaging? In particular, the consensus on Japan's slow change has not really examined the role of internal corporate change plans. Staff, especially middle management, are directly affected by organizational reform. How do they perceive new reform plans? What do the claims that Japanese organizations make to the public mean for middle management?

The theory of narrative management[97] has not yet been applied to Japan. This is a shortcoming in light of the considerable growth in the practice of crafting official corporate announcements. In order to explain the research questions, the theory of narrative management needs to be applied to Japan as there have been no previous studies published on narratives about organizational restructuring in Japan. What does narrative mean for Japan's firms? This is explained below, and the reasons why it is useful in this case are given.

## 2.4 What is narrative management?

While it is widely acknowledged that Japanese firms do not operate under the pressure of shareholder value logic, it is clear that there has been a recent upsurge in the use of US-oriented measures, at least in the public claims made by Japanese firms. Narrative management theory and 'continuity and change' are useful ways to understand the recent change in public claims made by Japanese organizations and are the main areas of literature used in answering these research questions. This section will introduce the developing debate on corporate narrative management. In the USA and the UK narrative management is essentially a tactic used to boost share prices and therefore augment shareholder value. Next, the literature on 'continuity and change' in

Japan is reviewed and discussed, suggesting that Japanese firms simultaneously change and yet also fail to change (they somehow persist with traditional ways of acting and operating).

### 2.4.1 Narrative management

This section first reviews the ways in which firms under pressure to deliver shareholder value frequently adopt employment downsizing as a form of narrative management. Second, it discusses how narrative management is developed owing to the pressure of financialization and shareholder value logic. In doing so, it discuss how narrative management may make sense in a Japanese context.

#### 2.4.1.1 Corporate narrative management: shareholder value logic and employment downsizing

It has been assumed among narrative management theorists that firms are compelled to enact forms of narrative management owing to the pressure of shareholder value logic. In recent decades the idea that shareholder value is the only valid target for corporate managers has been reinforced.[98] Through financialization, financial value (as reported in financial statements) is desperately pursued by the investment community, which puts huge pressure on management to prioritize shareholder value. Shareholder value comes to have ultimate authority over any other concerns a firm might have. According to shareholder value logic, stock price is the measure of a firm's success and investors expect managers to deliver profit growth. An increasing number of firms have adopted popular strategies such as Value-based Management, Economic Value Added and Shareholder Value Added, all of which are American in origin and popular among US firms. Firms adopt 'best practice' corporate strategies designed to help to satisfy the demands of capital markets and they need to employ management concepts that are similar to those of other firms in order to prevent their corporate reputations from being damaged.[99] In order to increase firms' comparative status in such financial indexes, shareholders rather than other stakeholders are now highly esteemed by management. Management strategy has changed from 'to retain and to reinvest' to 'to downsize and to distribute' in order to increase shareholder value. The concept of control has changed.[100] A firm's investment in plant and equipment has been replaced by leveraged buyouts, the repurchasing of stocks, restructuring and M&A, so that a firm can easily give stocks a lift. Using this new concept of control, management pursues numbers for short-term gains and is eager to create abnormally large value in the capital market.[101] Accordingly, shareholder value is all-important for management.[102]

Despite its popularity, shareholder value has a very ambiguous meaning, which makes room for firms to manipulate their strategies. Firms themselves decide on their own concepts of shareholder value, resulting in ambiguity. In the case of US and UK firms, shareholder value has strongly influenced modes of restructuring and is accompanied by the firm's own strategies, one of which is organizational restructuring. Shareholder value is abused to justify employment downsizing,[103] and as a result firms employ irrational employment downsizing.[104]

The originally expected result of restructuring is to improve performance through effectiveness, flexibility, and communication,[105] and for this purposes firms adopt downsizing, redundancy, delayering, outsourcing, and M&A.[106] Organizations employ downsizing strategies to achieve efficiency when their profitability and productivity are down. The adoption of employment downsizing is often announced in order to attempt to please market analysts and investors, demonstrating that a firm is reducing 'unnecessary' costs in order to increase profitability and generate higher stock returns.[107] Employment downsizing can easily be adopted by firms to improve their stock prices as labor costs account for a large part of production costs.[108] Thus, employment downsizing is abused as being a way of signalling to the investor community by organizations in order to increase their stock prices.[109] Even leaders of large firms, such as Jack Welch, CEO of General Electric (GE), admit to using employment downsizing in order to achieve higher stock prices.[110] Company takeovers are another example of a radical measure designed to generate higher stock returns. Long-term contracts between employers and employees are easily dissolved once a firm has been taken over.[111] When the sub-owner is a private equity firm, restructuring is often more drastic. This is because a hedge fund becomes part of the management team and tends to adopt drastic forms of restructuring. Private equity actors such as general partners (GPs) receive large amounts of capital from limited partners (LPs), and agree the period of time to invest, normally around five years, and the time to return the capital to LPs, around another five to seven years[112] In other words, GPs and LPs have to end their investments at specified times. At this point profits are then distributed from stakeholders to shareholders.

Such high priority on distributing of returns through reducing the number of employees has been very common in the stock market, especially in the USA. Stock price has been supported by continuous corporate downsizing in the recent bubble in the US stock market, unlike the US bubble in the 1920s and the Japan bubble in the 1980s.[113] This means that employment downsizing only benefits shareholders. Given that stock price is the measure of a firm's success, an organization has changed the original purpose of organizational restructuring from improving performance to cost-cutting. Thus new forms of restructuring easily destroy contracts with stakeholders, especially employees.[114] According to various perspectives, widely recognized common preconditions for financialization include consideration of shareholder value, emphasis on value investment, and rapid cost-cutting by management.[115] According to Sloan,[116] layoffs improve stock values in the short term. Employment downsizing is supposed to achieve efficiency in an organization by cutting bureaucracy and wastage, and speeding up decision making. Economists tend to suggest that corporate restructuring brings about 'improved management and increased efficiencies', which are finally beneficial to shareholders[117].

However, a large number of critics have argued for years that such employment downsizing does not deliver increased efficiency, although it is readily adopted (or at least announced) by firms. In the long term, downsizing has not brought about improved stock returns.[118] Financialized management seems to be only temporarily beneficial to firms. This is because financialized management is accompanied by managements' moral degeneration, which eventually affects the future of the firm, employees' motivation, and the relationship between employer and employees. First, it has been argued that focusing a company's energies exclusively on distribution to shareholders negatively affects that company's future.[119] Fligstein (1990) indicates that the concept of control has changed from pursuing a strategy that encourages employees to sell more products (marketing strategy) to pursuing a strategy of collecting assets that can rapidly increase profits. In other words, they do not sell their products but collect beneficial assets that can easily make profits. Such financialized management temporarily constructs shareholder value, but limits firms' long-term capacity for success. The frequent use of employment downsizing can have a negative impact on a firm's future. Labor costs can easily be cut as a 'quick fix'[120], and is no more successful than other forms of restructuring[121].

In addition, placing such great priority on distributing returns through a reduction in staff numbers threatens firms' employees, which potentially is a very dangerous impact of financialized management. Dramatic reductions in the number of employees, no pay rises and poor security of employment erode corporate cultures.[122] Layoffs particularly damage employees' well-being, and lower employee morale and motivation as survivors struggle to manage the same workload with fewer colleagues.[123]

Despite employees suffering as a result of layoffs, managers often benefit enormously from employment downsizing. New business models designed to eliminate the 'agency problem' by aligning top management compensation with share price performance has given huge incentives to senior executives to engage in downsizing. Under such circumstances, contribution to shareholders is not actually realized by management. Instead, top management gains from 'value skimming'.[124] In addition, the relationship between employers and employees is made worse by layoffs, although this is never precisely transmitted by the media.[125] Such unstable circumstances cause antagonism and alienation within the workplace, where employees cannot freely exchange ideas and knowledge.[126] Thus, financialized management damages management morale, which causes disorder and resentment among employees and eventually affects the future of the firm.

All employment downsizing seems to deliver a short-lived uplift in stock prices. Firms are keen to show how slim they are. However, the numbers quickly created through cost-cutting and announced to the public should be understood as part of a broader attempt at corporate narrative construction. The next section focuses on what happens within organizations that leads to the public claims and the role of corporate narrative management.

### 2.4.1.2  Corporate narrative management

As firms are keen to show how lean they are based on the ambiguous meaning of shareholder value logic they construct a narrative of corporate value, but their public claims rarely show what they actually do. Narrative is defined as the device which is used when corporate purposes are devised by CEOs of large organizations. CEOs in particular can play a vital role in the development and dissemination of narratives. This is because a trustworthy commentary made by a CEO can enhance a firm's strategic image, and the credibility of that strategy is crucial if it is to have a positive influence on stock prices.[127] Verbal and visual factors from firms prompt the audience to take part in story-telling.[128] In this respect the most influential person creates a narrative so that it can stimulate the audience's emotions. Thus narrative is fiction created by clever narrators, and may be distinct from reality.[129] Fiction constructed by firms has also been discussed in new institutionalism and symbolic management literature.[130] Westphal and Zajac argue that the symbols and substance of CEO compensation are not consistent when CEOs discuss returns to stockholders.

Yet the relationship between narrative context and organizational restructuring has received insufficient research attention to date. Perhaps the most important contributions to the field has been made by Littler[131] from the viewpoint of signalling theory and Froud et al.[132] on Ford, General Electric and Procter & Gamble from cultural economy theory. Both explore the Anglo-Saxon context; discussions that connect narrative management with organizational change in Japan are extremely scarce, yet it appears that similar trends of corporate narrative and signalling do apply in Japan. What roles narrative and signalling actually play in Japan is even less well known.

It is well known in liberal market economies that organizations employ downsizing strategies in order to try to boost efficiencies and cut costs when their profitability and productivities are down. Such organizations are regarded as failures by the financial markets and the announcement of restructuring usually carry negative connotations for the audience and for the capital markets. According to Higgins and Diffenbach,[133] strategy communication is important, especially for the big firms that are carrying out restructuring or deregulation in order to improve their relationship with the financial community. Indeed, although announcements about organizational restructuring usually has negative implications for the audience or a capital market, in more recent years such announcements are more commonly associated with the *upgrading* of stock prices on Wall Street.[134] Layoff and radical restructuring announcements by firms increase stock prices while announcements solely about financial losses decrease stock values.[135] When firms announce restructuring goals in advance, shareholders often react positively, but announcements about employment downsizing tend to be more drastic than actual downsizing, bringing us back to the gap between saying and doing in financialized economy. Littler calls this gap 'false signalling' and 'downsizing fraud'. In this case, organizations undergoing restructuring are incentivized to create narratives which target their investors and the wider investment community (such as business journalists and stock analysts), with the CEO often playing an important role as a narrative maker, quickly attracting audiences and creating shareholder value. The narrative by the CEO heightens investors' expectations.[136]

Both restructuring and corporate value are manipulated through financialization. Froud et al.[137] explain how the extremely high-profile CEO of GE, Jack Welch, continued to succeed in making the audience believe in the story about the corporate value of GE from the accountant's viewpoint. They explain that GE's weaknesses were carefully disguised by Welch's story about the conglomerate's corporate value. Welch also used ambiguous descriptions in his public announcements to conceal the fact that almost half of GE's turnover was not derived from its main products and services but from financial services and financial engineering. Through his narrative construction, the value of GE was shared even with its employees. Thus the most influential person in a company creates a narrative so that he or she can stimulate the audience's emotions.

Furthermore, a CEO's narrative is enhanced by the mass media. CEOs use the media as a tool through which to transmit their narratives.[138] This is because corporate narratives should be public information that is widely circulated and legitimized in public and expert discourse, and ultimately affects the behaviour of investors and the general public.[139] The mass media plays an important role in the improvement of the credibility assigned to a CEO's public announcements about organizational restructurings[140] and at the same time the CEO's managerial ability is also influenced by mass media. The media audience is composed of a wide variety of people, including professional financiers as well as financial planners, market analysts, actuaries, and insurance and mutual fund managers. For such audiences, the mass media always exerts considerable pressure on firms regarding the importance of financial value.[141] Televised coverage of the financial markets such as that provided by CNBC and Bloomberg does not provide the audience with advice about financial investment but rather with advertising.[142] The media plays an important role in creating, circulating, and legitimizing corporate rhetoric relating to the financial industry. In this regard, the relationship between the CEO and the media is important in order to make a corporate narrative work effectively. The narrative-maker CEO needs to get the mass media to understand, accept and circulate his or her narrative. Thus, narrative structure is formed by a corporate CEO who can quickly and effectively transmit corporate narratives via the mass media.

As explained previously, this concept of narrative management is at a rather early stage in its theoretical development; there have been a large number of studies based on a wide range of theoretical backgrounds. In particular there is some debate about the fundamental ideology about the existence of 'the economy'. There are two main approaches based on theorists' attitudes to the concept of the economy. One approach is concerned with the reality of the economy and questions its very existence. The other accepts the existence of the economy, and considers statistical data about how the economy works. Furthermore, there are two main approaches to financialization; 'political economy' and 'cultural economy'. The difference between the two theories lies in the way in which they recognize the nature of 'the economy'.

The concept that is assumed by political economy is made by economics, which does not consider the foundations, preconditions and structure that support the actual economy. The concept and the assumption of the economy itself began to be reconsidered and redefined by Callon.[143] While political economy assumes the existence of the economy itself, cultural economy does not. Although economics merely pays attention to expanding the explanation about economic measures such as profit, surplus, consumption, and so on, cultural economy starts questioning the ontological scope of 'economy' itself.[144] Aitken (2005) suggests that cultural economy is interested in how 'economic persons, processes or spaces' are made up or constructed. Cultural economy regards the economic as not 'material or naturally existing reality' but as a 'constructed realm'. In this sense, cultural economy posits no boundary between 'cultural' and 'economic', and thus theories of cultural economy focus on the gap between the 'real' economy and the 'created' economy. Thus the whole area of firms' narratives and performances fits rather neatly into 'cultural economy' discussions.

Among past studies on narrative management, however, there have been two common shortcomings: a lack of internal perspective and fixed assumptions.

First, the existing studies on corporate narrative management have only looked at the impact that narrative management has the perception of outsiders such as shareholders, the mass media, and financial analysts. So far insufficient analyses have focused on internal interpretations, although there are some notable exceptions such as Froud et al. (2006) on critical accounting and Lazonick and O'Sullivan (2002) on political economy. As discussed above, narrative management is accompanied by a gap between saying and doing. If management control is predominated by the maximization of shareholder value, employees are likely to be affected. Does a gap affect the perceptions of morality, loyalty and motivation of employees who work for organizations? How does a gap between saying and doing influence employees' daily behaviour? Second, to date the argument about corporate narrative has been based upon the implicit assumption that firms are incentivized to create their narratives for the financialized community with the aim of improving their share prices. Narrative management has been adopted by US and British firms which are under pressure to uphold shareholder values. In this sense, arguments about narrative management have not been applied to the cases of countries that are not affected by stock market capitalism. Froud et al.[145] indicate that the preconditions of financialization characterized by the UK and the USA have not been satisfied by Japan. Morgan and Takahashi[146] also show that there has been no significant movement towards shareholder value logic in Japan. To date, there has been no study about narrative management in Japanese firms. Yet financialized public communication strategy has developed rapidly in Japan, as explained in Chapter 1. Do we assume that narratives are unnecessary for (non-financialized) Japanese firms? If so, how can we explain the increase in the number of public announcements issued by Japanese firms? Drawing on the concept of narrative management but applying it not only to external audiences but also to internal audiences, corporate narrative management is defined as visual, verbal, and imaginary contexts which are constructed by organizations in relation to their planned goals and are accompanied by a gap between saying and doing.

To what extent is the above relevant to Japan? The following section examines narrative management in the context of Japanese organizational restructuring.

### 2.4.1.3 Narrative management in Japan

As suggested above, the argument about corporate narrative is based on the implicit assumption that a firm is incentivized to make narratives owing to stock market capitalism. For that reason, the concept of narrative management has not been applied to Japan. Indeed, there have been no discussions of this issue in Japan so far, because it is widely assumed that the country does not operate within the confines of stock market capitalism. Do we assume, therefore, that narratives are unnecessary for (non-financialized) Japanese firms?

It might be said that US-style narrative has reached Japan, especially since the Big Bang reforms. This is because news and business media have started to exert a strong and influential authority over the Japanese public. Prior to the bursting of the bubble, until the 1990s investors were unable to judge the significance of the stock price with the little information they had to hand when such assets were increasing in value. Japanese firms were reluctant to disclose much about their assets, which caused investors to expect that stock prices would rise more rapidly. It has been suggested that inadequate disclosure of financial information was one of the reasons for the speculative bubble to develop in Japan.[147] Today a great deal more information is released by Japanese firms and the mass media, aimed in particular at the investor community.[148] According to Morgan and Takahashi (2002), the Japanese business system has not been influenced by shareholder value, but some internationalized firms have experienced strong elements of financialization. In fact, Japanese firms seem to be making more public announcements. One such company is Nissan. Before the onset of Japan's 'lost decade' (i.e. the period of recession from 1991 to 2001) it was fairly rare for this company to make public announcements,[149] but in recent years Nissan has established a powerful relationship with the mass media and now has much higher expectations of its interaction with the public.[150]

Dore's work[151] suggests that Japanese firms are shifting towards stock market capitalism. If this is the case, does the increase in public communication within Japanese firms seek to increase shareholder value as it is designed to do in the US context? As stated previously, the author of this book is not aware that any previous work has been carried out specifically on narrative management and organizational restructuring in Japan. Drawing on the interview data, the introduction of narrative management in Japanese organizations is explored in Chapters 4–7, illustrating the forms that this narrative management takes, its stated purpose and goals for management, and the impact it has on internal members of the organization.

## 2.5 Debate on 'continuity and change' in the Japanese economy

As explained earlier, the bulk of the literature on Japan points to slow change in Japanese firms. Since 2003 a modest economic recovery has been observed. The Economic White Paper (2005) confirmed that the Japanese economy recovered without additional government expenditure from 2002 onwards. According to *The Economist*, 'Now the time for lecture is over. Japan is back. It is being reformed. It is reviving.'[152] One could make the argument that this slow and steady restructuring has proved to be a largely successful strategy. Such a moderate and contested understanding of reorganization calls attention to the issue of 'continuity and change' in Japanese firms, a theme that has been widely discussed in recent scholarly work about Japan. Most of them are again based on, or at least influenced by, old institutionalism and the VoC theory.

Jacoby (2005) and Vogel (2006) highlight the presence of a wide range of restructuring styles in Japanese firms. In *The Embedded Corporation* Jacoby argues that Japanese firms have not shown substantial signs of change but that US methods of reform are officially adopted, especially by firms that are under foreign control or those which have large foreign shareholdings. This idea is also supported by a number of other authors.[153] Witt[154] examines the Japanese business system holistically and evaluates continuity and change by drawing on the VoC approach (especially Redding's framework, considered to be a refined version of Whitley's).[155] He reveals that stockholders which are foreign-owned exert considerable pressure to instigate institutional change, but despite this there is limited change in corporate governance systems. Such limited institutional change and slow institutional adjustment is largely due to the highly coordinated business model. Vogel (2006) examines large Japanese firms including Nissan, Shinsei Bank, Toyota and Sony, mostly through official literature and through interviews with top leaders. He found evidence to confirm the pursuit of more aggressive reforms in foreign-owned firms such as Nissan and Shinsei Bank, whereas more cautious strategies were taken in largely poorly performing Japanese firms such as Mizuho, NEC and Mitsukoshi.[156] The latter firms are basically timid and retain national characteristics with regard to reform. Vogel argues that this is because foreign managers are able to enact more radical plans because they are not restricted by social and personal relations and norms. Vogel produces evidence of convergence and divergence within Japanese firms through showing 'the varieties of restructuring' across sectors and some Japanese firms, and insists that their reforms show distinctive variations within the Japanese model of capitalism.[157]

A common argument in the literature on continuity and change is that more change takes place in Japanese firms which are foreign-owned or have obligations to foreign shareholders. Vogel and Olcott[158] are especially clear on this with regard to Shinsei Bank. By many accounts (such as business and news media) the shift towards US-style management is having a harmful effect on the future of the bank. In 2004, four years after Shinsei Bank began operating, it was listed in the first section of the Tokyo Stock Exchange. It showed net losses of –¥60.9 billion in 2007, –¥143 billion in 2008 and –¥140 billion in 2009. As Shinsei Bank has not returned public funds borrowed from the Japanese government when LTCB went bankrupt, since March 2008 the government has become the second biggest shareholder.[159] In August 2011 the bank's stock price stood at its lowest ever level, at ¥88, having reached its highest level of ¥825 when it was first listed in March 2004. Shinsei's troubles have lent further credence to strong feeling in Japan that US-style reforms are socially illegitimate. The findings of both Vogel (and Jacoby) are somewhat dated as the data were gathered in 2000–04 when many Japanese firms were announcing their intention to reform. With hindsight it was perhaps too early to tell at that stage how these reforms would actually turn out.

Other literature suggests that a mixed strategy of convergence and divergence is applied within Japanese firms. In general, Olcott[160] agrees with Jacoby's and Vogel's argument but also points to continuity and change at local level. He analyzes Nissan and highlights the 'co-existence of change and continuity' in each company in his analysis, suggesting that most of the staff who perceived a significant change within Nissan simultaneously indicated the importance of the continuity of its traditional system. A much earlier study by Sato[161] also comes to a similar conclusion, showing that HR in Japanese firms covers two strata, regular and non-regular employees. Instead of maintaining the lifetime or secure employment system, instead Japanese firms have started to employ temporary or part-time staff who are flexible and can be dismissed whenever business is bad. That firms maintain long-term employment while simultaneously increasing the number of temporary workers can be said to show aspects of both continuity and change in the lifetime employment system. Much of the literature concludes that slow change is taking place, but Japanese firms may also be exhibiting forms of continuity and change. These perspectives indicate a new direction for future debate on Japanese organizational reform.

Some scholars have found that the Japanese model of continuity and change is changing through continuity rather than discontinuity. For example, Aoki et al.[162] explored the progress of Japanese firms that were restructuring and emphasize that such firms have reformed their corporate structures, board meetings and employment systems since mid-1990s. They used quantitative research on the characteristics of Japanese firms' corporate governance and internal structure and used cluster analysis on data collected from 723 firms listed on the Tokyo stock market. Their findings show that such reforms result in the situation where Japanese corporate governance has not converged toward US-style structure but towards a hybrid style that involves traditional Japanese characteristics such as long-term thinking. Their analysis shows that 67 per cent of firms are regarded as hybrid-style firms and are relatively profitable and suggest that firms that shift towards a hybrid-style system improve their efficiency.[163] Continuous slow change eventually has a striking effect on firms over a longer time frame. Other literature offers similar perspectives.[164] They indicate that continuous slow change eventually leads to substantial transformations. However, there again tends to be a lack of detail about what actually goes on within firms, and very little analysis of how insiders interpret the effects of these changes.

Furthermore, some very recent literature has developed the argument more forcefully, suggesting that continuity is less important than change.[165] Dore's works, especially his recent ones, insist that greater levels of transformation have been achieved in Japan than anticipated in previous studies (including his own).

Dore's work also shows that pressure from the ideology of stock market capitalism has been gradually imported and that established Japanese systems are actively threatened by the inclination towards US-style systems. Dore highlights several examples of the movement of Japanese firms towards stock market capitalism that have evolved in terms of Japanese trends of thought and law systems since 2000. Writing in a leading business journal, Dore[166] claims that the former prime minister, Junichiro Koizumi,[167] kick-started structural reform, with the result that since the 1990s the Japanese government has made changes to its corporate governance laws. Dore indicates that these progressive revisions in the law represent significant steps towards US systems. He also suggests that many Japanese firms are ready to embrace stock market capitalism and suggests that the Japanese stock market has already joined stock market capitalism or investor capitalism. He shows that institutional differences between US and Japanese business models were remarkable up to the 1990s but insists that the Japanese business model is now a thing of the past, although rather than following the US model it follows a neo-Japanese model. However, Dore's work is derived from a macro-level perspective and does not draw on empirical data taken from firms.

Olcott[168] indicates the shift of managerial ideology while focusing on the role of the CEO in Japanese firms. Taking Rakesh Khurana's book[169] about the rise of the charismatic CEO in US firms as his inspiration, Olcott examines the change in Japanese CEOs' behaviour. He indicates that the recent increase in the distribution of profits to shareholders and the reform of the board committee within Japanese firms are oriented towards the new ideology of shareholder value logic. He demonstrates that Japanese CEOs are more influenced by the movements of their stock prices while targeting new measures of success, and that CEOs admit to a greater focus on IR than previously (see Dore, and Lazonick and O'Sullivan).[170] One of the reasons for this is the increasing number of external media resources such as financial analysts. Nonetheless Japanese CEOs are portrayed as not really having changed their mindset away from internal stakeholders and towards external shareholders and the investment community. Likewise, Buchanan and Deakin (2009) suggest that steady change is taking place in the structure of Japanese firms. While indicating that such change is an extremely long process, they argue that Japanese firms are starting to show a convergence towards the US model. Like Dore and Olcott, the authors examine the impact of the change in corporate governance law. The passing of new laws cannot be said to directly affect Japanese firms but it does help to accelerate their restructuring through a wide variety methods (for example they provide a major impetus for firms to introduce external directors and a US-style corporate officer system).

As shown by Buchanan and Deakin, and Olcott,[171] the debate on continuity and change has been dominated by discussions about the high-level system of Japanese corporate governance.[172] The literature on corporate governance has increasingly highlighted the transformation of the Japanese business model. Their arguments are almost exclusively based on discussions about institutional arrangements and the legal reforms of the 2000s. Again, the institutional context does not completely explain actual internal changes. It is also necessary to examine how Japanese firms react to such external pressure. Buchanan interestingly shows a deeper viewpoint by exploring the role of newly appointed corporate auditors and external directors.[173] His evidence shows that external directors are not useful as they lack meaningful internal knowledge and are not in a position to judge effectively what is going on. According to Buchanan, 'truly independent external supervision is neither customary nor welcome at most companies'.[174] As suggested in other literature, Japanese firms have rather grudgingly adopted new systems of corporate governance, but the system does not really work, at least not in terms of bringing about US standards of corporate governance and investor-friendly transparency.

While the latest studies tend to argue that change rather than continuity has occurred, they base their discussions on an examination of senior management-level perceptions.[175] This is something of a shortcoming in the debate on continuity and change. Olcott's argument is based on data from senior management, such as the former and current chairmen and presidents of large Japanese firms. Buchanan and Deakin, like Olcott, only examine the interview data from the senior management group. Yet the role of top executives in the whole affair of Japanese corporate restructuring is only one role of many that could be interesting and enlightening. Middle managers are the ones who in practice implement restructuring plans.[176] We still know little about how middle managers – who are directly exposed to corporate restructuring – react to the development of new management strategies in their everyday work. Without consulting the views of middle management, the extent to which Japanese firms change remains rather unclear.

Thus, the debate on continuity and change has recently developed among the experts on Japan. However, as shown earlier, there are two quite prominent gaps in our knowledge among these studies that need to be filled by future research. First, the arguments of many authors are based on relatively old data gathered before 2004, when Japanese organizations had only just begun to announce their restructuring plans.[177] In order fully to understand Japanese organizational changes, we need to know how the processes and effects of these changes have turned out. Second, recent work has implied a greater degree of change within Japanese organizations, and have developed arguments based on data from Japanese firms.[178] The use of extensive data is helpful, and certainly takes us beyond the often highly abstract and stereotyped portrayals of Japan provided by much of the VoC literature. However, the data is mostly gathered from senior and especially top management. It is very easy for top management to announce organizational reform plans but much more difficult to implement change within organizations.[179] As indicated, it is also necessary for us to examine how middle management, which is heavily affected by new organizational strategy, perceives such restructuring.

Future research on the continuity and change debate and narrative management theory would be very useful if it took the form of empirical studies. The debate on continuity and change is a fruitful way of understanding how and why Japanese firms seem to be increasingly developing US forms of corporate messages, while remaining sensitive to questions of whether or not these US-style management approaches are being practically implemented within Japanese organizations. Corporate narrative management is a new research area in Japan, and therefore we need more empirical data. A multi-case study with an interview-based design provides a closer understanding of the structure of the dynamics of the Japanese style of narrative management. The four large Japanese organizations under study in this book – Nissan Motor, BTMU, Shinsei Bank and Yokohama City Council – all have different reform plans under different levels of pressure from external audiences. In what ways and to what extent do they reform, even though they use quite different reform methods from traditional restructuring methods? How and why have Japanese organizations selected new reform models and developed IR activities? How have the new reform methods been perceived by staff? In order to address these research questions, interview data and official documents such as annual reports, websites and business magazines were obtained.

In Chapter 3 these interview data are analyzed and discussed in order to obtain answers to the research questions posed in the study. Nissan Motor, Bank of Tokyo-Mitsubishi UFJ and Shinsei Bank are analyzed in Chapters 3–5, and Yokohama City Council in Chapter 6. Chapter 7 seeks to clarify what the issuing of public statements and narratives means for Japanese organizations.

## Notes

1  See Hall and Soskice (2001); Streeck and Yamamura (2001); Whitley (1999).
2  See, for example, Hall and Soskice (2001).
3  See Noguchi (1995).
4  See Amable (2003).
5  See Dore (2000).
6  Ibid.
7  See Jacoby (2005).
8  See Gerlach (1992).
9  See, for example, Hall and Soskice (2001).
10  See, for example, Krippner (2005) and Stockhammer (2004).
11  See Stockhammer (2004).
12  See Dore (2000).
13  See Lazonick and O'Sullivan (2000).
14  See Jacoby (2005).
15  See Amable (2003).
16  See Hall and Soskice (2001).
17  See O'Sullivan (2000).
18  See Dore (2000).
19  See Zysman (1983).
20  See Noguchi (1995).
21  See Gerlach (1992).
22  Ibid.
23  See Lincoln and Gerlach (2004).
24  See Gerlach (1992).
25  See Dore (2000).
26  Corporate stock ownership increased from 15.5 per cent in 1949 to 66.0 per cent in 1991, while individual stock ownership declined from 70.0 per cent to 23.2 per cent (Okumura 1999).
27  See Aoki (1988).
28  See Vogel (2006).
29  See Gerlach (1992).
30  See Dore (2000).
31  See Hall and Soskice (2001).
32  See, for example, Aoki (1996).
33  See, for example, Whitley (1999).
34  See, for example, Dore (2000, 2002); Matanle (2003); McCann *et al.* (2004, 2006); Morris *et al.* (2006); Noguchi (2002).
35  See, for example, Graham (2003); Dore (2005, 2006, 2008); Ahmadjian and Robinson (2001).
36  See Dore (2000, 2002); Gedajlovic and Yoshikawa 2005); Hasegawa and Hook (2002); Morgan and Takahashi (2002).
37  See, for example, Aoki (1988); Dore (2000, 2002); Sato (1997); Witt (2006).
38  Ibid.
39  See Noguchi (2002).
40  See, for example, Aoki (1996); Witt (2006).

41   See Witt (2006).
42   See, for example, Aoki (1986); Matanle (2003); McCann *et al.* (2004); Morgan and Takahashi (2002); Sato (1997).
43   See, for example, Dore (2000); Matanle (2003); McCann *et al.* (2006); Nishihara (2002); Noguchi (2002).
44   See Noguchi (2002).
45   See, for example, Dore (2000) and Graham (2003).
46   See Graham (2003); Jacoby (2005).
47   See Jacoby (2005).
48   See, for example, Amable (2003) and Whitley (1999).
49   See Witt (2006).
50   See Matanle (2003); McCann *et al.* (2006).
51   Ibid.
52   See Matanle (2003).
53   See Vogel (2006).
54   See Matanle (2003).
55   See Dore (2000).
56   See Noguchi (2002).
57   Bank of California merged with Union Bank to become Union Bank of California in 1996, when Mitsubishi Bank merged with Tokyo Bank.
58   See Bank of Tokyo-Mitsubishi UFJ annual report (2008: 8, 9). The report is distributed by the firm to all shareholders with a dividend after every accounting date.
59   See Sato (1997).
60   Toyota cut its temporary workforce at its plants by 20 per cent in 2008. Nissan cut its temporary workforce at its plants by 780 from November 2008 to March 2009. See http://www.j-cast.com/2008/11/04029658.html (accessed 30 March 2012).
61   See Vogel (2006).
62   See Abegglen (1958).
63   See Gerlach (1992).
64   See Koike (1983); Aoki (1988).
65   See Aoki (1988); Goto (1982).
66   See Osano and Tsutsui (1986); Sheard (1986).
67   See the RIETI website. Available at http://www.rieti.go.jp/jp/publications/act_dp 2005.html
68   See Robinson and Shimizu (2006).
69   In 2006.
70   In 2001.
71   In 2008.
72   See Dore (2000) and Noguchi (2002).
73   See Olcott (2008).
74   See http://web-japan.org/trends/business/bus050905.html#pagetop (accessed 30 August 2005).
75   See Witt (2006) and Olcott (2008).
76   See, for example, Whitley (1999) and Amable (2003).
77   See, for example, Ahmadjian and Robinson (2001); Dore (2005, 2006); Graham (2003, 2004); Olcott (2009).
78   See, for example, Dore (2008, 2011).
79   See Munakata (2002).
80   See Graham (2003) and Yashiro (2006).
81   See Graham (2003).
82   See Graham (2004).
83   See Nishihara (2002) and Watanabe (2002).
84   See Watanabe (2002).
85   See Ikeda (2002).

86   See Morgan and Kubo (2005).
87   Cabinet Office, Government of Japan (2009).
88   See Sekiguchi (1996).
89   See Ahmadjian and Robinson (2001).
90   See Dore (2003).
91   See Dore (2003) and Lazonick and O'Sullivan (2000).
92   Ahmadjian and Robinson (2001).
93   See Olcott (2008).
94   See, for example, Hassard *et al.* (2009); McCann *et al.* (2010); Olcott (2008).
95   See Froud *et al.* (2000).
96   See Aoki and Dore (1996).
97   See Froud *et al.* (2000).
98   See Dore (2000).
99   See Nicolai *et al.* (2010).
100  See Fligstein (1990).
101  See Froud et al. (2000).
102  See Aglietta (2000).
103  See Williams (2000).
104  See, for example, Erturk (2008); Engelen (2003) and Capelli (1997).
105  See Kim (1994).
106  See Kanter (1992); Hassard *et al.* (2009); Worrall *et al.* (2004).
107  See Littler (2006).
108  This is further accelerated through the new group of intermediaries such as pension funds that inflate capital markets, encouraging firms to choose takeovers and/or other forms of radical restructuring (Toporowski 1999).
109  See Lazonick and O'Sullivan (2000); Littler (2006).
110  See Barley and Kunda (2004).
111  See Shleifer and Summers (1988).
112  See Kaplan and Schoar (2005).
113  Shareholder value logic does not necessarily cause a speculative bubble (Lasonick and O'Sullivan 2000).
114  See Froud *et al.* (2000).
115  See ibid. and Morgan and Takahashi (2002).
116  Sloan (1996).
117  Shleifer and Summers (1988).
118  Even for short-term employment downsizing does not produce more improvements to stock returns than the average in the same industry (Cascio 1998). Also see Cascio (1993, 2002); Littler (2006); Druckman *et al.* (1997).
119  See, for example, Engelen (2003); Fligstein (1990); Lazonick and O'Sullivan (2000); O'Sullivan (2000).
120  Cascio (2002).
121  See Froud *et al.* (2000).
122  Engelen (2003).
123  Sennett (1998) and Hassard *et al.* (2009).
124  Erturk (2008).
125  Cappelli *et al.* (1997).
126  Engelen (2003); Cappelli *et al.* (1997); Hassard *et al.* (2009).
127  Higgens and Bannister (1992).
128  Jameson (2000).
129  Stark (2003); Froud *et al.* (2000); Boje (2001); Collins (2008); Gabriel (2000, 2004).
130  For example, Westphal and Zajac (1994, 2001); Meyer and Rowan (1977).
131  See Littler (2006).
132  See Froud *et al.* (2000).
133  Higgins and Dzjkzbach (1989).

134   See Kim (1994).
135   See Worrall and Cooper (1998) and Druckman *et al.* (1997).
136   Khurana (2002).
137   Froud *et al.* (2000).
138   Ibid.; Khurana (2002).
139   Pollock and Rindova (2003).
140   Higgins and Dzjkzbach (1989).
141   Engelen (2003).
142   Clark *et al.* (2004).
143   Callon (1988).
144   Amin and Thrift (2004).
145   Froud *et al.* (2000).
146   Morgan and Takahashi (2002).
147   Miwa (1990).
148   Dore (2006, 2008); Noguchi (2002).
149   Shigeki *et al.* (1990).
150   Magee (2003).
151   Dore (2006, 2008).
152   http://www.economist.com/node/4454244
153   Ahmadjian and Robinson (2001); Vogel (2006); Witt (2006).
154   Witt (2006).
155   Redding (2005).
156   Vogel (2006: 157–204).
157   Ibid. (2006).
158   Ibid; Olcott (2009).
159   Shinsei Bank annual report (2007). Further information is provided in Chapter 6.
160   Olcott (2008).
161   Sato (1997).
162   Aoki *et al.* (2007).
163   At the same time Aoki *et al.* (2007) indicate that this new type of system is not necessarily effective for the motivation of employees.
164   For example Katz (2003); Matanle *et al.* (2006).
165   E.g. Buchanan and Deakin (2009); Dore (2006, 2008, 2009, 2011); Olcott (2009).
166   Dore (2008: 46–49).
167   Junichiro Koizumi held office from 2001–06.
168   Olcott (2009).
169   Khurana (2002).
170   Dore (2003, 2009); Lazonick and O'Sullivan (2000).
171   Buchanan and Deakin (2009); Olcott (2009).
172   Also Aoki (2007); Buchanan (2007); and, to a large extent, Jacoby (2005).
173   Buchanan (2007).
174   Ibid.: 7.
175   For example Buchanan and Deakin (2009); Dore (2006, 2008, 2009, 2011); Olcott (2009).
176   See, for example, Graham (2004); Hassard *et al.* (2009).
177   See, for example, Ahmadjian and Robinson (2001); Jacoby (2005); Vogel (2006).
178   Such as Buchanan and Deakin (2009); Dore (2009, 2011); Olcott (2009).
179   Cascio (1998).

# 3　Nissan Motor

## An ongoing and sophisticated narrative management strategy

### 3.1 Introduction

This chapter investigates what Nissan's new restructuring plans mean for its employees, especially mid-level managers. What do these mid-level managers at Nissan really think about the supposedly radical changes implemented by top management? Do they agree with the need for change, and have they had any input into it? To what extent have the changes affected their working lives and their attitudes towards their work and to Nissan itself? Through positing and answering these questions the chapter develops the argument that Nissan has not implemented as much change as it claims to have done.

As discussed in the previous chapter, much of the literature on Japanese restructuring argues that US-style management strategy is incompatible with Japan's complex and highly embedded institutional structure. However, Nissan, which was faced with near-bankruptcy until its alliance with Renault in 1999, announced perhaps the most famous of all US-style restructuring plans in Japan. Launched with a great fanfare, it was known as the Nissan Revival plan (or NRP), and included downsizing during 2000–01.[1] Following the NRP, Nissan persisted with further high-profile reform plans, namely Nissan 180 (2002–04), Nissan Value Up (2005–07), and GT2012 (2008–12). However, what has been the effect of these high-profile change programs? To what extent has Nissan implemented US-style restructuring, and in particular, how do middle management perceive Nissan's seemingly endless reform plans?

After some initial public hostility to the changes, it has become the generally accepted public view that the US-style management approach actually rescued Nissan, and that similar reforms are needed in other traditional and slow-moving Japanese organizations. However, based on the viewpoints of the middle managers interviewed for this study, it seems that these dramatic reforms actually serve to conceal the fact that there has been only limited real change within Nissan. Nissan's new restructuring plan is a part of its narrative management, designed to show the outside world that Nissan is changing, yet in practice it still clings to its traditional business methods.

## 3.2 Nissan's new reform plans

Before examining Nissan's new reform plans information about the company is provided in section 3.2.1 in order to set the context for the ensuing analysis.

### 3.2.1 Nissan corporate information

Since the company's foundation in Yokohama City in 1933 the Nissan brand has gained a huge reputation in the Japanese community. Nissan has the second largest share of the domestic automobile market in Japan and the sixth largest in the world. It has a workforce of 30,718 employees.[2] While Nissan is noted by industry insiders as possessing a higher quality of technology than that of Toyota, its sales have historically lagged behind Toyota, largely because of Toyota's dealership dominance. By 1970 Nissan's market share in Japan was close to Toyota's, but a decade later Toyota had outstripped Nissan.

Following the bursting of the bubble the early 1990s Nissan was saddled with approximately ¥4.3 trillion of debt, accruing about ¥100 billion in interest payments, equivalent to the company's consolidated operating income.[3] In other words, Nissan found itself in the unenviable position of running a business solely to pay the interest. Nissan slipped down to third place in the Japanese rankings during the 1990s (with Honda taking second place). Although Nissan implemented its restructuring plan in 1991, it was faced with near bankruptcy until it formed an alliance with Renault in 1999. Renault invested ¥585 billion in Nissan in order to acquire 36.8 per cent of its shares, and injected ¥643 billion in total. To represent the interests of Renault, Carlos Ghosn[4] was appointed CEO. He has been CEO of Nissan since 1998 – a very long tenure for such a high-profile position in the world of business.[5] Carlos Ghosn has also been CEO of Renault since 2005. Toshiyuki Shiga, a Nissan 'company man' became Chief Operating Officer of Nissan. As the largest shareholder, Renault had acquired 44.3 per cent of Nissan's shares. While participating in the management in Nissan, it announced major restructuring plans in 1999, just after the alliance. Nissan's board was reduced to ten members, with one of these being an outside director. An audit committee was also introduced, with three of the four auditors coming from outside Nissan.

This alliance between a Japanese and a foreign-affiliated firm was one of the first to occur in Japan. It surprised Japanese society, mainly because Nissan belonged to Fuyo, one of the Japanese *keiretsu* groups, which evolved out of the Yasuda *zaibatsu*, which had been dissolved after the Second World War. Mitsubishi, Mitsui, Sumitomo and Yasuda comprised the largest *zaibatsu* groups[6] at that time.

The popular Nissan brand has been carefully maintained since the alliance with Renault. Nissan has emphasized that cooperation and synergies result from the alliance. According to the company's 2008 annual report:

The Alliance is a partnership based on trust and mutual respect. The transparency of the organization ensures clear decision-making for speed, accountability and high standards of performance. Weaving the strengths of Nissan and Renault together creates synergies through common structures, cross-company teams, shared platforms and components.[7]

Nissan's profits have increased significantly since the alliance with Renault, and the media and public have called this transformation a V-shaped recovery. In 2007 the company's profits dropped for the first time since the alliance, due to low domestic demand, and in 2007–08 Nissan reported a net deficit, of ¥233.7 billion, for the first time since 1999. However, since that time Nissan has continued to improve its financial performance. Nissan's stock price has increased since 1999, except during the crisis period of 2008–09. Following the alliance, the highest share price was ¥1,508 in 2007 and the lowest was ¥306 in 2009.

Nissan uses US-style business language aimed at the investor community. Nissan's vision and values are based on currently popular US-style business strategies, employing a Value-Based Management (VBM) approach and drastic serial restructuring announcements. Although there is a consistent argument that Japanese firms have not been influenced by shareholder value logic,[8] Ghosn has clearly created shareholder value based on VBM at Nissan and has helped to legitimize the practice across corporate Japan.

### 3.2.2 Nissan's US-style reform plans

According to Nissan's 2005 annual report stock price is the central measure of a firm's success:

> The sole objective function of a public company is to create growing sustainable value. Nissan is no exception; our market capitalization, which is the value of what our shareholders own, has increased from ¥1.2 trillion at the end of fiscal 1999 to 6.3 trillion at the end of fiscal 2005. We approach shareholder value creation in a systematic manner, and have implemented Value-based Management (VBM) as the strategic tool to achieve long-term value creation …
>
> Nissan's share performance since 1999 has been, in large part, a measure of our effectiveness in implementing VBM. Management systems are now fully consistent with VBM. And a value creation mindset is now pervasive throughout the company.[9]

The language here is striking because it introduces an abundance of new terms: a value creation mindset, VBM, and shareholder value creation. All of these meet the preconditions for financialization: shareholder value, value investment and rapid cost-cutting.[10] VBM is a management approach that has become very popular among US firms. A firm tries to link its strategy to indexes such as EVA and SVA, so that it can improve its shareholder value.[11] It can be expected that a reward system will be introduced in recognition of employee achievement, so that employees can share this VBM knowledge and directly contribute to shareholder value creation.[12] VBM involves three steps: choosing value, making value and communicating value,[13] and Ghosn's reform plans consistently connect to shareholder value maximization through employees' adoption of key values, a performance-based pay system, and a clear investor communication strategy. The 2005 annual report reflects this policy:

> VBM at Nissan:
> Our VBM has two stages. We first try to maximize our intrinsic value or the present value of risk-adjusted, expected future free cash flow. Through investor communications, we then try to manage the expectations of the capital market in order to ensure that our market value matches with our intrinsic value ...
> For example, under Nissan Value-Up we focus on key value drivers, such as profitability, growth, and investment efficiency. The other two steps, performance measurement and compensation system, are defined by our commitments. But whether maximizing our intrinsic value in the first stage leads to maximizing shareholder value depends on the second stage, investor communications. Obviously, if the improvement in intrinsic value is not reflected in the market value, it does not reward shareholders at all. Therefore, the role investor communications play in our VBM is significant ... Since we believe that our share price is the most objective measure of our future performance, we use that feedback at the highest levels of the company.[14]

At Nissan shareholder value is constructed through profit-making and increased communication with investors or the capital market, while employees' pay scales are based on a calculation of their direct contributions to that profit-making. Nissan's VBM aims to boost their share price. Nissan's new management approach imitates popular US strategies by targeting the company's shareholders in its public claim.[15]

Under the VBM approach, Nissan's top management further deploys a rolling program of drastic restructuring (see Table 3.1).

*Table 3.1* Nissan restructuring plans since 2000

| *2000–01* | *2002–04* | *2005–07* | *2008–12* |
| --- | --- | --- | --- |
| Nissan Revival Plan (NRP) | Nissan 180 | Nissan Value-Up | GT2012 |

The first restructuring plan promised drastic changes within the company:

> There is no problem at a car company that good products can't solve; product development will be at the heart of Nissan's revival." Thus Nissan's Chief Operating Officer, Carlos Ghosn laid out the Nissan Revival Plan on 18 October 1999. These words emphasized that the dramatic, far-reaching changes to reshape Nissan have product development and sales growth at their heart. While cost-cutting will be the most dramatic and visible part of the Plan, executives know the company cannot save its way to success. By achieving its three commitments, Nissan will return to sustainable, profitable growth – the ultimate target of this comprehensive Plan. And, in a balanced alliance with Renault, it will stand strong as a major global player in the world automobile industry...
>
> Mr Ghosn was straightforward in assessing the need for dramatic change. Nissan, he noted, is in tough shape. "The company has been losing market share since 1991", he said. "It has been struggling with profitability over the same period, and has been, and remains, a highly indebted company."[16]

Ghosn's public statements emulate US-style business phraseology such as 'the need for dramatic change', and 'rebuilding the corporation'. These public claims suggest that the case of Nissan contradicts the findings of past studies, which showed that there had been a minimal shift towards stock market capitalism in Japan.[17]

This section showed how the alliance between Nissan and Renault brought US-style business language to Japan. The following sections will explore interview data from mid-level Nissan managers in order to investigate the local and practical effects of VBM as it was rolled out. Viewed from the level of middle management, Nissan's dramatic apparent shift towards shareholder value is actually much less significant than it might appear.

## 3.3 External and internal acceptance of Nissan's new reform plans

The attempts by Nissan to completely transform itself into a US-style investor capitalism enterprise can be viewed as being radical and controversial in a business environment as cautious as Japan's, so how has Nissan's US-style business strategy been perceived by external and internal audiences? Given that this alliance between a Japanese and a foreign-affiliated firm in 1999 was the first of its kind in Japan, Nissan's reform plans have had a far-reaching impact on Japanese society. Nissan's reform plans were initially repudiated by external audiences, but later were regarded to have been hugely successful and accepted as having been entirely necessary. This is especially striking given the way in which the Japanese mass media initially criticized Nissan's attempts to de-institutionalize traditional Japanese management. Later the media focused on the advantages brought about by the restructuring, and this swing from rejection to acceptance appears to have occurred also among Nissan's staff.

This section will explore the reaction of outsiders (such as the investor community) to Nissan's restructuring. It will then offer a closer examination of the views of employees (Nissan middle managers) about what these changes mean for the everyday functioning and behaviour of the firm.

### 3.3.1 External acceptance that influences the mass media

Nissan's US-style reform plans have strongly influenced Japanese society. Ghosn's high profile, as well as his unusual and controversial reform strategies, have garnered considerable media attention. In this interview a senior manager who had worked in Nissan's PR department, describes how the company's reform plan had become the centre of attention.

> The mass media takes a close interest in Nissan, which is lucky for Nissan. The media is interested in a firm where the work looks interesting. When I worked in the PR department, I felt that Nissan was attracting the mass media more than Toyota or Honda, or what we actually did.

This middle manager recognizes that Nissan does attract the mass media. Indeed, the media pays close attention to Ghosn's public claims. Here are two examples from one of Japan's leading business journals:

> CEO Carlos Ghosn who arrives from Renault announced big reform plans on 18 October 1999. Only six months after his arrival in Japan he launched his reforms: five plants to be closed, 21,000 employees laid off, and the *keiretsu* connection dissolved. Why is he employing such drastic restructuring, which has never before been adopted by a Japanese firm? … According to colleagues, Ghosn stated that he intends to go back to Renault in two or three years' time. He is reforming Nissan for the short term.
>
> (*Weekly Diamond* 1999a: 52)

> The Nissan Revival Plan introduced by Carlos Ghosn incorporates the same drastic tactics that he implemented at Renault, and the company is also cutting its ties with the *keiretsu*. His ideology justifies abandoning the weak.
>
> (*Weekly Diamond* 1999c: 17)

Ghosn's radical reforms were the target of blistering criticism by the mass media, which fixated on the single point that he had cut the cost of HR for short-term gain. The media chiefly focused on Nissan's employment and asset downsizing – closing plants, reducing the workforce, shrinking and transforming suppliers and eliminating non-core assets. Later Ghosn would be known as 'the cost-cutter'.

However, the media began to view him in a new light when the NRP finished one year ahead of schedule. By 2001 Ghosn was considered to be a successful leader.

> Nissan accumulated ¥684.4 billion in (consolidated) losses in 1999, the largest ever in the manufacturing sector. In the following year, however, the company made a record ¥331.1 billion in profits. Ghosn, who came from Renault, rapidly put Nissan on the road to recovery. He was called in as a cost-cutter, but is now the highest-profile company president from a foreign country.
>
> (*Weekly Diamond* 2001a: 144)

Thus it can be seen that perceptions of Ghosn dramatically and rapidly changed from negative to positive. At the time of writing he has received even higher plaudits from the public, which calls him 'a superhero for Nissan'.[18] Ghosn has become a celebrated turnaround specialist – a remarkable leader who successfully revived the public image of Nissan and became 'a corporate saviour'.[19] Thus Nissan's reform plans received strong social acceptance, which in turn benefited the company's business. For example, Interbrand, one of the best-known international global branding consultancies, has ranked Nissan highly in its index of car manufacturers since it was first listed in 2003. (see Table 3.2).

According to Interbrand:

> There are three key aspects that contribute to the assessment: the financial performance of the branded products or services, the role of brand in the purchase decision process and the strength of the brand ... Brand Strength Score is comprised of 10 components, one of which measures the degree to which a brand feels omnipresent and how positively consumers, customers and opinion formers discuss it in both traditional and social media.[21]

*Table 3.2* Interbrand brand performance

| Year | *Global best brand: Nissan* |
| --- | --- |
| 2003 | 89th (enters the rankings for the first time) |
| 2004 | 90th |
| 2005 | 85th |
| 2006 | 90th |
| 2007 | 98th |
| 2011 | 90th |

Source: Interbrand[20]

As a positive public reaction is one of the criteria for its ranking, strong social acceptance of the US-style business strategy contributed to status enhancement and brand recognition for Nissan. The new, post-reform Nissan enjoys strong public support, which has clear advantages for the brand.

Interbrand takes financial performance into consideration when assessing companies for its rankings, and Nissan has continued to record a profit since it started its reform plans (see Figure 3.1): ¥331.0 billion in 2000, ¥372.2 billion in 2001, ¥495.1 billion in 2002, ¥503.6 billion in 2003, ¥512.2 billion in 2004, ¥518.0 billion in 2005, ¥460.7 billion in 2006, ¥482.2 billion in 2007 (Nissan annual reports 1999–2008).

In addition, Nissan's stock price has continued to increase since the company began its restructuring plans in 1999, except, of course, in 2007/08, when Japan and much of the global economies suffered from the effects of the recession.

Nissan's stock price has been consistently higher than that of Toyota and Honda. As of January 1998 the company's stock price stood at its lowest ever level, ¥380, reaching its highest level of ¥1,508 in January 2007. It has been stable at a level of around ¥822 since July 2011. These figures are evidence that Ghosn's radical US-style reforms have helped to win strong external support and acceptance for Nissan.

### 3.3.2 Internal acceptance of Nissan's reform plans

After a difficult start, Nissan managed to achieve strong external and internal acceptance and understanding of its reform plans. In other words, Nissan's

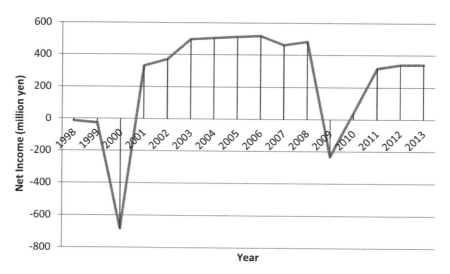

*Figure 3.1* Nissan's net income (1997–2010)
Source: Tokyo Stock Exchange

US-style reforms have been welcomed by its employees. Although it has been suggested by some academics that it is difficult for Japanese salarymen to adapt to new management systems,[22] even the new business language introduced by the new regime became fashionable within the workplace. For example, as part of VBM 'commitment management' (organizational commitment) was introduced, and the phrase has become very popular among employees; even the public has become enamoured of it.[23] This management strategy is designed to enhance employee motivation.[24] Every employee is given 'commitments' and his or her pay is monitored in relation to these commitments:

> The other two steps, performance measurement and compensation system, are defined by our commitments. Each top-level commitment in the business plan is backed by specific commitments at every level of the organization. Everyone throughout Nissan knows what he or she must achieve. Close monitoring of performance creates an objective basis for a pay-for-performance compensation system. Our compensation system has played a key role in cultivating the value creation mindset in our company.[25]

Nissan has therefore changed its pay system to a Western-style system based (supposedly) on promotion according to merit rather than seniority. Some academics have observed that reward systems have changed in other Japanese companies too,[26] but this is rare. The following interviewee, who had worked at one of Nissan's plants, explained that the rank-and-file workers had begun to use the term organizational commitment.

> We have developed organizational consciousness thanks to his [Ghosn's] introduction of commitment management. When I worked at one of Nissan's plants before, we tried to achieve our own commitments. Through 'commitment', we could move in the same direction as the firm. We used the term 'commitment' even when we were at an after-work party in the *karaoke* shop. For example, we said 'each person has to sing a song today, which is our commitment'. I think that it is important for staff to share such essential terms of the firm as a common language. It is also easy for the management to unify employees and their ways of thinking.

It seems that even in their private lives, Nissan staff, including plant workers, use fashionable business terminology. Nissan's language is highly influential to them and appears to have contributed to a sense of organizational unity. The influence of its message reaches far beyond the workplace.[27]

Other research has suggested that Nissan's staff admire and trust Ghosn and his package of reforms.[28] According to one interviewee:

I am glad that I chose to work at Nissan because I could see how Nissan changed before and after the arrival of Ghosn-san. With my own eyes I saw that Nissan was going bankrupt but then it recovered. For me it was a positive experience to see and feel how Ghosn-san improved Nissan. Whenever I hear news about other firms going bankrupt, I do think that the reason must be the CEOs. Whether a firm can change or not depends on its CEO.

Employees think that the changes wrought at Nissan were the result of Ghosn's policies and that he was crucial to Nissan's recovery. They appreciate Ghosn, and he is much liked by employees, according to the comments from the following interviewee:

Ghosn-san is popular, especially with the employees who work at Nissan's plants. I had worked at Yokohama plant before. Whenever Ghosn-san visits the plant, they ask him to sign autographs and shake hands.

Following considerable initial hostility, Ghosn now seems to be genuinely respected and trusted by the firm's employees. He is treated like a superhero. The middle manager interviewed for this research calls him 'Ghosn-san', which means he is now regarded as a close friend of Nissan's employees. Normally Japanese salarymen call the head of an organization 'Mr CEO' to maintain distance and show respect.[29] Staff perceive Ghosn as a trustworthy and approachable person. Nissan's employees generally do not appear to feel antagonized or alienated as a result of organizational reform.[30] They are not confused by the new management system, as previous research has shown that staff in traditional Japanese firms usually are[31] and do not seem to be upset by the top management's high bonuses, ranked the highest among listed firms in Japan.[32] The average annual earnings of a Nissan executive in 2005 amounted to five times as much as that of a Toyota executive.[33] Nissan's executives earned ¥0.3 billion each while Toyota's executives received ¥62 million. This figure is 41 times as much as the annual earnings of the rest of the firm's staff; on average Nissan's employees earn ¥7.3 million a year.

It is clear that Nissan's US-style business tactics have earned strong external and internal support. The next section will explore this validation in more detail and the extent to which Nissan has changed under Ghosn's leadership. One aspect of how Nissan manages to gain external acceptance and how it manages to earn internal cooperation will be described.

## 3.4 Nissan's narrative management

This section will look at how Nissan has actually implemented its new approach to reform. In particular it focuses on the way in which it accomplishes employment downsizing and VBM. This section also explains how Nissan secured and sustains external and internal understanding of its reform plans. First, how did Nissan gain understanding from its external audience when discussing the extremely sensitive issue of employment downsizing within Nissan? The internal audience's understanding of the way in which VBM was adopted within Nissan will be discussed later.

### 3.4.1 Narrative management and employment downsizing

How has Nissan managed to win widespread external acceptance despite facing initial strong criticism from the media and the general public? Research on public companies worldwide suggests that information about corporate organizational changes is seldom broadcast by media outlets in exact detail.[34] How accurately did the mass media communicate the details of Nissan's reform package? What specific methods did Nissan use to secure social acceptance of a radical new organizational approach? This section explores these points through examining interview data gathered within Nissan.

Nissan has attempted to control the impact of its public messages carefully. Although these public messages were designed to have broad impact and to highlight the need for radical change, up-to-date and correct, the actual details of the reform package were deliberately sketchy, or omitted altogether. Only the vaguest details about what specifically would be done at Nissan were provided to the news media. We can learn more by looking closely at the messages publicly disclosed by Nissan. In its annual report for 1999 Nissan provided explicit details about the NRP:

> The Nissan Revival Plan is designed to rebuild Nissan from a multi-regional organization to a true global company. In announcing the Plan, company leaders made three firm commitments:
>
> - To return to profitability by 2000
> - To achieve consolidated operating profit of 4.5 percent by 2002
> - To reduce net automotive debt from ¥1.4 trillion to less than ¥700 billion by 2002.[35]
>
> Main restructuring measures
>
> 1 Reduction of 21,000 employees that occupy 14 per cent of the total labour force by March 2003 (from 0.148 million to 0.127 million employees).
> 2 Closing three assembly plants and two power train plans aimed at reduction of 30% of surplus produce by March 2002. Reduction of the number of car platforms from 24 to 15.
> 3 Reduction in purchasing costs by 20 per cent and reduction of the number of existing suppliers from 600 to less than 114 by March 2002.
> 4 Selling stocks and assets belonging to Nissan's *keiretsu* firms.[36]

However, the report states only why Nissan is going to reform, and provides no details about how it will carry out its reforms. Succeeding annual reports for 2000 and 2001 failed to include information about the program of layoffs that received such negative media attention. Public statements made around this time also gave scant detail on these areas. What actually happened with respect to downsizing according to Nissan's restructuring measures? According to the middle managers who had experience of Nissan before the new reforms started:

> We are committed to cutting the number of the employees every year. Even so, we employed an early retirement system during 1999–2001. Now we are employing fewer a lower number of new graduates than the number of employees who retired.

> We still offer lifetime employment. The age limit is 60 years, but those who are at manager level and beyond retire at 50 or 55 years of age and are then relocated to Nissan's affiliate firms.

It appears that the traditional Japanese employment system has not really been affected by Nissan's reforms. The company achieved downsizing through an early retirement system, similar to that used in traditional Japanese firms. This evidence supports the views of academics[37] who indicate that an early retirement system is the main method of reducing the headcount in Japan. An early retirement system is never regarded as a form of downsizing.[38] In 1999 Nissan announced its intention to reduce its workforce of 39,969 by 21,000 before 2003, and although the number of staff has decreased, by 2003 the headcount had fallen by only 7,480 (see Table 3.3).

As Table 3.3 shows, Nissan has in fact slightly increased the number of its employees since 2003. Clearly Nissan's restructuring was not as drastic as reported by its PR department and the Japanese media. There is a gap between saying and doing in Nissan's very limited use of employment downsizing. This is an example of downsizing fraud[39] and mirrors almost exactly the findings about Ford Motor Company[40] and other case studies, in that the overall employment numbers remain extraordinarily stable despite endless downsizing announcements. The mass media has duly overreacted to Nissan's 'over-announcement'. Thus, Nissan has maximized the quantity and minimized the quality of the information about its reform plans to the public. It can be said that Ghosn and Nissan's top management are successful and sophisticated operators of image restructuring.

This is Nissan's narrative management strategy in a nutshell. Specifically, the mass media plays an important role in this narrative construction. Nissan aims to make the public create and circulate stories, rather than the firm always making and circulating the stories. Now, the firm does not receive criticism, but elicts much higher expectations from the public. This is its public narrative construction. Nissan uses the media for its narrative.[41] Here a

*Table 3.3* Nissan's workforce (1999–2008)

| Year | Total workforce |
| --- | --- |
| 1999 | 39,969 |
| 2000 | 39,467 |
| 2001 | 32,707 |
| 2002 | 30,747 |
| 2003 | 30,365 |
| 2004 | 31,128 |
| 2005 | 31,389 |
| 2006 | 32,177 |
| 2007 | 32,180 |
| 2008 | 32,489 |

Source: Toyokeizai 2000–2009

member of Nissan explains how the company's new reform plans depend on effective PR:

> PR is cost-effective. We shifted the budget from the marketing depart-ment to the PR department. There is strong evidence that Ghosn increased the value of the Nissan brand when we successfully turned around the business. How did we do that? We sent the same ques-tionnaires to employees and customers alike. Other surveys are run by third parties; Interbrand is one of the methods we use to find out about Nissan's image. The commitment of our PR department is that the amount of media reporting has to be more than that of Toyota or Honda when basically we do not spend any money on making public announcements.

If a firm can find another marketing strategy that just as easily produces profitable assets for its shareholders, it will adopt this new strategy.[42] Nissan carefully limits and controls the information that is released to media outlets, and is putting increasing effort into managing its PR in order to encourage the media to boost Nissan's reputation. In fact, the firm only disclosed the full details of the layoffs resulting from NRP in 2001, once the plans had been fully implemented and the desired results achieved. Ghosn's book, *Renaissance*,[43] explains the rationale behind the success of NRP:

> When the NRP was announced in 1999, much of the focus from media was on what Nissan had to do to streamline its business – closing plants, reducing headcounts. In response to their voices, I kept considering care-fully employees' difficulties without sleeping or resting. As a result, the total number of affected employees was 5,200. Among them 3,248

employees transferred to other Nissan factories and 420 changed to Nissan's affiliated firms. The number of retired persons was 1,300, 100 of them reached retiring age and 1,200 choosing to leave. For 1,200 people I tried everything to find other jobs.

(Ghosn 2001: 265, 266)

Nissan's US-style reform plans garnered strong external support through its active use of corporate communications and PR. Indeed, this support has been sustained as a result of the continuing narrative management strategy employed by Nissan's PR department since 1999.

Since that time, similar restructuring plans became more widespread in large Japanese firms such as Recruit Holdings, NTT DOCOMO, Sumitomo 3M[44] and HOYA. This has spread even into Japanese local government, such as Yokohama City Council, which called their reform plan the Yokohama Revival Plan, after the NRP, in 2002 (see Chapter 6).

Interestingly, however, in Nissan's case, such bombastic announcements about corporate change do not really tally with the actual scale of employment downsizing, which has remained very limited as shown above. Nissan employed a sophisticated narrative management strategy towards the mass media. The company's public communications clearly have an ever more important role to play. In particular, Nissan manipulates the quality, quantity and timing of the information released to the media, a fact that the employees also seem to recognize. What Japanese organizations choose to disclose is an important part of organizational change, and is similar to the experience of large firms in Anglo-Saxon contexts.[45]

### 3.4.2 Nissan's Narrative Management: Value-based management

This section focuses on Nissan's new management system called Value-Based Management (VBM). To what extent has Nissan actually implemented VBM within the firm? As explained previously, Nissan has adopted commitment management, which is integral to VBM and seems to have become accepted and circulated by Nissan staff. Exploring how VBM was adopted helps us to understand how Nissan has maintained internal cooperation for its US-style reforms.

Under commitment management, the pay system changed from a traditional seniority-based structure to a more Anglo-Saxon-style annual salary scheme. Employees' pay depends on whether or not staff satisfy their commitments.[46] Nissan states that employees' annual pay can increase by 20–30 per cent if they meet their commitments.[47] How has VBM been received by Nissan's staff, who were more used to a traditional seniority-based wage system? The quote below gives an indication of staff feelings:

We like Ghosn-san and Nissan's rescue plan. Ghosn-san is popular owing to his new-style reform plans, externally and internally. On the contrary, I do not feel that there have been major changes here. That's why we have never been worried so far.

While this interviewee clearly accepts Ghosn and Nissan's management approach, s/he indicated a lack of drastic change within Nissan. Several other interviewees gave similar responses, noting that no really drastic reforms have been carried out at Nissan. For example, some feel that commitment management is little different from what has always gone on in the firm – i.e. heavy workloads and strong commitment to the company's goals.

> What have Nissan not changed? Fundamentally Nissan plants have not changed. They do not need to change, although there have been some minor changes. It is at senior manager level and above that change needs to occur. Our commitments are greater than those of the other employees. Having said that, this situation does not seem to have changed. When I came to Nissan twenty-five years ago, general managers had a heavy workload. I think that it is the same for all other automobile and manufacturing firms, primarily because they are required to sell as many products as possible.

One middle manager said that performance management really only applies to staff at senior middle management level or above. Another interviewee agreed:

> Even if I achieve my commitments, nothing happens to my pay. The pay-for-performance compensation system only applies to those who are at senior or general manager level or above owing to their heavier commitments. A large number of employees are not at general manager level because it is difficult for Nissan's employees to be promoted to even manager level. Their remuneration is based on age. All employees receive increases of ¥10,000 per month, so nothing has changed there, despite the fact that we are all supposed to embrace 'commitment'.

The performance management and new pay systems apply only to those at general or senior manager level or above. It is generally recognized in the Japanese manufacturing industry that firms put more pressure on higher-level positions such as general and senior manager, in order to drastically reduce costs.[48] Ono Taichi, who created the Toyota production system, indicates that cost reduction is a key way to produce profits,[49] and the higher positions have more responsibility to make profits. There are just under 1,500 employees[50] at senior manager level at Nissan, which is only 5 per cent of all Nissan staff. Therefore, 95 per cent of Nissan's staff have not really been affected by the VBM performance management system.

Since 2005, when Nissan introduced commitment management, the average annual salaries for Nissan staff has not changed. For example, employees' average annual salaries amounted to ¥7.30 million in 2006, ¥7.29 million in 2007, ¥7.22 million in 2008, ¥7.13 million in 2009, ¥7.28 million 2010, ¥6.27 million in 2011 and ¥6.84 million in 2012.[51] This suggests that Nissan has changed the quality and quantity of tasks for employees in different managerial positions. Nissan has, therefore, opened up a gap between saying and doing in terms of not only employment downsizing but also the performance and pay systems. Most literature on Japan suggests that many of the traditional systems are still in place.[52] It seems that Nissan has not reformed as drastically as it announced and in fact has been somewhat slow to implement change.

The process of organizational change is complex and subtle, and can perhaps best be understood by detailed studies of employees' opinions. Despite the gap between saying and doing, Nissan's staff have a good understanding and acceptance of the company's new plans (see above). How did the company achieve this? First, Nissan has a highly developed internal information strategy. The firm carefully chooses the terms to be disclosed to its staff. When doing so, it sometimes slightly changes some of the terms from those used in its public announcements. For instance, the guiding principles or the Nissan Way have been delivered to employees only since 2006. The aim was for the Nissan Way to be commonly adopted across Nissan's global workforce. In 2008 workers at the Nissan plants in the United Kingdom and Japan were both using this company paper. Some interviewees said that they carried with them a short leaflet explaining the Nissan Way. The leaflet contains the following text, which is an excellent example of corporate internal narrative management:

> The Nissan Way is a set of guiding principles that shapes how everyone at Nissan should carry out their day to day jobs. It is made up of five Mindsets and Actions. The Mindsets refer to our overall approach to work, and the Actions outline how we should behave or act. The idea behind the Nissan Way is to provide a simple 'best practice' guide that everyone in the Company, across all functions and grades including Nissan's management team, can bring into their everyday work.
>
> By all Nissan employees working in the same clear, consistent direction we will have a stronger, more focussed company. This will benefit our customers through better products and services, and also our Company in terms of profits, which provides a prosperous future for *all staff*.
>
> Nissan's management team recognizes the benefits of the Nissan Way and is committed to using the mindsets and actions to make positive changes. Please take time to learn the Mindsets and Actions and think about how you can use the Nissan Way in your job.[53]

The Nissan Way does not make any reference to shareholders, whereas the term appears frequently in the company's public announcements. Instead, Nissan refers to 'all staff' here. Nissan explains that what Nissan staff do for profit eventually benefits the staff too. It avoids making any links to its shareholders despite its emphasis on the importance of shareholders in its public announcements (see above or the Nissan annual report 2005: 2). Nissan manipulates the nuances of its public messages, and relays a subtly different message to its staff.

Nissan further strengthens its internal narrative management by its practice. To emphasize the importance of its staff the company aims to deliver its message to all its employees (including the blue-collar workers) before delivering it to outsiders. These two employees are surprised by what Nissan frequently says to those on the front line:

> Messages from Ghosn-san come down to me and other workers who work at the plants. I am glad that the CEO's messages reached everyone in the company, even plant workers. This is a big change since I started working here.

> One of the most suprising things that I have noticed since joining Nissan that Ghosn-san relays messages to all of the company's employees via television. When this happens the production lines in the factories and work in the offices come to a standstill. Messages are delivered at year end in particular.

Nissan's messages are relayed to all of its employees and this provides them with an equal opportunity to heed the firm's messages. According to the manager of the PR department, who deals with the disclosure of the firm's messages to its employees, Nissan has pledged to disclose public information to its employees before broadcasting it to the mass media. This helps to build Nissan staff's trust in senior management, as the following interviewee explains:

> As promised, Ghosn-san now passes information to all employees before it is published in the media. I mistrusted him before because the media often wrote differently from what Ghosn said to us. In this point I feel that he respects his employees and we can trust him.

Ghosn has become close to Nissan's staff. They have come to trust him and as a result are more likely to believe management's messages. This is noteworthy as it is unusual for a traditional Japanese CEO to be close and visible to their blue-collar workers.[54] By prioritizing its employees, Nissan has successfully breached the cultural barrier between the top floor and the company's employees.

In addition, Nissan has changed its internal strategy since 'Nissan 180' started in 2002. Information is tactically relayed to the staff by Ghosn himself. According to a correspondent who has dealt with disclosing the messages from Nissan, information is transmitted as text and video.

Before Ghosn discloses information to outsiders he transmits it to employees via the intranet, which is only available to our employees. His messages are always uploaded onto the intranet. Basically we put the text and video messages from Ghosn there. Also we receive monthly progress reports about whether the reform plans have been achieved or not. When we achieved 'Nissan 180', we celebrated this successful achievement, and Ghosn himself came onto each floor to thanks us for a job well done. The live video of this scene was also streamed via the intranet.

This way of doing things makes Ghosn visible and not the traditional 'hands off' CEO, especially as he transmits the information himself. Ghosn's role seems to have developed into that of an out-and-out performer within Nissan. Nissan seems to take seriously the relationship between the leader and the led.[55] The same interviewee said that information is relayed by Ghosn in Japanese:

He speaks in Japanese to say Konnichiwa [hello] to employees. Whenever he makes a speech at a welcoming ceremony for new employees or he visits a department or section, he brings a note written phonetically in the Roman alphabet, so that he can speak Japanese. This is because he tries to be close to employees.

Through speaking Japanese, Ghosn provides a sense of affinity to his workforce and to the wider Japanese society. Ghosn demonstrates the fact that he is a Japanophile on the front page of his books by wearing a *kimono*, a traditional form of Japanese clothing.[56] He has at least attempted to show some affinity and respect towards Japanese culture as a foreign CEO.[57]

Indeed, unlike Nissan's public claims, the internal messages seem to take on board many aspects of traditional Japanese work culture. Japanese institutionalized cultural pressure clearly seems to influence Ghosn's actions. In this way, the visible messages and actions contribute to sustaining internal acceptance.

The effects of this sophisticated internal and external narrative management seem to be widespread and effective for Nissan. While strong internal support is maintained, Nissan middle managers join Nissan's reform scheme and help to spread its message. Staff have transmitted Nissan's story themselves. The following interviewee, who came to Nissan in 2004, heard from a colleague about what Ghosn did at the plant.

The CEO, Ghosn himself, visited the Tochigi plant. I heard indirectly that he listened to the opinions of plant workers. This stuck in their minds. While I was working there, one particular employee, a very energetic man who was more than fifty years old, took Ghosn-san round the plant. The man was impressed by the fact that Ghosn was prepared to listen to his opinions. He kept telling me that 'the CEO came here and listened to me'. He listened to the field operatives, and that information has been relayed to other employees since his first visit.

Ghosn's site visits in order to hear his employees' opinions about Nissan's reforms are becoming legendary, and have been relayed and shared among Nissan salarymen. Nissan often includes phographs of Ghosn's visits to plants in its public narrative management. For example, in his book (Ghosn 2001) shows him shaking hands and talking frankly with front-line workers. The captions attached to the pictures suggest that he was warmly welcomed by them.

Nissan's middle managers help to make the company's public narrative work. Nissan's strategy of visible messages and actions encourages staff to take part in the firm's story making. Internal acceptance contributes to the sustaining of the publicly supported narrative, now that Nissan staff have also joined the narrative management effort. It is important that employees accept and contribute to Nissan's narratives if they are to become credible and sustainable. According to the interviewees, Nissan's staff seem to be genuinely engaging with the company's internal strategy. It appears that long-sustained internal support of Nissan's US-style reform follows from its careful and sophisticated efforts at internal and external narrative creation. Its extra effort behind the use of VBM management has encouraged staff to join Nissan's narrative management. Nissan's careful attention to employee-focused strategy helps Nissan staff to deal with Nissan's new organizational activities.

## 3.5 Lessons from Nissan Motor: on-going and sophisticated narrative management

Following its alliance with Renault in 1999 Nissan introduced popular US-type reform plans. However, in terms of employment downsizing and VBM these reforms have not been as drastic as the company's public announcements suggest. Employees have identified a significant gap between saying and doing and hence a clear case of narrative management[58] or false signalling[59] at Nissan. This case shows that Nissan's restructuring plan is a part of its wider narrative construction.

The number of firms adopting employment downsizing in Japan has increased owing to institutional pressure,[60] but in truth this downsizing occurs only in the public statements made by top management and has no internal perspective. When focusing on the experiences of workers and managers themselves, previous discussions about slow change in Japanese organizations[61] are seen to be basically correct. Change has not been nearly as pronounced as it appears when looking only at external statements.

Although Nissan's reform plans were initially viewed negatively by the public, Ghosn later received strong support from society. External support eventually came through Nissan's PR strategy. Nissan manipulates the impact of its messages on society through controlling the quantity and quality of the messages when making disclosures to the media. Nissan has deployed a sophisticated PR strategy aimed at the mass media. Nissan's reform plans have now been widely acknowledged as a successful strategy among Japanese firms. Public communications have become increasingly important at Nissan, as it has in other Japanese firms,[62] and cutting-edge Japanese firms such as Nissan are clearly involved in making forms of narrative management or signalling. In doing so, their behaviour and aims are not dissimilar, in many ways, to large Anglo-Saxon firms.[63]

When making its narratives, Nissan's public announcements do not articulate how their reform plans will be carried out within the firm.

Among its the company's many restructuring plans, this research examined employment downsizing and VBM in particular. The HR system in Japanese firms tends to stay somewhat unchanged as many researchers agree.[64] Nissan, like many Japanese firms, values its HR and this is reflected in its retaining of lifetime employment and the seniority-based pay system. Indeed, although Nissan announced that its workforce would be reduced by 21,000 in its NRP, the number of employees has hardly changed since Nissan started its reforms (see above). This is a clear and powerful example of downsizing fraud taking place in Japan, just as it has done widely in liberalized and financialized economies such as the USA or the UK.[65]

Also, commitment management and a merit-based pay system, both part of VBM, seem to have been rather superficially introduced. The system has been only applied to those few staff above senior management level. A much more traditional seniority-based pay system is still adopted towards the remaining 95 per cent of staff (including middle management). Thus, Nissan's US-style restructuring plans in terms of employment downsizing and VBM is a part of Nissan's narrative management. Although this backs up the findings about slow change that appear in previous literature on Japan, it does not really support studies that suggest that foreign-owned firms have implemented more aggressive restructuring than Japanese firms.[66] Nissan has certainly altered and augmented its IR activities under foreign owners and investors, but in doing so it seems to deploy a sophisticated narrative management strategy in order to provide a smokescreen, thus enabling the company to continue with largely traditional ways of operating and restructuring.

This view is also supported by Nissan's internal discourse. Nissan's internal messages are quite different in tone from its external messages, suggesting that the firm still conforms to the Japanese corporate tradition of favouring employees over investors. Having said that, this internal communication has encouraged employees to understand and accept its reform plans. Although there is a gap between Nissan's saying and doing, its reform plans (for example commitment management) have proved surprisingly popular among Nissan's staff. Employees appear to have accepted Nissan's restructuring plans and to have joined in the process of the narrative management. Nissan's visible messages and actions towards its staff contribute to the building of a lasting internal understanding. The company has earned and maintained internal support over a long time period, and its strong levels of internal focus aid this. It also contributes to employees' involvement with its broader process of narrative management. Meanwhile, even the wider Japanese society now appears to admire Nissan's seemingly endless reform plans.

In other words, external and internal audiences have favourably received and helped to develop Nissan's narrative management. It seems likely that this carefully crafted narrative management will continue in the foreseeable future.

Although actual reforms at company level are relatively minor, the development of this highly sophisticated internal and external relations program in itself represents an important form of change in Japan. This new dynamic – the perceived necessity for a vastly augmented and vastly more sophisticated form of corporate storytelling – is an important manifestation of ongoing changes in Japanese corporate governance and Japanese capitalism, an issue which will be explored in more detail in the concluding Chapters 7 and 8. For the moment, however, it is important to draw from the Nissan case the main finding that the development of these new forms of corporate communication has been largely successful: the message has been accepted and circulated by both internal and external audiences. This success is largely due to the sustained efforts of Nissan's narrative-makers, and especially by the efforts expended on internal acceptance.

The next chapter will examine the reform plans of Bank of Tokyo-Mitsubishi UFJ (BTMU). BTMU is one of the most traditional firms in that it belongs to the biggest Mitsubishi *keiretsu* group. The bank, however, has recently announced US ways of restructuring. This will again be examined through interview data, and a discussion will ensue about the nature of BTMU's narrative – how it is constructed, how it has been accepted or resisted. The next section will draw further arguments from this case as to the nature and meaning of emerging Japanese forms of narrative management.

## Notes

1　Nissan annual report (1999).
2　Non-consolidated basis figure. The consolidated basis figure was 175,766 at 31 March 2009. See http://www.nissan-global.com/EN/COMPANY/PROFILE/
3　Nissan annual report (1999).
4　Globally and in Japan Carlos Ghosn is considered to be an iconic successful business leader. Yet he had to follow a tough road before he came to be widely accepted by the Japanese public. Ghosn's US-style reform plans came under fire when he first arrived at Nissan as COO in 1999. Since then, he has published numerous books (twenty-two in Japan alone) about his experiences and journey to becoming a successful leader. The name Ghosn has become a synonym for successful leadership. These books have become bibles for Japanese businessmen, and Ghosn is regarded as an opinion maker.
5　A passage in one of Ghosn's books includes his declaration of his long-term vision: 'The CEO, Louis Schweitzer, disclosed that Ghosn will take on the position of CEO when Louis retires. However, "I will never leave Nissan until I can achieve

Nissan's goals." A president should not leave a firm until he or she achieves a firm's goal, which is my own individual philosophy. I am trying to help Nissan to make lasting profit' (Ghosn 2001: 265, 266). This demonstrates his commitment to Nissan.

 6  The Japanese group was comprised of fifteen *zaibatsu*; Mitsubishi, Mitsui, Sumitomo, Ayukawa, Asano, Furukawa, Yasuda, Okura, Nakajima, Nomura, Shibusawa, Koubekawasaki, Riken, Nichitsu and Niso.
 7  Nissan annual report (2008: 7).
 8  See, for example, Froud *et al.* (2000); Morgan and Takahashi (2002).
 9  Nissan annual report (2005: 2).
10  See Froud *et al.* (2000).
11  See Stewart (1991).
12  See Martin and Petty (2000).
13  See Koller *et al.* (2010).
14  Nissan annual report (2005: 2, 3).
15  Nicolai *et al.* (2010) purport that capital markets have begun to follow a similar management strategy.
16  Nissan annual report (1999: 4, 5).
17  See, for example, Morgan and Takahashi (2002).
18  See Magee (2003) for further details. Ghosn has also published nine books about how he successfully accomplished NRP. His success story was later published in *Manga*. For example, a comic-book version of *The True Story of Carlos Ghosn* was written by Togashima and Toda in 2002. The authors state that 'two years after Ghosn came to Nissan, its commitment was met one full year ahead of schedule and Nissan is moving with surprising speed towards recovery. Ghosn is the most notable leader in the world. There is an answer to Japanese economic regeneration in this book' (Togashima and Toda 2002: 1).
19  See Khurana (2002).
20  http://www.interbrand.com/ja/best-global-brands/best-global-brands-2008/best-glob al-brands-2007.aspx  and  http://www.interbrand.com/en/best-global-brands/Best-Global-Brands-2011.aspx
21  http://www.interbrand.com/ja/best-global-brands/best-global-brands-methodology/ Brand-Strength.aspx
22  See, for example, Graham (2003).
23  Sixty-one books about commitment management have been published in Japanese and in translation since 2001.
24  See Katzenbach (2001).
25  Nissan annual report (2005: 2).
26  See, for example, Matanle (2003); Nishihara (2002).
27  See, for example, Graham (2003).
28  See Olcott (2008).
29  See Mehri (2005).
30  Engelen (2003), Capelli *et al.* (1997), Hassard *et al.* (2009) for a US perspective on this.
31  See Graham (2003).
32  Nissan has been ranked in first place in terms of the disparity between the annual earnings of the company's top executives and the remainder of its employees (*Weekly Diamond*, 13 September 2008: 106). Their annual pay is 37.5 times as high as those of the rest of employees.
33  *Weekly Diamond*, 16 September 2006: 59.
34  See, for example, Capelli *et al.* (1997).
35  Nissan annual report (1999: 4, 5).
36  Ibid.: 3, 4, 5.
37  See, for example, Matanle (2003); McCann *et al.* (2006).

38  See, for example, Matanle (2003).
39  See Littler (2006).
40  See Froud *et al.* (2000).
41  See, for example, Froud *et al.* (2000); Khurana (2002).
42  See Fligstein (1990).
43  Ghosn, C. (2001) *Renaissance: Challenge to Reform.* Tokyo: Diamond sha.
44  Recruit Holdings, NTT DOCOMO and Sumitomo 3M also adopted commitment management.
45  See Baumol *et al.* (2003); Littler (2006); Froud *et al.* (2000).
46  Nissan annual report (2005: 2).
47  According to Nissan's COO, Toshiyuki Shiga. See http://www.fujixerox.co.jp/sup port/xdirect/magazine/rp0701/07011a.html#pageTop
48  See Ono (1978).
49  Ibid.
50  There are 1,500 employees above manager level. See http://business.nikkeibp.co. jp/article/topics/20070510/124461/?P=1
51  Toyokeizai (2005).
52  See, for example, Morgan and Takahashi (2002).
53  I was given a copy of the leaflet by an HR director at Nissan's Sunderland plant when I visited in September 2008.
54  See Dore (2006).
55  See Goffee and Jones (2006).
56  See Ghosn and Ries (2003) *Carlos Ghosn Talks about his Management Style.* Nihonkeizai Shinbunsha: Tokyo).
57  His private life has been written about in a number of books. His wife, Rita Ghosn, also published a book, in Japanese, about Ghosn's family values. According to her, the Ghosn family has lived in Tokyo since 1999, when Ghosn came to Nissan as COO, and she introduces the family as Japanophiles. Through such detailed and extensive forms of media management, Ghosn came to be widely acknowledged as not only one of the 'celebrity business elite' but also a well-known and popular figure among the general Japanese public. Ghosn is thus most unlike the typical traditional Japanese CEO, who tends not to have a high profile (Dore 2006).
58  See Froud (2006).
59  See Littler (2006).
60  Such as in Ahmadjian and Robinson (2001)'s 'new institutional' analysis.
61  See, for example, Aoki (1996); Dore (2000); Morgan and Takahashi (2002).
62  See, for example, Dore (2011); Olcott (2009).
63  See, for example, Froud *et al.* (2000); Littler (2006).
64  See, for example, Aoki (1986); Matanle (2003); McCann *et al.* (2004); Morgan and Takahashi (2002); Sato (1997).
65  See Baumol (2003); Littler (2006).
66  See Jacoby (2005) and Vogel (2006).

# 4   Bank of Tokyo-Mitsubishi UFJ
## Brand-led narrative management

## 4.1. Introduction

This chapter examines the case of Bank of Tokyo-Mitsubishi UFJ (hereafter BTMU). BTMU, which has been highly valued as a trustworthy firm by Japanese society is part of the Mitsubishi *keiretsu,* which historically maintains the authority of the Mitsubishi brand. The Mitsubishi *keiretsu* has shaped its business strategy[1] and there have long been institutional restrictions within the Mitsubishi *keiretsu* group that limit the prospects for drastic change.[2] BTMU could, therefore, be expected to keep a low profile within such a historically embedded institution. Yet this case study reveals that the bank is increasingly showing signs of following US ways of restructuring, and that it engages in complex and increasingly dramatic forms of narrative management. Its restructuring message has also 'sold' surprisingly well with wider Japanese society. However, similarly to Nissan Motor (see Chapter 3), close examination of the interview data reveals that the outcome of this case shows few signs of change within the bank; there is once again a distinct gap between saying and doing. This chapter reflects a quite unique process of organizational change and narrative management: in this case maintaining the credibility of the Mitsubishi brand is given far greater priority than implementing the publicly announced reform plans. In contrast to Nissan, BTMU's narrative focuses much more strongly on the *keiretsu* brand, and is thus a more historically constrained and more institutionally embedded form of narrative management.

## 4.2 BTMU's US-style reform plans

The following chapter explains that BTMU, as a highly respected organization with considerable financial power, adopted a steady, trusted and quite traditional Japanese strategy of reform and narrative making. In contrast to other financially weaker companies (such as the almost bankrupt Nissan), the bank has had less incentive to respond rapidly to the recent fashion for the US-style high-risk, financialized approach aimed at the investor community. Nevertheless, BTMU has announced new restructuring plans that include more US-style reform measures. BTMU has found it necessary recently to change its strategy towards a much more intense focus on external audiences, and thus has become a more visible public firm than previously. This section first provides background information about the bank, and second describes and explains the background to BTMU's restructuring plans.

### 4.2.1 BTMU

BTMU[3] is a pre-war *zaibatsu* firm and is the main financial organization in the Mitsubishi *keiretsu* group (alongside such giants as Mitsubishi Motor Corporation and Mitsubishi Heavy Industries Ltd). BTMU comprises 33,827 employees (as of 2011), and Mitsubishi UFJ financial group, led by BTMU, is currently ranked as the biggest bank in Japan (see Table 4.1).

Prior to the merger between Bank of Tokyo Mitsubishi and UFJ Bank into BTMU in 2006, Bank of Mitsubishi merged with Bank of Tokyo in 1996 to form Bank of Tokyo Mitsubishi (BTM) in order to strengthen its market share (see Table 4.2). The Mitsubishi firm is very well known and highly valued and trusted by the Japanese public, despite the scandals at Mitsubishi Motors.[5] (In 2000 and 2004 Mitsubishi Fuso failed to announce that its automobiles were needed to be recalled for safety reasons.[6])

As a Mitsubishi *keiretsu* firm, BTM has built up high levels of trust within Japanese society since the pre-war era. Although the Mitsubishi *keiretsu* system was established after the Second World War, it actually has a longer tradition that predates it. Mitsubishi *zaibatsu* was founded by Yataro Iwasaki in 1873. Mitsubishi *zaibatsu* was one of the biggest three *zaibatsu:* Mitsui, Mitsubishi, and Sumitomo. When Japan was occupied by the USA after the war, the use of the name *zaibatsu,* which referred to big Japanese monopolistic enterprisers run by prominent families, was prohibited. Mitsubishi *zaibatsu* had to change its name and be separated into smaller units. The term *zaibatsu* had become commonplace in Japan because it was representative of a large, authoritative group with a long tradition, and had won the Japanese

*Table 4.1* Consolidated assets of domestic large financial groups in Japan (as of December 2008)[4]

| Name of financial group (FG) | Consolidated assets (trillion yen) |
|---|---|
| 1. Mitsubishi UFJ FG | 198.89 |
| 2. Mizuho FG | 157.19 |
| 3. Mitsui Sumito FG | 116.18 |
| 4. Risona HD | 39.21 |
| 5. Sumitomo Trust Bank | 22.79 |
| 6. Chuo Mitsui Trust and Banking | 14.64 |
| 7. Shinsei Bank | 12.23 |
| 8. Aozora Bank | 6.35 |

people's confidence. Therefore, after the occupation ended in 1952, they began to use the name again, although *keiretsu* has come to predominate as the alternative system to *zaibatsu* because of changes in the business environment. The Mitsubishi *keiretsu* network was instrumental in helping the Japanese economy to develop after the Second World War and grew large and influential. The authority of the Mitsubishi *keiretsu* has developed over time and institutional relationships have been formed among the group.[7]

As one example of an institutional relationship, only elite internal candidates can become presidents of BTMU. Only staff who graduated from Tokyo University can be considered as candidates for president as they are trained in the management of the Mitsubishi *keiretsu* group.[8] Furthermore the Mitsubishi *keiretsu* has a strong relationship among the *keiretsu* group. Bearing witness to this is the fact that BTMU has maintained the ratio of cross-shareholdings in order to strengthen relationships within the *keiretsu*. In 2008 the biggest shareholders were composed of seven Japanese firms: The Master Trust Bank of Japan (which owns 6.92 per cent), Japan Trustee Service Bank (4.86 per cent), Mitsubishi UFJ Financial Group (4.54 per cent), Nippon Life Insurance Company (2.57 per cent), State Street Bank and Trust (3.39 per cent), Meiji Yasuda Life Insurance Company (1.27 per cent), Toyota Motors (1.37 per cent). Five of them share stocks within the Mitsubishi *keiretsu* group. (In the case of Toyota BTMU is the main bank).

Fundamentally all of the remaining Japanese banks faced a turning point when the bubble burst in Japan in the early 1990s. They were saddled with huge non-performing loans while being under pressure from globalization, as well as from the long drawn-out stagnation, deflation, and de-regulation of the Japanese economy. As one of the ways to reform, a large number of banks chose to merge with domestic banks. Bank of Sanwa merged with Bank of Tokai to become UFJ bank in 2002. UFJ bank (which was ranked as the fourth biggest Japanese bank), underwent another merger with BTM (which was ranked as the biggest bank) in 2006, because UFJ bank had been suffering from severe deficits drawn from a very large volume of bad loans among the biggest Japanese banks. BTM was also affected by the long Japanese

*Table 4.2* History of BTMU

| 1800s | 1996 | 2002 | 2006 |
|---|---|---|---|
| Bank of Mitsubishi (since 1880) | Bank of Tokyo-Mitsubishi (BTM) (since 1996) | | Bank of Tokyo-Mitsubishi UFJ (BTMU) (since 2006) |
| Bank of Tokyo (since 1946) | | | |
| Bank of Sanwa (since 1877) | | UFJ bank (since 2002) | |
| Bank of Tokai (since 1877) | | | |

Source: BTMU.

recession, but it had the fewest non-performing loans among the major Japanese banks. Indeed, BTM has shown stable financial results over the past ten years. BTMU essentially rescued UFJ bank, and left the Mitsubishi name on the first line of the new corporate name. After this merger, most of the board positions were occupied by senior figures from BTM, and UFJ Bank was obliged to adopt BTM's internal systems (according to interview data from a branch general manager[9]).

Even though it was heavily supported by the strong Mitsubishi brand, BTMU announced a US-style restructuring plan. It was listed in the New York Stock Exchange in 2001. Its major restructuring included changes to the system of corporate governance from 2001 onwards. Three non-executive directors were introduced (there are 17 board members of BTMU in total). Three of the five audit committee members are recruited from outside the company. As the following sections will demonstrate, public statements made by BTMU increasingly emulate US-style business language.

### 4.2.2 BTMU's US-style reform plans

Public statements by BTMU increasingly reflect US-style language aimed at the investor community. BTMU has showed signs of following the currently popular strategy of US-style management that has been introduced into Japanese firms (at least in their official announcements and documents). Based on the interview data gathered at BTMU, staff have acknowledged BTMU's imitative behaviour:

> My firm is undertaking organizational restructuring based on the US approach. I feel that the bank just follows a current social trend that has encouraged firms to carry out employment downsizing based on an US-style business model.

BTMU also makes very explicit references to US-style governance in its public claims. The following corporate review in the 2006 annual report is one of such example:

> Regarding financial performance, our goal is to achieve earnings, financial soundness and long-term growth that are on par with the leading financial institutions in Europe and the United States ...
>
> Our capital policy will maintain the proper balance among measures to distribute earnings to shareholders, raise our equity capital and make strategic investments aimed at growth. The full repayment of public funds gave us flexibility on raising dividends, repurchasing stock and taking other *shareholder-oriented actions*. We will frequently review the amount of dividends based on operating results, dividends at other major Japanese companies and large European and US banks, and other factors.

Above all, we will aim to allocate earnings in a manner that is best suited to increasing *shareholder value* over the long term.[10]

BTMU was the only bank to fully return public funds to the Japanese government as of March 2006, and the firm then indicated that it would focus on shareholder-based management strategy. Next the bank announced the development of its corporate governance system. The extract from the company's annual report (below) highlights the fact that following the listing of its shares on the New York Stock Exchange in 2001 Mitsubishi Tokyo Financial Group (MTFG) has pursued US methods of corporate governance and transparency:

> Maintaining the objectivity and transparency of corporate decisions is a priority at MTFG. Along these lines, we are implementing strict corporate governance. We have, for instance, invited outside directors to join MTFG's board of directors, while BTM and MTBC are similarly reforming their boards. We are also putting into place a Compliance Advisory Committee of outside lawyers, accountants, and business executives to monitor our management of MTFG.
>   MTFG's distinction, meanwhile, as the only Japanese banking group listed on the New York Stock Exchange, subjects it to that market's disclosure rules and therefore brings more transparency to our operations and results than those of our competitors.[11]

This announcement shows that the bank is trying to demonstrate that it has a closer convergence with US-style corporate governance than other Japanese banks. The bank also emphasizes this point in its 2006 annual report as follows:

> We have a corporate governance system that meets the high standards required by our New York Stock Exchange listing. Our financial soundness is thus accompanied by reliable management systems.[12]

Interestingly, however, the statements read differently in the English and Japanese versions of official documents. For instance, we can see the difference between the following two messages about the appointment of outside directors.

The English version reads thus:

> We have appointed several outside directors to the Board of Directors. Furthermore, as a measure to enhance supervision of management by outside parties, we have introduced a voluntary system of board committees comprised mainly of outside members and chaired by an outside

director, such as the Internal Audit and Compliance Committee, the Nomination Committee and the Compensation Committee.[13]

The Japanese version reads thus:

Three of our seventeen directors have been appointed from outside the company.[14]

The message about outside directors in the English version does not give the number of outside directors, but that the Japanese version[15] does. In the case of Shinsei Bank (see Chapter 5), at June 2008 eleven of its fourteen board members were outside directors,[16] while only three out of seventeen board members were drawn from outside BTMU. The Japanese firms listed in the first section of the Tokyo Stock Exchange are required to appoint at least one outside director under a law introduced in 2006.[17] BTMU has satisfied the requirements of the new law but the bank is also listed on the New York Stock Exchange, and listed firms are required to appoint half of their board members from outside.[18] The appointment of three outside directors by itself cannot give foreign investors the impression of advanced governance. In the meantime, BTMU is deliberately presenting an image about its more developed stage of Americanized governance to the Japanese audience. As the literature[19] suggests, Japanese firms are beginning to introduce external board members. Yet it is almost impossible to bring in outside directors, as Japanese firms tend towards cronyism.[20] It seems that BTMU has been particularly influenced by institutional pressure and is attempting to become more transparent and investor friendly – at least this is certainly the image it is trying to convey through its emerging IR strategy.

Furthermore, BTMU's shareholder-oriented tactics can be seen in statements made in 2002 about its restructuring plans designed to improve shareholder value, when it acknowledged the need for 'aggressive' and 'rigorous trimming' of personnel and branches:

Our Medium-Term Business Plan recognizes the need to improve operating profit. Among the critical ways that we will do this is by rigorously trimming our operating costs and non-core assets.

- We seek to reduce our full-time domestic staff to approximately 18,000 people by the end of fiscal 2004. By the end of fiscal 2001 we had trimmed our staff by more than 1,000, to 21,385 personnel.
- We are also aggressively trimming our branch network in Japan. By the end of fiscal 2004 we expect to have pared approximately fifty branches from our domestic network. In fiscal 2001 we closed thirty-three branches in Japan, bringing our domestic group network to 351 branches by the end of the period.

- We are, in addition, targeting reductions in our non-core real estate assets, including corporate recreational properties. In fiscal 2001 we closed, sold or outsourced approximately ¥10 billion of our non-core real estate assets.[21]

The bank announced asset and employment downsizing in 2002. However, in 1998 the bank reported its worst ever financial performance with a net loss of −¥0.19 billion. During this period BTMU and other banks had been suffering from the need to settle non-performing debts. Although twenty-one Japanese major banks started receiving public funds in 1998, the bankruptcies continued; some of the biggest major banks, Long-term Credit Bank, Nippon Credit Bank and Hokkaido-Takushoku Bank, collapsed in that year. In 1999 further public funds to the tune of ¥7.4 trillion were injected into fifteen major banks.[22] BTMU received public funds in 1998 and in 1999. In keeping with Japanese firms' reluctance to instigate reform plans, BTMU[23] did not start restructuring at that time. However, BTMU announced organizational restructuring for the purpose of contributing to the raising of shareholder value in 2002. In January 2003 BTMU returned all public funds to the government.[24] This was much earlier than other major banks (such as Mitsui-Sumitomo Bank, Mizuho Bank and Risona Bank), which did not return borrowed funds to the government until 2006. Thus, BTMU has shifted its focus towards the investor community and adopted US-style reform measures after its recovery from non-performing loans.

BTMU has increasingly shown signs of following policies with US-style management. Again, BTMU's public claims seem to clash with the arguments of past Japanese studies about the slow and traditional ways of restructuring among Japanese firms. One of the reasons is the changing of the law, as recent literature on Japan indicates.[25]

Have the new reform plans actually brought about change within the bank? The next sections will examine data gathered at BTMU regarding BTMU's new reform plans as well as looking at the specific details of how its shareholder-oriented actions and its employment downsizing were enacted.

## 4.3 External and internal acceptance of BTMU's reform plans

As described above, BTMU has developed policies that demonstrate a strong degree of US-style business strategies. How have the Japanese public and corporate bankers reacted to BTMU's new restructuring plans, given that the company is still to a large extent constrained by it's highly traditional background? Interestingly, BTMU's reform plans appear to have received strong external comprehension and support, and this section will demonstrate that this is because the IR developed by BTMU was carefully crafted to connect with long-standing social trust traditionally extended to the Mitsubishi corporate brand. With the Mitsubishi brand behind them, BTMU's approach is trusted and the new US-style reforms are relayed to audiences in ways that remain concordant with the familiar messages from Mitsubishi. Moreover, while its new approach has been externally well understood, it also appears to have been internally understood and validated by employees, and this in turn adds further support to the project for change.

### 4.3.1 External Acceptance of BTMU's Reform Plan

As part of its US-style management strategy, since 2002 BTMU has publicly announced employment downsizing plans aimed at reforming its cost structures. BTMU's public statements increasingly incorporate US language aimed at the investor community. An example of this appeared in the bank's annual reports for 2003 and 2004:

> We have adopted *a more aggressive management approach* intended to increase profits and reduce costs.[26]
>
> Reducing our operating costs is an indispensable element of our strategy to increase our profits, and costs in all aspects of our operations are being rigorously reviewed as we pursue our cost cutting targets. In the year under review, we reduced staff to approximately 20,000 and reduced the number of domestic branches and other offices to 335. As a result of these and other measures, we cut our expense ratio under Japanese GAAP by 4.3 points year-on-year to 47.4%. As well as reductions in the number of branches that we operate, we are also *realizing synergies* between Group members; and by September 2003, BTM[27] and Mitsubishi Securities had combined operations in 27 branches. Through aggressive reform of our delivery channels, including expanded utilisation of ATMs [automatic teller machines] and Internet delivery channels, we aim to further reduce our costs while maintaining the high quality and wide range of financial services that our customers expect.[28]

Those messages indicate that the bank focuses on cost reduction in terms of the number of employees, branches and other assets. The Japanese business media seems to react positively to such aggressive messages. The following media report clearly suggests that BTMU is attempting to emulate US-based globalized banks such as Citigroup, which are supposedly the 'best in the world':

> The firm first reduced costs by restructuring into divisions. It has closed 37 branches and 82 ATMs over the past three years. In late 2001 in particular it made tremendous efforts to cut costs. It saved billions of yen in advertising expenses compared to previous years. Also the number of cars used by branch managers for business purposes was decreased. The firm's costs were reduced from ¥231.7 billion to ¥211.6 billion over two years.
>
> BTMU is aiming to be the best bank in the world, like Citibank. As the best Japanese bank, BTMU is driving the Japanese financial sector, so the public thought that the bank would not need to introduce reforms. Now BTMU is actively determined to become the best bank.[29]

The media reported that BTMU had reformed sufficiently well to be able to function effectively amid tough global competition. Although Nissan Motor's reform plans were heavily criticized by the public in 1999 (see Chapter 3), BTMU's reform plans had a higher degree of social acceptance, possibly because Nissan's reforms had come earlier, and the use of such radical plans had since become popular in Japan.

In particular, BTMU has used less PR in its reform plans than Nissan, which was an early and major adopter of active public communication strategies. Yet BTMU has managed to win strong support from its external audience, just as Nissan did. Why is this?

Despite BTMU's limited use of public communications, the media is highly attuned to stories about Mitsubishi and always reports on its restructuring plans. The following reports from mass media reveal how deep the social acceptance of BTMU is, mainly as a result of the long-standing importance of the Mitsubishi corporate brand in Japan.

> BTMU has a strong reputation because of the association with the Mitsubishi brand. This credibility has attracted deposits, which can generate further profits under its reforms. With the Mitsubishi brand, BTMU has been a winner among Japanese banks, so we thought that the bank did not need to reform. Yet the bank has now started an aggressive reform plan, which has good implications for its future given that BTMU is aiming to be the best bank in the world.[30]
>
> BTMU aims to become one of the top ten financial groups in the world with regard to total current market price during 2006. BTMU, which is part of a big *keiretsu* group, has set itself a magnificent objective, which has sent shockwaves throughout the financial sector in Japan.[31]

The public shows understanding and raised expectations of BTMU's reform plans based on the value of the Mitsubishi brand. To some extent such social support for the BTMU brand means that there is less incentive for BTMU to reform as drastically as it had previously announced. BTMU's financial performance and net income have been stable in for the past ten years (see Table 4.3).

One of the interviewees for this research has worked at the bank for more than twenty years, He said that as a result of BTMU's strong social reputation the public is always interested in BTMU and try to find out more about the bank themselves:

> The Mitsubishi brand has been built up since the Mitsubishi *zaibatsu* was founded by Yataro Iwasaki. Mitsubishi's tradition, history and success have been publicized to the public via TV documentaries, books and so on. The Mitsubishi brand is rooted in the Japanese consciousness. Even recent activities are transmitted by them. When we publish annual reports, CSR reports and so on, the public quickly becomes familiar with

them. When I talk to my customers, they are already very well informed about the bank. I always feel that what we say and do is very influential within the wider Japanese society and the Japanese economy.

The success story of the authoritive Mitsubishi brand has been transmitted to the wider society since the pre-war era and Mitsubishi's brand value is derived from the pre-war *zaibatsu* firms. The Mitsubishi brand is based on a powerful sense of corporate history and tradition, which has been believed, respected and shared by the Japanese society for many years. The bank does not need to make public announcements because people are already very aware of the Mitsubishi brand. At least 100 books[32], [33] have been published about Mitsubishi over the past 80 years, which is considerably more than those about Nissan. A wide variety of authors such as historians, novelists, business researchers and academics have written about the Mitsubishi *keiretsu, zaibatsu*, and Mitsubishi's founder, Yataro Iwasaki. Many describe Yataro Iwasaki as a successful and charismatic leader.[34] These business history books are widely read by Japanese salaryman. Peter Drucker (2004)[35] compared Iwasaki to the US business titans such as J. P. Morgan, Andrew Carnegie and John D. Rockefeller. In addition, stories about Mitsubishi and Iwasaki's success were published as *Manga*. [36] Thus Iwasaki and the Mitsubishi brand image are glorified and continue to be publicly shared.

Owing to its high social status that has been built up over a long period, BTMU does not have the incentive to use PR as much as other firms. Rather, BTMU may be more deliberate in its public disclosures to prevent its long-lasting and strong social reputation from being damaged.

Thus, external acceptance of BTMU's new reform plans is closely related to the Mitsubishi brand, the power of which gives BTMU management

*Table 4.3* BTMU's financial performance (2000–10)

| Year | Financial performance (¥) |
| --- | --- |
| 2000 | 174 billion |
| 2001 | 225 billion |
| 2002 | –92 billion |
| 2003 | 359 billion |
| 2004 | 227 billion |
| 2005 | 1.114 trillion |
| 2006 | 494 billion |
| 2007 | 669 billion |
| 2008 | 550 billion |
| 2009 | –366 billion |
| 2010 | 342 billion |

Source: BTMU annual reports for 2000–10.

considerable room to manoeuvre. This case shows that BTMU attracts media and public attention not primarily through its active disclosures but rather through maintaining the Mitsubishi brand value. The way in which BTMU adopts IR is different from Nissan, which is a somewhat more high profile organization, with more of a global orientation and a very well-known international CEO, and which had to extricate itself from considerable financial distress. In spite of this, BTMU has certainly placed greater importance on IR. As is the case at Nissan, IR play an important part in organizational change, but in the specific case of BTMU, it takes on a different form, reflecting the *maintenance* of the brand value, rather than the firms' creation of an entirely new story.

### *4.3.2 Internal acceptance and validation*

While BTMU's reform plans have been well understood externally, they also appear to have been internally understood and validated. Interview data gathered at BTMU regularly demonstrated that staff understand public announcements about BTMU's adoption of US-style management:

> The term 'US-style management' has become popular in society. We learnt something about this and employ some terms. BTMU is a public firm, which means that we need to make a profit. We have to think of shareholder value, stock price, ROE and so on. We get our salaries, so I feel that we need to make efficient use of capital contributed by shareholders.

Insiders are highly cognizant of the current trend for financialized governance in Japan. Given this new knowledge, staff are in agreement with BTMU's US-style reform plans:

> The message from my bank includes the term 'shareholder value'. BTMU implies that the value depends on whether a shareholder wants to keep holding the firm's stocks or not. The value is also created by a dividend and a share price. Capital contributed by a shareholder is very important. Following the sub-prime crisis, the US government injected public funds into public banks. Likewise, we cannot operate unless there we have sufficient capital, so it is important for our business that the shareholders retain our stocks. Naturally we try to meet their expectations.

> Nobody doubted that employees own the firm, but now we commonly think that shareholders own the firm. Of course, there have been a lot of improvements that we have not introduced for shareholders yet. Yet the top management started to move in a new direction, 'shareholder value',

which is one of the most important things that public firms should do under increasing external pressure.

These staff members have noticed that the bank's efforts on behalf of its shareholders are inadequate. Yet BTMU bankers show their understanding about the growing importance of shareholder value and support their new management's attempts to deliver value for shareholders. BTMU's public announcements about shareholder value creation have filtered through well to internal staff, even though past studies have indicated that it is difficult for Japanese employees who work under the traditional Japanese HR system to adapt to a US-style management system.[37]

So how and why has BTMU secured internal support for its new reform plans? How have the plans actually been put into practice within the bank? This point is addressed in further detail in the following section.

## 4.4 BTMU's narrative management

This section will show how BTMU has influenced its staff to understand and generally accept its new reform plans, and will also explore how BTMU (one of the oldest pre-war *zaibatsu* firms) has carried out its supposedly radical reforms within the bank. Internal data shows that BTMU does not need to change as drastically as its public announcements suggest, owing to its strong social credibility achieved through the Mitsubishi brand. BTMU is offering a public narrative of organizational change, while leaving its main operations largely unchanged. This is another example of corporate narratives acting as a smokescreen behind which little really changes. In other words, the corporate narrative of change is a means by which the organization can claim to have changed while remaining largely unreformed.

### 4.4.1 BTMU's narrative management: employment downsizing

Similarly to Nissan, when BTMU disclosed its organizational reform plans it released only the most sketchy details. BTMU did not disclose how the bank planned to downsize in its annual reports but indicated the probability of a large number of lay-offs. How did these its drastic reform plans in 2002 revealed significant facts:

> The firm's early retirement system ceased to operate after 2004. The firm asked all employees over the age of 45 years to retire early voluntarily in exchange for an additional pension package. To date, we have never felt that the bank has drastically reformed.

> The bank is so conservative that it did not cut the number of employees. Instead it simply cut the number of branches. It temporarily employed an early retirement scheme for those over the age of 45 years. In any case all

employees have to move to the bank's subsidiary and affiliated firms within the Mitsubishi *keiretsu* at around that age. My bosses went to the subsidiary firms at 45. This means that an early retirement scheme at the age of 45 actually does not mean anything.

According to those bankers, the firm employed an early retirement scheme, which is one of the main ways of downsizing in many Japanese firms.[38] Drastic employment downsizing was not carried out by the firm,[39] and a voluntary early retirement scheme is not regarded as employment downsizing in Japan.[40] Voluntary early retirement at the age of 45 years is meaningless as staff have to leave the bank at that age anyway; this is implicit in the system at BTMU. BTMU has never disclosed that it expects its employees to retire at the age of 45 years, and this might provide the firm with the incentive to conceal its adoption of an early retirement scheme. In 2002 the bank announced a decrease of approximately 20,000 employees by the end of 2004, as shown in section 4.2. However, the workforce has not decreased since 2002 (see Table 4.4). The numbers increased significantly in 2006, when Bank of Tokyo-Mitsubishi merged with Bank of UFJ. Employment numbers fell back slightly after 2008, but certainly there is no sign of the mass lay-offs that were announced in 2002.

It appears that BTMU is offering a public narrative of downsizing and cost control while actually continuing much as before; this is a now familiar case of false signalling designed to follow institutional pressures and to impress the business and investor community, but without causing massive internal disruption.[42]

Information about increasing recruitment was also manipulated by BTMU. According to one manager who worked at BTMU headquarters, 'Recently the firm has increased the number of workers at retail branches. I think that around 1,000 staff join as mid-career workers every year'. Even when the firm dramatically increased the number of employees during 2005–08, it chose not to disclose this fact in its annual reports. BTMU actually increased the number of employees in most years (See Table 4.4), and it appears to be

*Table 4.4* Number of employees at BTMU (2002–10)[41]

| Year | Total number of employees |
| --- | --- |
| 2002 | 34,846 |
| 2003 | 37,380 |
| 2004 | 36,624 |
| 2005 | 37,754 |
| 2006 | 57,600 |
| 2007 | 60,291 |
| 2008 | 58,725 |
| 2009 | 55,650 |
| 2010 | 55,300 |

deliberately providing very selective information, emphasizing drastic reforms to the cost structure. Thus there is a clear gap between saying and doing in terms of employment downsizing, and an obvious use of false signalling. BTMU's reform plan for employment downsizing is clearly a part of its narrative management providing the smokescreen effect needed to shield the reality of little actual change.

### 4.4.2 BTMU's narrative management: shareholder-oriented actions

In this section, shareholder-oriented action, one of BTMU's new plans for reform, is examined, along with whether its staff accept and engage in the bank's shareholder-oriented actions.

BTMU's internal discourse about its restructuring plans, like Nissan's, delivers a different message from the message relayed to its external audience. The bank has introduced Mitsubishi brand management and has endeavoured to get its staff on board and the public has accepted the bank's restructuring plans based on its corporate brand authority. Internally BTMU shows the beneficial impact of the Mitsubishi brand on its financial performance, and makes full use of internal newsletters which are distributed exclusively to BTMU employees. In one such newsletter from 2001[43] the bank emphasizes that it continues to realize the importance of upholding the Mitsubishi brand.

> 'Brand' has received attention as a key word in corporate restructuring. About 20–30 per cent of a company's corporate value (stock price) is enhanced by brand value. Here, Professor Kunio Ito, a corporate brand management specialist, explains the concept.
> A 'corporate brand' is a corporate asset that improves corporate value. A corporate brand establishes a bond between a firm and its shareholders and customers. As the market becomes more competitive, 'brand' becomes an important management resource and its value needs to be enhanced. This is an important component of corporate restructuring.[44]

BTMU indicates the importance of the Mitsubishi brand value to the last. Through its use of academic theory, the bank internally announces the close connection between the Mitsubishi brand and the company's share price. The newsletter refers to Ito's book, *Corporate Brand Management* [45]. In his book, Ito explains that if customers' and investors' expectations of a corporate brand continue to be satisfied, it helps to achieve stable profits and share values over the long term. In other words, Ito argues that a corporate brand plays a central role in enhancing share price. The bank tries to validate its brand management through showing the theoretically supported effect on shareholder value of maintaining the Mitsubishi brand value. This particular newsletter also highlighted the bank's listing in the New York Stock Exchange. The bank attempts to control its internal environment so that staff can understand what the bank says and does. Recent literature examining

Japanese firms' use of IR[46] concluded that more changes have occurred in Japanese firms than previously. Yet Japanese firms' internal discourse (which is not really discussed in detail by existing literature) shows a rather different picture.

BTMU's internal discourse is strongly characterized by a focus on brand management. Interestingly, the following interviewee, who has worked for over twenty years at the bank, pointed out that brand management has been central to BTMU and its predecessors for decades:

> How do you create shareholder value? The long-term method leads to increased shareholder value. Neither thinking of stock price on a short-term basis nor the US CEO's way of managing suits Japanese firms, and employees will not follow in such circumstances. In the case of the Japanese firms, a new person does not join a firm as the CEO; rather, an existing employee, who has worked under lifetime employment, is promoted to CEO. Executives one level below the CEO ensure that the CEO does not take short-term steps, because they need to consider their own interest in the firm's future.
>
> We do business by building on our corporate brand or corporate name. The Mitsubishi Committee on Public Information is careful to manage the Mitsubishi brand not as a bank but as a Mitsubishi *zaibatsu* within the Mitsubishi *keiretsu* group. Whenever I am talking about financial products I can't use the name Mitsubishi, unless that Committee permits it. Bankers from the Bank of Mitsubishi are especially protective of the brand. Employees need to follow the rules in order not to cause any trouble for other firms belonging to the Mitsubishi *keiretsu*. We therefore cannot do anything that might compromise the brand.

The interviewee spoke about the power of the Mitsubishi brand heritage. The brand is closely policed by the Mitsubishi Committee on Public Information. The Mitsubishi brand is a more important factor for the firm than simply making profits.[47] The Mitsubishi committee is composed of 40 firms who are members of the *Kinyōkai* (a monthly CEO meeting within the Mitsubishi *keiretsu* group). Table 4.5 lists the *Kinyōkai* members.

The Mitsubishi Committee has the following principle, which has been in place since its inception:

> Our aim is to establish trust and goodwill between us and our customers. We seek to improve the image of the Mitsubishi group and contribute to the development of society. For mutual education we have interchange between the Mitsubishi group firms.[49]

Mitsubishi's image is the most important factor for the Mitsubishi group. This principle was actually created by Koyata Iwasaki, one of the founders of the Mitsubishi *zaibatsu*:

The Mitsubishi group's members, many of which are affiliated and wholly owned subsidiary companies, strategically represent a diversified business matrix. The common philosophies are the Mitsubishi Principles. The Principles are the management philosophies created by the fourth president, Koyata Iwasaki, and are inherited like an unbroken string of traditions.[50]

The philosophy of the 'unbroken string of traditions' has been shared within the Mitsubishi *keiretsu* group, and is used as justification for bank insiders to prioritize protecting the Mitsubishi brand over improving shareholder value. The Mitsubishi brand is protected by the Mitsubishi *keiretsu* group and all staff take lifetime employment for granted. In this sense, as part of the Mitsubishi group, BTMU may be under less external pressure to change the firm than other organizations, especially those experiencing or having experienced acute financial distress (such as Nissan and Shinsei Bank).

In order to protect the Mitsubishi brand, staff at BTMU have been asked to take a conservative approach to business. This is evidenced by a comparison between interview data of a former Bank of Mitsubishi banker and a

*Table 4.5* Mitsubishi committee[48]

| Mitsubishi committee members | | | |
| --- | --- | --- | --- |
| The Bank of Tokyo-Mitsubishi UFJ | Mitsubishi Fuso Truck and Bus Corporation | Mitsubishi Shokuhin | Mitsubishi UFJ Securities Holdings |
| Mitsubishi Kakoki Kaisha | P.S. Mitsubishi Construction | Mitsubishi Rayon | Mitsubishi Estate Company |
| Mitsubishi Corporation | Mitsubishi Aluminum | IT Frontier Corporation | Mitsubishi Precision |
| Mitsubishi Heavy Industries | Mitsubishi Steel | Toyo Engineering Works | Kirin Holdings Company |
| Mitsubishi Chemical Corporation | Mitsubishi Gas Chemical Company | Nippon Yusen Kabushiki Kaisha (NYK Line) | Mitsubishi Space Software |
| Mitsubishi Motors Corporation | Mitsubishi Plastics | Asahi Glass | Mfg Mitsubishi Paper Mills |
| Tokyo Marin & Nichido Fire Insurance | Meiji Yasuda Life Insurance Company | Astomost Energy Corporation | Mitsubishi Materials Corporation |
| Mitsubishi Nuclear Fuel | Mitsubishi Ore Transport | Dai Nippon Toryo | Mitsubishi Electric Corporation |
| Nikon Corporation | Mitsubishi UFJ NICOS | JX Holdings | Mitsubishi Research Institute |
| Mitsubishi UFJ Lease & Finance Company | Mitsubishi UFJ Trust and Banking Corporation | Mitsubishi Auto Leasing Corporation | Mitsubishi Logistics Corporation |

UFJ banker. A Bank of Mitsubishi manager was asked about the differences between both banks:

> We never visit customers' homes for business in early morning (8 am) or late evening (9 pm), although the bankers at UFJ Bank do. We have an easy time of it. This conservative approach helps to maintain the credibility of our bank. Through the Mitsubishi corporate value, our daily work is never as tough as it is at other banks.

Staff are not under pressure to work hard and achieve the tough goals. However, the banker from UFJ bank said:

> The Mitsubishi Bank has the backing of the Mitsubishi group, while UFJ Bank is not included in a *zaibatsu*. We do not have customers who regularly choose us unless we do things differently from other banks. As a result we have to employ a more aggressive way of doing business.

The Mitsubishi brand is renowned as part of a big *keiretsu* group and customers choose Mitsubishi almost by default, out of public respect for the brand. As a result, a conservative approach has been allowed to develop for insiders. As a result, the credibility of the brand confers considerable advantages to the staff. This banker referred to the advantage of the brand thus:

> Whenever I exchange business cards with clients, they easily open their minds, respect me, and quickly trust me, which makes it is easy for us to talk shop. I have felt the value of the corporate name.
>   Our predecessors did not dabble in new forms of businesses and kept things as before, which led to us reaching the number one position in the banking sector in Japan. We have not taken any chances so far, which is our corporate culture. It is a fact that we are the strongest *zaibatsu* group. We can make profits without dabbling in new forms of business, though there may be some kind of emotional dependence on this. Although UFJ Bank does not have the backing of Mitsubishi, it had bad deficits through engagement with more risky businesses. If UFJ Bank needs to do ten different types of business, my firm [BTMU] only needs to do seven, which is enough for our business.

This BTMU banker enjoys the strong public trust accorded to the Mitsubishi brand. With the backing of the Mitsubishi story, the bank can do business more easily. As a result of the strong external credibility of the Mitsubishi brand, staff do not need to do anything special to gain a lead for the firm. Here, protecting the brand value is beneficial enough for its business.

  In fact brand management appears to be a long-lasting tradition within the whole Mitsubishi group. Interestingly, the Mitsubishi committee indicates the importance of 'the Mitsubishi group's DNA' as follows:

As the activities of Mitsubishi group companies become global in scope, it is important to firmly instil the Principles globally as the group's basic philosophy and values, to guide its activities across all nationalities and regions. I believe that the business activities of Mitsubishi group companies have fostered stakeholders' trust – the Mitsubishi brand has become synonymous with reliability, as well as with sincerity and integrity. I have received a similar affirmation of this point overseas as well. The reliability we have built up over many years is indeed one of the Mitsubishi group's unique strengths. By increasing our understanding of the culture and history of the Mitsubishi group, we must work to ensure that we pass down the Mitsubishi group's DNA, as expressed in the Principles, to the next generation all around the world.

In closing, by sharing this timeless philosophy and acting on it, I am sure that the Mitsubishi group can conduct activities that lead to a brighter future for societies, nations and the world at large.[51]

It is not shareholder value but the Mitsubishi group's DNA that the Mitsubishi Committee actually monitors. Interview data has shown that the Mitsubishi philosophy of maintaining a trusted corporate brand for its public audience is the number one priority for BTMU. This indicates that the Mitsubishi group's DNA or the unbroken string of traditions appears to be strongly shared among BTMU's staff. In this sense, it seems that the DNA has been passed down and penetrated over time and developed through complex iterations of the Mitsubishi brand management. This implies that BTMU's public announcements about the creation of shareholder value are far removed from actually engaging in US-style shareholder value management forms and actions.

We can see the difference between the net incomes of Bank of Tokyo Mitsubishi and UFJ bank in Table 4.6, suggesting that this expert brand management has an important effect on the bank's performance.

The table shows that prior to its merger with BTM, UFJ bank suffered large losses each year from 2001 to 2005, whereas Bank of Tokyo-Mitsubishi had demonstrated more stable financial performance before the merger. In 2008 it was ranked as top of the Japanese financial sector (see Table 4.1) and the *Keiretsu* system is an important feature in its business.[53]

The following interview data also indicate that there is little in BTMU's US-style reform plans to threaten the traditional ways of working for staff. Staff have already enjoyed considerable benefits from the existing brand management strategy. The following interviewee made an interesting point about this:

We know that BTMU began to talk about shareholder value more often than ever before. This is, of course, important. However, what we have to do every day never changes. Our way is always conservative. That's why we can work here in peace and quiet. This is the most important thing for the BTMU bankers, who have to work for their whole lives. If the top management was totally committed to the new ideology, as they officially said they were, we would all go into a panic and never support it.

This interview data shows that staff prefer an unchanged and peaceful work environment and do not want change. In fact, little change has occurred under BTMU's new reform plans and the gap between saying and doing is actually welcomed by insiders. Why are staff so opposed to organizational change? The Mitsubishi brand value already benefits the bankers' daily work and allows staff to maintain a conservative approach. Moreover, at a deeper level, staff indicated that they are proud to work at a bank which adheres to a traditional approach. This interviewee showed strong satisfaction at working under the socially legitimized Mitsubishi brand.

> Whenever I do business, our company name provides a sense of security for customers. The Mitsubishi brand gives me a sense of security. I enjoy working here. I feel warmth from a bank with a proud tradition that has been maintained by the strong Mitsubishi *keiretsu* network. We benefit greatly from the Mitsubishi brand that has been built up by our senior bankers over time.

Another banker who has worked at the bank since the Bank of Mitsubishi days made a similar point about the brand:

> I did not intend to work here this long when I started working here. Everyone knows about my firm with the highest brand value. With this value, we are often admired, respected and trusted by outsiders. I am very happy to work at this kind of big firm.

Staff claim that they can do business more satisfactorily owing to the Mitsubishi brand. Even after the bank announced the adoption of its US-style reform plans, employee work satisfaction levels have been protected. Thus, staff do not need to change and do not lose any benefits that they have enjoyed so far as a result of BTMU's restructuring plans. The supposed switch

*Table 4.6* Net incomes of Bank of Tokyo-Mitsubishi and UFJ Bank[52]

| Year | Bank of Tokyo-Mitsubishi (¥) | UFJ Bank (¥) |
|------|------------------------------|--------------|
| 2001 | 225 billion | 220.1 billion |
| 2002 | –92 billion | –1,114 billion |
| 2003 | 359 billion | –625.6 billion |
| 2004 | 227 billion | –375.5 billion |
| 2005 | 1.114 trillion | –681.9 billion |

to US-style business models has not in fact affected the staff and so they do not appear to exhibit radically changed or reduced work satisfaction levels.

## 4.5 A lesson from BTMU

This chapter has shown that BTMU, as part of the Mitsubishi *keiretsu* group, is under considerable institutional restraint when it comes to radical reform. It has made increased reference to its US-style reforms in its public statements aimed at the investor community. However, interview data shows that BTMU has not carried out drastic reforms, especially in terms of employment downsizing and shareholder value creation. There is thus a large gap between saying and doing. BTMU's restructuring announcement is a part of its narrative management designed to show the public that the organization has changed and is changing; yet below the surface, little substantial change is occurring. Moreover, the ways in which the narrative is told are also conservative. BTMU's narrative of change is itself couched in terms of the traditions of the Mitsubishi brand.

The plan includes US ways of restructuring and the public announcement shows that 'the bank takes shareholder-oriented actions, aiming to allocate earnings in a manner that is best suited to raising shareholder value over the long term'.[54] However, this study shows that BTMU's new plans are constituted by a rather unique set of processes. Given the strength of the Mitsubishi brand, the public is always interested in BTMU and is willing to find out the latest information about the bank by themselves. This is rather different to the situation at Nissan. The bank's authority, established around a famous corporate brand, is based on the long-term success, history and tradition of the Mitsubishi *keiretsu* group. These elements have been transmitted, shared with, and glorified by the wider Japanese society since the pre-war era. BTMU attracts media and public attention not through its actual disclosures but rather by ensuring and maintaining the authority of the Mitsubishi brand story over time, so it does not have the incentive to actively adopt a public communication strategy.

Nevertheless, public communication is becoming a very important part of organizational change. Previous studies have suggested that IR has been the main factor in instigating change within Japanese firms, and this case shows one of the ways in which IR can be conducted in Japan. It is important to note that public communications can include a wide range of strategies and IR strategies appear to be developed differently depending on the differing historical contexts, and differing demands and audiences that organizations face.

This study specifically examined the employment downsizing and shareholder-oriented actions in the reform plan, and interview and document data shows that genuine employment downsizing has not actually been carried out at BTMU. The bank claimed in its 2001 annual report that it planned to reduce its staff by 20,000 by 2004 but this has not occurred. Although an early retirement scheme has been adopted, instead there has been an increase in the number of staff overall. The bank maintains the principle of lifetime employment, and the literature indicates that it is normal for Japanese firms to protect their employees' positions.[55]

In addition, institutional restraints make it harder for BTMU to reform. Shareholder value creation, as described in the 2001 annual report, has not been prioritized by the bank's employees. Instead, it is clearly more important to maintain the credibility of the Mitsubishi corporate brand. This has actually been justified and described as the Mitsubishi group's DNA within the Mitsubishi *keiretsu* group. The relationships among the *keiretsu* group are still strong and they influence organizational behaviour. This is a strong institutional restraint, which prevents radical reform.

The analysis shows that BTMU's restructuring plans, particularly its employment downsizing and shareholder-oriented actions, are part of its narrative management. This means that BTMU has shown little change and only a small shift towards shareholder value ideology.

The recent development of IR in Japanese firms has convinced many researchers that more radical forms of change have finally reached Japan,[56] but this study suggests that such organizational reform is not actually taking place.

Nonetheless, the new reform plans have been accepted by the internal audience. Past studies[57] have suggested that the Japanese salaryman finds it hard to absorb new management strategies, and while BTMU staff fit this pattern in that they basically resist organizational reform, the US-style shareholder value-added management referred to in its public claims has been grasped by BTMU's staff. This is partly because BTMU adopts a careful internal discourse and has outlined its new plans to staff. It delivers its messages internally about theoretical connections between the new restructuring plans and traditional brand management.

Research has focused on the extent of change in Japanese firms,[58] but in this case staff and the external audience both show understanding about the new reform plans and accordingly have developed narratives about BTMU's performance through its strategy for validation and justification. Insiders appear to have accepted this reform plan and continue to support the narrative seven years after BTMU's reform plans were announced in 2001, and after three changes of president.

Although the case of BTMU shows that the US-style reform plans are part of narrative management, it also shows that the bank has definitely advanced and built on its IR strategy. Its organizational change has been backed up and sustained in the long term by internal understanding; in other words, internal support is important for the process of organizational change. Moreover, the kind of narrative pursued by BTMU also differs from Nissan's in its much more traditional form of maintaining a traditional brand, rather than building a new organization. This difference reminds us of the importance of multiple forms of narrative existing within the Japanese business system. While all corporate narratives exist largely for the same reason (to inform audiences and to persuade audiences them that firms' courses of action are legitimate and necessary), firms are under quite different types of pressure, have different leadership and work under a variety of institutional possiblities and constraints.

The next chapter will look at Shinsei Bank's reform plans. Shinsei Bank was one of the most traditional banks in Japan as it was state-owned. However, it was taken over by a US hedge fund which announced very radical US-style restructuring. Its reform plans will again be examined based on interview data. The Shinsei narrative is wholly different from that of Nissan and BTMU, and considerably less successful in terms of persuading internal and external audiences of the value of its reform efforts, or even the value of Shinsei itself as a corporation.

## Notes

1  See Gerlach (1992).
2  See, for example, Aoki (1996); Hall and Soskice (2001).
3  Part of Mitsubishi UFJ Financial Group.
4  *Mainichi*, 26 April 2009. Available at http://mainichi.jp/select/biz/news/ 20090426ddm002020164000c.html
5  The entire Mitsubishi group strongly supported Mitsubishi Motors. BTMU financed them to sustain the name value of the Mitsubishi *keiretsu* even after Mitsubishi Motors failed to link up with Daimler Chrysler in 2000, leaving Mitsubishi Motors facing bankruptcy (Sankei Shinbun Syuzaihan 2002: 268). Mitsubishi Heavy Industries and Mitsubishi Electric Corporation (Mitsubishi Denki) carried out research and development on behalf of Mitsubishi Motors (ibid). Mitsubishi Corporation (Mitsubishi Shoji) supported Mitsubishi Motors' business in other countries.
6  *Yomiuri*. Available at http://www.yomiuri.co.jp/atcars/news/20040312ve03.htm (as of 11 March 2011).
7  The history of the firm makes it hard for contemporary leaders of Mitsubishi to maintain a high profile. For example, Shigemitsu Miki took up his post in 2000. (He was promoted to chairman of Mitsubishi-Tokyo Financial Group in 2004 and has been a board member since 2008). As president he has a much less visible public presence than Nissan's Ghosn or Yokohama's Nakada, both of whom became high-profile spokesmen for their organizations and advocates for wider changes to Japanese capitalism. Miki does not often appear in public, and the Mitsubishi corporate brand is very familiar to the Japanese public. Owing to the Mitsubishi brand, successive presidents of BTMU do not have the incentive to frequently appear in the public on behalf of the firm. It would be insulting to historical memory to try to usurp Iwasaki. Over the course of several leadership positions, they seek to maintain the authority of the Mitsubishi brand. This places strong institutional restraint on the possibility for radical reform.
8  For example, the previous president, Shigemitsu Miki, was recruited by the bank of Mitsubishi in 1958 after graduating from university, and became President in 2000. He had worked at Mitsubishi as a career banker for more than forty years. His is a classic example of a Japanese salaryman working at one firm for the whole of his career, under a guaranteed lifetime employment system and no external labor market for management talent (Graham 2003; Dore 2000). Among such salarymen, he is in a career elite as only the bankers who graduated from Tokyo University can become candidates for the presidency of BTMU, according to insiders interviewed. According to a manager at HQ: 'The bank is too big for

every banker to be promoted to a high position. Only alumni from Tokyo University can become executives. President Miki in particular has won praise and when he started working at the bank of Mitsubishi it was obvious that he was a likely contender for the position of president in the future'. Clearly Miki was considered by bank insiders as a leading contender for the presidency since he started working at the bank.

9  11 December 2008.
10  Mitsubishi UFJ Financial Group annual report (2006: 8, 9, 10). Available at http://www.mufg.jp/ir/annualreport/2006mufg/pdffile/cr_all.pdf
11  Mitsubishi-Tokyo Financial Group annual report (2001: 7). Available at http://www.mufg.jp/english/ir/annualreport/backnumber/
12  Mitsubishi UFJ Financial Group annual report (2006: 7, 8). Available at http://www.mufg.jp/ir/annualreport/2006mufg/pdffile/cr_all.pdf
13  Mitsubishi UFG Financial Group (English website). Available at http://www.mufg.jp/english/profile/governance/
14  Mitsubishi UFG (Japanese website). Available at http://www.mufg.jp/profile/governance/
15  Ibid.
16  Shinsei Bank annual report (2008). Around 78 per cent of the board is made up of outside directors.
17  See Kanda (2009).
18  See Kuronuma (2009).
19  See, for example, Morgan and Kubo (2005).
20  See Buchanan (2007); Tamura (2002).
21  Mitsubishi-Tokyo Financial Group annual report (2002: 6). Available at http://www.mufg.jp/english/ir/annualreport/backnumber/
22  *Mainichi* newspaper. Available at http://www.mainichi.co.jp/life/money/invest/030129-1.html (accessed March 2012).
23  As of 1998 the firm was known as Bank of Tokyo-Mitsubishi (BTM).
24  *Nikkei* newspaper. Available at http://www.nikkei.co.jp/sp1/nt32/20030818AS1F1800718082003.htm (accessed March 2012).
25  See, for example, Dore (2008); Morgan and Kubo (2005).
26  Mitsubishi-Tokyo Financial Group annual report (2004: 4). Available at http://www.mufg.jp/english/ir/annualreport/backnumber/
27  Bank of Tokyo Mitsubishi.
28  Mitsubishi-Tokyo Financial Group annual report (2003: 7). Available at http://www.mufg.jp/english/ir/annualreport/backnumber/
29  *Weekly Diamond* (2003b: 52, 53, 55).
30  Ibid.: 55.
31  Ibid., (2004a: 18).
32  See the latest book Hiroshi Okumura (2004) *What Is Mitsubishi?* Tokyo: Ota Syupan.
33  Excluding books about other firms who also belong to the Mitsubishi *keiretsu* such as Mitsubishi Motors and Mitsubishi Electronic.
34  See, for example, Shin Shimaoka (2010) *Iwasaki Yataro: Founder of Mitsuibishi,* Tokyo: Kawade Shobo Shinsha; Akira Nakano (2010) *Iwasaki Yataro and Mitsubishi's Corporate Policy,,* Tokyo: Asahi Shinbun Syupan; Atsushi Kawai (2010) *Iwasaki Yataro and Four Generations,* Tokyo: Gentosha; Yu Tateishi (2009) *Iwasaki Yataro,* Tokyo: PHP Kenkyusho; Fujiyoshi Sakamoto (1986) *Iwasaki Yataro's Unique Management Style: The Charismatic Founder of Mitsubishi,* Tokyo: Kodansha.
35  Drucker (2004) *Peter F. Drucker on Management,* Harvard Business School Press, Harvard.
36  Hiroshi Motomiya's *Salaryman Kintaro* Manga series (see Matanle *et al.* 2008).
37  See, for example, Graham (2003).
38  See, for example, Dore (2000); Matanle (2006); McCann *et al.* (2006).

39 See Morgan and Takashi (2002); Vogel (2006).
40 See Matanle (2006).
41 Toyokeizai (2002).
42 See Littler (2006).
43 The PR department publishes a newsletter monthly which is distributed only to the bank's staff. The author was given copies by interviewees at the bank.
44 Mitsubishi-Tokyo Financial Group annual report (2001: 37, 38). Available at http://www.mufg.jp/english/ir/annualreport/backnumber/
45 Ito, K. (2000) *Corporate Brand Management: Competitive Advantage*. Tokyo: Nihon Keizai Shinbunsha.
46 See, for example, Dore (2008); Olcott (2008).
47 A notable example of this occurred when BTMU financed Mitsubishi Motors in order to sustain the brand value of the Mitsubishi *keiretsu* even after Mitsubishi Motors failed to link up with Daimler Chrysler in 2000 and was faced with bankruptcy. Strategy follows the lead of the Mitsubishi brand.
48 Mitsubishi Public Affairs Committee. Available at http://www.mitsubishi.com/mpa c/j/companies/index.html
49 Ibid.
50 Ibid.
51 Ibid.
52 Toyokeizai (2001).
53 See Aoki (1988); Goto (1982).
54 Mitsubishi UFJ Financial Group annual report (2006: 8, 9, 10). Available at http:// www.mufg.jp/ir/annualreport/2006mufg/pdffile/cr_all.pdf
55 See Sato (1997); Vogel (2006).
56 See, for example, Morgan and Kubo (2005); Olcott (2009).
57 See, for example, Graham (2003).
58 See, for example, Dore (2008); Morgan and Kubo (2005).

# 5    Shinsei Bank

## A financialized, Anglo-Saxon style of narrative management

### 5.1 Introduction

This chapter looks at Shinsei Bank. Shinsei Bank is a relatively new firm which was formed from the remnants of Long-Term Credit Bank (LTCB), a state-owned firm founded in 1952 and recognized as one of the most stable and conservative of Japanese banks. However, Shinsei Bank (*shinsei* means 'reborn') has come to symbolize the intrusion of US-style restructuring, since it was established in 2000 following a takeover of the failed LTCB by a US investment fund, Ripplewood Holdings. Much of the existing research on Japan suggests that firms under foreign control have engaged in more drastic reform measures.[1] The interview data gathered at Shinsei Bank also demonstrates that US-style methods of restructuring have actually been implemented by the new management. There has been more change than continuity at Shinsei Bank, which might lead observers to think that there has been less of a gap between saying and doing than at Nissan and BTMU, which have not engaged in such far-reaching reform. However, the actual details of reform have – once again – been different from that which Shinsei has announced in public. In the case of Shinsei Bank, there is strong evidence of an undisclosed business model behind the official reform plan. The outcome of this case is that Shinsei Bank's new restructuring plan is another example of a company's narrative management, but in this case the gap between saying and doing is much more similar to that found in US or Anglo-Saxon forms of financial narrative management strategy.[2] Interestingly, despite this being in many ways the most accurate form of narrative management, the chapter will go on to explain that in this case the narrative is much harder for internal and external audiences to accept than was the case at Nissan and BTMU.

### 5.2 Shinsei Bank's new reform plans

This section provides general information about Shinsei Bank and discusses the bank's attempts to incorporate US management styles into its restructuring plans.

### 5.2.1 Shinsei Bank

Shinsei Bank is a large Japanese financial firm with 5,245 employees.[3] It has recently been ranked as the seventh largest in the Japanese financial industry (see Table 4.6). Shinsei Bank commenced operations in 2000 after LTCB was taken over by Ripplewood Holdings following LTCB's bankruptcy in 1998. The bank was acquired by Timothy C. Collins, CEO of Ripplewood together with J. C. Flowers & Co. LLC[4] in 2000. Ripplewood also bought out four more Japanese firms from 2000 to 2002. It took over LTCB in 2000, bought stocks of Niles Parts Sales (owned by Nissan) in 2001, and took over Nippon Columbia in 2001. In addition, in 2002 it effected a merger of Marantz Japan and Denon Consumer Marketing Co. (which belonged to Nippon Columbia and was listed on the stock exchange as D&M Holdings). Furthermore, it acquired Phoenix Seagaia Resort in 2001. Collins resigned from the board of Shinsei Bank in 2007 and subsequently withdrew all investments from the bank. J. C. Flowers & Co. LLC and affiliates are now the largest shareholder with 32.6 per cent of Shinsei common shares. Foreign shareholders now own 62.4 per cent of all shares.

LTCB was one of the most prestigious firms in Japan. Its brand name had a huge influence on the Japanese economy given that as a state-owned firm it played an important role in contributing to the growth of the Japanese economy. A position at LTCB would have been highly sought-after among new graduates. As it was hard to gain entry to LTCB, successful employees were proud to work for the bank and were very loyal to it[5]. As we shall see, such unity and staff loyalty seems not to be inherited by Shinsei Bank.

The new management approach brought in by the US hedge fund marked a radical shift of direction for Shinsei. The new bank comprises a commercial bank and an investment bank, and is expanding its retail and investment operations[6]. Each business department, such as investment banking, consumer finance, retail banking, is independent of the HR department,[7] and this allows each department to assume responsibility for its own personnel management.[8] In addition, the composition of its board is different from other Japanese firms. Around 78 per cent (11 out of 14 members) of the Shinsei board is composed of directors from outside the bank.[9] This ratio is much higher than that of Japanese firms listed in the first section of the Tokyo stock exchange, as only 45 per cent of them had introduced outside directors in 2008.[10] Furthermore, to date the top positions have been taken by outsiders. For example, since the takeover all the CEOs have been invited to join the bank from outside: the first CEO, Masamoto Yashiro[11] (incumbent from 1999–2004 and 2009–10) was previously chairman of Citicorp Japan; Thierry Porté,[12,13] (2005–08) was president of Morgan Stanley Japan; and Shigeki Toma[14] (2010–)was vice-president at Isuzu Motors. None of these CEOs have remained in post for long, and each has announced different restructuring plans. However, they have all showed an affinity for US methods of corporate reorganization such as Shareholder Value Added (SVA). Shinsei brought in these different executives and US-influenced management styles as part of a deliberately radical shake-up plan. The next section will discuss this in detail.

Four years after Shinsei Bank began operating in 2004, the bank was listed in the first section of the Tokyo stock exchange. Although LTCB recorded net losses of –¥14.8 trillion in 1998 and –¥1,010 billion in 1999, Shinsei Bank was to enjoy handsome profits from 2001. However, from 2007 onwards the bank has suffered very heavy net losses. Flowers blames excessive investment in the USA and the European Union as the reason for the recent negative earnings.[15] Furthermore, when its consolidated net losses reached –¥143 billion in 2009, Shinsei Bank reached an agreement for an alliance or business merger with Aozora Bank, which was also burdened with reduced profits.[16] The predecessor of Aozora Bank was Nippon Credit Bank, which was a state-owned firm like LTCB. It too went bankrupt in 1998 just after LTCB's collapse, and since 2003 the major shareholder has been the US hedge fund Cerberus Capital Management.[17] Although the new bank planned officially to commence operations in October 2010, Shinsei Bank, which has made consecutive losses, had no choice but to approve resolutions to terminate the alliance agreement with Aozora Bank.[18]

### 5.2.2 Shinsei Bank's US-style reform plans

This section will introduce Shinsei Banks's new reform plans. When Shinsei Bank began operations in 2000 it revealed its US-style management strategy. Meanwhile, the Japanese government had just introduced its Big Bang reforms, which marked a significant liberalization of Japan's insurance and banking industries. Firms that introduced US-style management reforms were officially approved by the government. For its part, Shinsei Bank adopted SVA. According to its annual report:

> We believe that we have made the right choices to position our business for future growth by strategically focusing our business around the customer. Our goal is a bold one – to become the fastest-growing, highest-returning financial services firm in Japan by creating *value for our shareholders* through the provision of the right solutions to meet our customers' ever-evolving needs.
>
> To achieve this goal, we are now working on optimizing our operations including cost rationalization and have introduced Shareholder Value Added (SVA) as one of the measures better to allocate our capital. We will continue to focus on expanding our quality customer base organically while actively pursuing M&A opportunities to grow our business in the right areas.[19]

This unusual but cutting-edge strategy was new to Japan. Furthermore, this Japanese version of the bank's message shows that Shinsei is emphazising to its Japanese audience that it seeks to create value for its shareholders. However, when we look at the same section in the English version of the bank's 2008 annual report, it emphasizes the goal of improving value for customers as well as shareholders:

> Our goal is a bold one: to become the fastest-growing, highest-returning financial services firm in Japan by creating *value for our customers* through the provision of the right solutions to meet their ever-evolving needs.[20]

Interestingly, Shinsei chose to use the term 'value for our shareholders' when addressing its Japanese audience. This could reflect a current fashion in Japanese society where the term 'shareholder value' has become increasingly popular; an increasing number of people recognize the importance of shareholders in Japan[21]. Or perhaps Shinsei is trying to be deliberately provocative in order to boost a radical shake-up of the Japanese market.

In particular, Shinsei has sought to deinstitutionalize traditional Japanese HR practices.[22] While past research has shown that HR in Japanese firms has remained fairly static,[23] it has also been suggested that it is very difficult for Japanese firms to maintain traditional employment systems.[24] Shinsei announced the introduction of a new HR policy in its 2000 annual report as follows:

> Accompanying the recommencement of its activities, the Bank is undertaking a thorough reform of its human resources policies as part of overall activities to enhance its operating infrastructure. The aims of the new human resource policies will be to create a new corporate culture and promote a renewed awareness of the roles and objectives of corporations ...
>
> With the aims of better motivating staff members and promoting greater emphasis on profitability in its operations, the Bank has introduced personnel evaluation on the basis of performance for all employees ...
>
> Authority for personnel matters will be delegated to Groups, to the greatest extent possible, and the heads of the Groups will make decisions regarding employment, job assignments and transfers, evaluation, compensation, and other matters. Thereby, the Bank will enhance its capabilities for meeting customer needs responsively and appropriately ...
>
> To facilitate entry into new areas and strengthen capabilities in strategic businesses, the Bank is aggressively recruiting external personnel with sophisticated professional knowledge and skills, especially in such advanced fields as financial products, risk management and IT.[25]

HR departments (or personnel divisions) in Japan traditionally wield strong authority on personnel matters, which hinders drastic employment downsizing[26]. However, Shinsei's policies represent a major departure from traditional HR systems, removing a considerable amount of clout from personnel departments and encouraging mobility in employment, the adoption of a merit-based pay system and the hiring of external staff[27]. It has been agreed by academics that there has generally been no deinstitutionalization of the traditional Japanese system, especially with regard to HR practices[28]. The bank has announced that the old Japanese lifetime employment system associated with LTCB will be abolished by the newly formed Shinsei Bank.

This section showed that the US company, Ripplewood, brought in a deliberately radical shake-up plan in an attempt to break with traditions that still feature strongly throughout Japan[29]. Ripplewood has sought to integrate US-style strategy into its restructuring plans. Internal data obtained at Shinsei Bank will be analyzed below to provide the detail about its new reform plan, especially SVA management.

## 5.3 External and internal scepticism about SVA management

SVA management is an important aspect of Shinsei Bank's reform plans. How has the Japanese public, which lent public funds to Shinsei, reacted to this new approach? Furthermore, have staff at Shinsei Bank accepted or rejected its new reform plans? Shinsei's plans received strong criticism from Japanese society during 2000–02. This social reaction was very similar to the case of Nissan. It gradually came to earn external understanding, but unlike Nissan Shinsei could not maintain this social understanding in the long term. Social support for Shinsei was only temporally earned, and there is again today a strong sense of scepticism about the Shinsei approach. This section will show that a lack of current external support seems to result from a lack of public communication. Public rejection is due to influence by mass media reports on the bank. A firm's PR activity may be an important element of organizational change as corporations struggle to obtain support from society as a whole for their reform processes. Likewise, staff are also sceptical about Shinsei's reforms. External and internal reactions will be discussed below.

### 5.3.1 External scepticism about SVA management

Shinsei's US-style restructuring plans have received strong criticism from Japanese society since 2000. The media described Ripplewood as *Hagetaka* which in Japanese means 'concession hunters,' looking to feed off the bodies of failed Japanese institutions. (In Germany, private equity partners were famously described as 'locusts' by Social Democrat politician Franz Müntefering in April 2005.) Although the bank's profits began to increase, Shinsei encountered heavy criticism from the Japanese public. According to one media story:

Shinsei Bank has been overrun by foreign high-fliers: this concession hunter or vulture has caused further recession in Japan.

LTCB was taken over by Ripplewood, one of the most stupid events from a historical point of view. After LTCB went bankrupt, it made a contract with Goldman Sachs. It ate out of Goldman Sachs' hand, and LTCB was sold to Ripplewood at only ¥1 billion in spite of there having been an injection of ¥7 trillion of public funds into LTCB when it was nationalized. In addition, this takeover was carried out on the condition that the government would buy any debts if the price was reduced by 2003. Under this warranty for latent defect, Shinsei Bank easily extracts money from its customers. For example, one of the most popular department stores in Japan, Sogo, which had tried to reform itself, was driven to bankruptcy because Shinsei Bank stopped lending money to it. As a concession hunter or vulture Ripplewood pursues only profits for itself, without thinking of the Japanese economy, and this has caused further recession.

The Japanese nation is being exploited by Ripplewood. The company should take heed of our strong arguments in order to reform Shinsei Bank.[30]

Thus, it can be seen that Ripplewood and US-style restructuring have been rejected. Despite the fact that ¥7.8 trillion of public funds were injected into LTCB to counteract its non-performing loans,[31] the US hedge fund took it over at only ¥1 billion,[32] which drew strong social criticism. Even so, it is clear that the bank has managed to produce good results. Shinsei Bank cleaned up its balance sheet, which led to a reduction in the number of negative claims. Total non-consolidated claims decreased from ¥1,113 billion in 2002 to ¥97.3 billion in 2004.[33] Furthermore, it has maintained a higher net income since the takeover. Its net losses amounted to ¥14.8 trillion in 1998 and ¥1,010 billion in 1999, and by 2001 it was bringing in handsome profits of ¥90.4 billion. It remained in profit, ¥61.2 billion in 2002, ¥53.0 billion in 2003, and ¥66.3 billion in 2004.[34] Shinsei had taken a very decided turn for the better as a result of US-style restructuring (as did Nissan).

Nonetheless, neither the media nor the bank's existing customers were prepared to accept that the bank's transformation was socially legitimate according to former Shinsei and LTCB banker:

> The new management ignores customers who are inexperienced in an English inscription. Some of LTCB's former customers left Shinsei Bank because they did not like the methods used by Shinsei. Clients have said that they liked LTCB but do not like Shinsei Bank.

The new US style of management has not proved popular with old LTCB customers. Japanese society seems to be uncomfortable with US methods. This viewpoint is also supported by the case of Nissan. Nissan was also faced with this kind of strong social criticism when it announced the NRP in 1999. Both firms' approaches were rejected simultaneously by the public. Shinsei was described as a vulture, and Nissan as a cost-cutter.

However, Shinsei's approach gradually came to be socially accepted. Shinsei bankers (former LTCB banker) noticed a shift in social perception, as explained by this interviewee:

> Shinsei Bank suddenly started to gain a reputation that was as good as Nissan's three or four years ago. The public, which had strongly criticized Shinsei Bank from 2000, came to value the bank more highly. A larger number of customers opened accounts with the bank. Shinsei Bank also ranked high in a social survey about the increase in the number of new graduates wanting to work at the bank. Shinsei's stock price rose rapidly after it was listed. It felt like a kind of bubble in its social reputation. This marked the peak of the bank's popularity in 2005.

As explained above, the social status of Shinsei Bank actually began to improve. Indeed, since 2003 Shinsei Bank has won many awards from third parties: *FinanceAsia*'s Best Local Bank (Japan) award for the second year running in July 2003, *The Banker*'s 2003 Bank of the Year for Japan award in September 2003, and *International Financing Review (IFR)*'s 2003 Best Securitization Deal and Team award in December 2003.[35] In February 2004 the bank was listed in the first section of the Tokyo Stock Exchange. Shortly afterwards, the bank won *EUROMONEY*'s Best Bank in Japan award in 2004 and 2006, and was ranked first in the *Nihon Keizai Shinbun* (Nikkei) customer satisfaction survey in August 2004, 2005 and 2006.[36]

Having initially rejected Shinsei's methods, the mass media also started view Shinsei Bank as a business with a future. For example, one of the most popular business magazines discussed the bank thus:

> Shinsei Bank will be listed again on 19 February 2004. The public is beginning to put its hope in Shinsei's future. Many securities companies are now receiving inquiries about the bank.[37]

As Shinsei Bank accomplished its aim to list its stock on the Tokyo market, this raised the public's expectations. In consequence Shinsei Bank marked the peak of its stock price, ¥825 in 2004, when listed in the stock market and its price remained high until 2006 (¥824 in 2006).[38]

Public expectations and a higher stock price fundamentally were supported by Shinsei's US-style management. The following interviewee, a former Shinsei banker, explained the benefits of the new management strategy.

> Customers have a good image of Shinsei Bank. The bank was popular with high interest rates and convenient services. We made profits through providing unconventional products. Thus, Shinsei Bank became very well

known. Otherwise, the bank might not occupy such a high position within the industry.

Now other Japanese banks are adopting some of our new services such as telephone banking, internet banking, longer opening hours, and so on, all of which were introduced by my bank for the first time in Japan.

Shinsei Bank launched its internet banking services, extended its retail branch opening hours from 3 pm (when Japanese banks normally close) to 7 pm, and began offering a 24-hour/365-day ATM service in 2001 for the first time in Japan[39]. All city banks, local banks and some trust banks have now reformed their traditional systems and have launched similar services following Shinsei's lead; among the city banks, Mizuho Bank and Sumitomo Mitsui Banking Corporation launched these services in 2005 and Bank of Tokyo-Mitsubishi UFJ followed suit in 2006. Progressive services and products were introduced, which garnered profits for the bank and further boosted its reputation among the wider Japanese society. Indeed, the bank maintained higher net incomes; ¥66.4 billion in 2004, ¥67.4 billion in 2005 and ¥76.0 billion in 2006.[40] These underlying factors contributed to Shinsei's social enhancement. Furthermore, the public, which had criticized Shinsei Bank even when it was recording handsome profits during 2000–02, began to accept the bank when it contined to record similar profit levels during 2003–06. This continuing financial success contributed to growing public acceptance.

Shinsei's level of public communication was much lower than Nissan's, but the common point between them is that they both seemed to bring rich profits into a failing and moribund Japanese economy. This continuing financial success fundamentally helped Shinsei's new approach to earn social support. However, as we shall see below, this external support did not last long.

Although Shinsei Bank had gradually gained social support for its reform plans during 2004–06, it external acceptance took a turn for the worse from 2007 onwards. This point was indicated by insiders (former LTCB banker) as follows:

> Shinsei Bank came into the limelight some time ago, but now its social reputation is lower than ever. We have breached the Securities Exchange law and the advertising law for the past few years, and this might be one of the reasons for this decline in popularity. In addition, Shinsei did not achieve good business results in 2007.

This shows that the employee had recognizes that society's expectations of the bank had reached a low ebb. Shinsei Bank itself admitted to failing to meet expectations. Shinsei Trust & Banking was ordered partly to suspend its business and retail product promotion practices following questioning by the regulators.[41] This was in relation to an advertisement run by the bank in 2006 which caused consumer misunderstanding; hence the bank received a cease and desist order from the Japan Fair Trade Commission in 2007.[42] In addition, Shinsei Bank showed a loss (–¥60.9 billion) in 2007, the first recorded loss since it started operations in 2000.[43] Having borrowed public funds in order to rescue LTCB from bankruptcy Shinsei Bank was ordered by the government to improve its business.[44] It showed further net losses of –¥60.9 billion in 2007, –¥143 billion in 2008 and –¥140 billion in 2009. As of August 2011, the bank's stock price was at its lowest ever level, ¥88, having reached its highest level, of ¥825, when it was first listed in March 2004. There is thus a strong feeling that the US-style reform approach was simply not working in Japan.

Once Shinsei Bank revealed net losses in 2007, the media quickly started criticizing the bank once more. For example, unflattering reports appeared about how Shinsei Bank scraped together a net income of ¥60.1 billion for fiscal year 2008. As one news outlet reported, 'Shinsei Bank sold the head office at the end of the fiscal year, in March. Otherwise the bank would have gone into the red for two consecutive years. Consolidated profit for 2008, ¥60.1 billion, was derived from selling the office at ¥61.7 billion'.[45] The mass media again began to criticize Shinsei's management. Its net losses of 2007 received a lot of bad media attention. According to one of Japan's premier business magazines:

> Shinsei Bank has always ranked high in customer satisfaction surveys, but now its retail department has gone into the red. The bank received public funds, but it has not made good use of them. Its business was aborted during the planning stage.[46]

Shinsei's new business model was described in the press as 'vicious tyranny,' and it was suggested that the company was being exploited by the overpaid US staff brought in by the new management. Although many business magazines praised the bank in 2004, by 2008 the plaudits were replaced by criticisms.

> After LTCB went bankrupt, it was reborn as Shinsei Bank under a US hedge fund. Eight years have passed since then. Shinsei Bank is now listed on the stock exchange, and it has been acclaimed as good example of corporate regeneration. However, its staff are united in their resentment of CEO's vicious tyranny. Shinsei Bank, which restarted as a new bank, has never been rewarded.
>
> The bank received a 'Best Bank in Japan' award from the British magazine *Euromoney* but this award does not reflect the reality of the situation there.[47]
>
> Since 2007 Shinsei Bank has not come out of the red. Nevertheless, CEO has continued to employ foreign financial high-fliers at absurdly high remuneration levels. Shinsei Bank paid for luxury residential apartments for them. They were extremely well-treated by him.[48]

Both magazines blame CEO for the bank's difficulties. They report that CEO and his high-ranking colleagues are directly responsible for the bank's heavy losses. One of the reasons for this kind of criticism might be the perceived abuse of ¥336.9 billion in public funds. Despite the fact that Shinsei recorded a net loss in 2007, 2009 and 2010 and twice was ordered to improve the business by the government,[49] the top management still continues to be paid huge salaries and annual bonuses (discussed further below). This echoes two British banks, Lloyds Bank and Royal Bank of Scotland, which received massive public bailouts. The perceived greed of the top management causes great public dissatisfaction. Existing customers are easily influenced by such negative media comments and began to show their distrust of Shinsei out of sympathy with the media. The following interviewee (a former Shinsei and LTCB banker), believes that customers accepted the media's attitude because of the low levels of trust between the bank and the public:

> Many of our customers withdrew all their deposits from their accounts when they expired. The same thing happens whenever the media makes negative comments about Shinsei Bank. It was painful for me to work at this kind of firm. I could not trust Shinsei Bank either. I agreed with the newspaper reports.

One way for Shinsei to improve its relationship with its customers might be for it to engage in more active PR. However, Shinsei does not often make public announcements, unlike Nissan, so there is little opportunity for outsiders to understand the management's vision for Shinsei. Media articles do not include Shinsei's viewpoints. Another interviewee (former LTCB banker) highlighted this as a fault in the bank's public communication strategy:

> I think that there has been a lack of public expectation of Shinsei Bank. Outsiders can't understand Shinsei's vision. Even we do not know what the bank is doing. I guess outsiders won't know more than I do about the bank. Unlike charismatic CEOs of other firms, Shinsei's CEO has not behaved enthusiastically towards outsiders. It is our weak point that we do not make strong public statements. LTCB did not need external actions because it had long-term social credibility.

Shinsei's spokesmen rarely appear, so the public is ill informed about the company. Outsiders can discover Shinsei's message and image only through its annual reports. Although a firm might not necessarily need a spokesman, Shinsei's reform plans at least need to be understood by outsiders without ambiguity. The interview data shows that the public is influenced by media comment, so the way in which the media judges and transmits Shinsei's new approach to reform is an important key to securing and sustaining external understanding. Attempts to improve Shinsei's public image are an important part of its restructuring.

This section showed that Shinsei's use of SVA management has not, in the end, earned social support. At an earlier stage Shinsei Bank came to be gradually supported by the public and later secured external acceptance. The fundamental factors behind Shinsei's strong profits seemed to help it to secure external support. However, it could not maintain social support in the long term, suggesting that showing a new reform plan by itself is not sufficient to gain external support. Among the reasons for this failure is the bank's weak business results and its limited efforts to engage outsiders. The mass media is one of the key audiences for external acceptance. In the case of Shinsei Bank, the analysis suggests that media reporting has played a powerful role in the bank's failure to gain external acceptance for its reform plans. There has been insufficient research in the literature about Japan on the role of corporate public communications. Recent literature[50] indicates an increased use of IR by Japanese firms. Shinsei also has also employed IR in order to explain its new reform plans to the investor community, but this analysis suggests that this usage has been quite limited and this has probably played a role in the company's failure to secure internal or external support for its reform measures.

### 5.3.2 Internal scepticism and disagreement

This section discusses how internal staff at Shinsei Bank have reacted to its SVA management. Similarly to external reactions, the bank's staff are profoundly sceptical about the new reform policies. They have lost their loyalty to the bank. The ambiguity of organizational identity after the M&A activity undermines institutional trust, in a similar way to that suggested by prior work.[51] It is certainly difficult for the employees who had been trained and worked at LTCB under the traditional management to cope with the new systems.[52] Shinsei mid-career worker, expressed the same concerns. This banker came to Shinsei Bank without having first worked at LTCB:

> The management just focuses on earning profits. The biggest shareholders are investment funds, who think only of numbers. Cosmetic gestures and reality are different. In a normal situation profits are earned for a big shareholder, normal shareholders and customers in a balanced manner. That balance is broken in a clear-cut way by the management. Above all, the benefits for customers and normal shareholders are not protected by them. Shinsei Bank focuses only on specific stockholders, who are foreign executives and who receive million-dollar salaries for working there.

Even newcomers to the bank, who had not experienced working life at LTCB, have expressed concerns about the hedge fund model. Staff clearly feel controlled by the biggest shareholder. They also wonder if profits are withheld from stakeholders by the management. There is a real doubt that SVA management has genuinely been carried out by Shinsei Bank. SVA management appears not to have secured internal acceptance, and many staff feel deeply uncomfortable about the new approach.

Why do staff at Shinsei Bank so strongly reject its new forms of business management? The next section examines internal refusal to embrace Shinsei's SVA management in detail.

## 5.4 Shinsei's narrative management: SVA management

Why is this approach so unpopular among the bank's staff? It is obviously not easy to accept, especially by former LTCB bankers whose business had been allocated by the government since 1952.

This section examines how Shinsei Bank has implemented its reform plans internally, particularly SVA management. It will also look at why Shinsei never managed to secure internal understanding for its plans. Shinsei has not been able to manage and overcome staff scepticism about its SVA management. The general consensus is of unsound management practices and undisclosed business models behind SVA management. Shinsei's new business management behaviour of necessity includes a gap between saying and doing; it is a part of the firm's narrative management. This gap has not been tolerated or validated by internal employees.

Employment downsizing and the role of poor customer treatment will be examined below.

### 5.4.1 Shinsei's narrative management: employment downsizing

Although Shinsei adopted SVA management, SVA essentially serves as an ideological shield behind which a quite different business model has been running. In order to earn profits quickly, Shinsei has not implemented an official lay-off system; rather it has adopted an unofficial lay-off system. First, Shinsei announced an early retirement system during 2008 owing to heavy damage from the sub-prime crisis.

> Expenses were aggressively managed through the Voluntary Early Retirement Program (VERP) offered to select employees at Shinsei Bank and Shinsei Financial, which together resulted in over 1,000 staff VERP acceptances. We expect the majority of restructuring charges associated with these programs to be recovered in fiscal year 2009 through a reduction in personnel expenses going forward.[53]

The total number of the employees who left Shinsei voluntarily reached 1,000 in 2009. However, the number of employees has not actually declined, and has in fact increased since 2010 (see Table 5.1).

It seems that Shinsei did not carry out employment downsizing after all, resulting in another instance of false signalling. Large Japanese firms' lay-off announcements are often overstated, which is supported by other cases such

*Table 5.1* Number of employees at Shinsei Bank (taken from Toyokeizai 2008–11)[54]

| Year | Number of employees |
| --- | --- |
| 2004 | 2,380 |
| 2005 | 5,013 |
| 2006 | 5,120 |
| 2007 | 5,281 |
| 2008 | 5,346 |
| 2009 | 5,245 |
| 2010 | 6,116 |
| 2011 | 5,718 |

as Nissan, which avoided disclosing the adoption of an early retirement system.[55] The reason is that voluntary early retirement programs are not regarded as equivalent to downsizing.[56] Despite this, Shinsei Bank officially announced that it had adopted a voluntary early retirement program. Why? The following data from former Shinsei bankers clearly prove clearly that the management was using undisclosed measures to reduce its headcount.

> I left Shinsei Bank in 2008. I could not achieve the commitment and my bonus was halved. Then the firm asked me to leave, so I started looking for another job.

> There was an early retirement system in operation. My boss did not vote for that system, but afterwards his bonus was very low, which indicated that the firm wanted him to quit. Then he had to move to another firm, a consumer finance firm.

There has been no public announcements about this unofficial lay-off system. This is an example of downsizing fraud.[57] HR practice in Japanese firms has shown little sign of change even after takeover by US firms,[58] but this does not seem to apply to Shinsei Bank, which represents a very tough Anglo-Saxon form of employment system, almost the antithesis of a traditional Japanese firm. Having said that, the bank's labor costs have increased: ¥42.9 billion in 2006, ¥59.7 billion in 2007, ¥62.7 billion in 2008, ¥64.5 billion in 2009 and ¥64.8 billion in 2010. The number of staff has increased (see Table 5.1). Shinsei could additionally hire new bankers. Most interviewees mentioned that there are always newcomers at the bank and there is always someone leaving. For example, a former Shinsei banker who had already moved to another firm by the time that these interviews were conducted said that "new staff join Shinsei Bank throughout the year but rarely stay for long – two or three years at most'. This contradicts the goal of the bank's reform plans to improve shareholder value. It is more akin to an 'undisclosed business' model along the lines indicated by Froud et al. (2006) suggesting that financialized management is accompanied by a gap between saying and doing. Shinsei's employment downsizing is part of its narrative management.

Such tactics, associated with 'value skimming' for top management,[59] aroused staff anger. According to two previous employees who were dismissed under the unofficial lay-off system:

> I do not know who owns the firm. The CEO was always changing and quitting. I am wondering if no top management takes the firm seriously. I suspect that Shinsei Bank is where foreign businessmen come to earn good money because they arrive, earn a pile of money and then leave. They are never laid off. Even when the bank is showing a deficit, their salaries are never cut, while ours are reduced. All of the other employees are unhappy about this.

> The management team (those at top, executive and general manager level, for whom salaries are extremely high) is composed of those who come from outside the firm. They are never restructured. They quit in a few years once they've made their profits. We get the impression that a lot of money is taken by them.
> They just think in terms of short-term profit. For that reason, they simply cut the number of workers in order to turn a profit for a single year. We all think that you don't need to cut five workers when one of the top team is cut. The labor union complains about this, but the largely foreign management is never cut.

Shinsei's staff are angry that employee numbers are cut while top executives' posts remain intact. The bank has recently been ranked eighth in terms of disparity between the annual earnings of top executives and the rest of employees.[60] Their annual pay is 10.8 times as high as those of the rest of employees (see Table 5.2).

This data is based on annual earnings during 2007, when Shinsei Bank reported a net loss for the first time since the bank started. Folkman *et al.* (2007) point out that firms have a business model that enriches the management layer through restructuring. The undisclosed business model partially works by increases in staff workload, 'sweating' the internal assets, as suggested by Baumol *et al.* (2003). Employment downsizing increases the amount of pay available for senior management members, which triggers antagonism and alienation between top management and the rest of a firm's employees, according to the literature.[62] This can certainly be applied to the case of Shinsei Bank. It is not rare for the executives of foreign-affiliated firms to receive higher salaries than those of Japanese firms. However, the point that dissatisfies Shinsei bankers is that the firm's executives have not endured the pain of recovery from bad situations together with the employees. This has raised a question about whether profit is not for the customer, employees or

*Table 5.2* Executive earnings in relation to employee earnings[61]

| Ranking | Company name | Average annual income: executives (A) in ten thousands of yen | Average annual income: employees (B) in ten thousands of yen | (A)/(B) times |
|---|---|---|---|---|
| 1 | Nissan | 26,782 | 714 | 37.5 |
| 2 | Sony | 28,986 | 958 | 30.3 |
| 3 | Fanuc | 16,269 | 1,002 | 16.2 |
| 4 | HOYA | 10,300 | 654 | 15.7 |
| 5 | Sumitomo Realty and Development | 10,110 | 652 | 15.5 |
| 6 | Nippon Steel Corporation | 11,018 | 750 | 14.7 |
| 7 | Daito Trust Construction | 11,780 | 861 | 12.9 |
| 8 | Shinsei Bank | 9,913 | 918 | 10.8 |
| 9 | Yamada Denki | 4,036 | 409 | 9.9 |
| 10 | Sumitomo Metal Industries | 7,050 | 740 | 9.5 |

shareholders but only for the top executives, who instruct the public that 'customer focus, integrity, accountability, teamwork and community' are Shinsei values (see below). Only executives seem to have job security and high bonuses. Shinsei bankers seem to regard this as an exploitation of the firm and its customers for the enrichment of top executives, the new global financial elites.[63] Although Shinsei announced its intention to pursue US-style reform plans, SVA management has acted as a smokescreen to hide its undisclosed business model. Exploring this undisclosed business model sheds light on management's apparent moral degeneration and self-serving behaviour which has led to a massive loss in internal acceptance.

### 5.4.2 Shinsei's narrative management: the role of poor customer treatment

Management's apparent moral degeneration behind an undisclosed business model has fostered severe internal disagreement with Shinsei's approach. This section examines the role of poor customer treatment. How has Shinsei implemented its reform plans in terms of customer treatment behind SVA management?

Surprisingly, the new strategy for customer treatment is associated with the staff's profound scepticism about Shinsei's public claims about shareholder value creation. According to a former Shinsei banker:

> Despite Shinsei's official announcement about customer-oriented service, the management places most value on profit making rather than

customer satisfaction. Looking at the long term we should create a lot of fans, which is important for the future of Shinsei Bank.

This interviewee discussed Shinsei's lack of attention to the needs of existing customers as the bank focuses on chasing profits based on short-term thinking. Staff are sceptical of pursuing nothing but profit. Another former LTCB banker also questioned management's goals:

> The management has a foreign business model. They have officially said that we must place a great deal of importance on our customers, but what they ask staff to do is different from the official messages. They focus only on customers who can meet the requirements of the business model, and so they ignore the rest of the customers. We question what the president said.

Staff regularly highlighted a gap between management's saying and doing in the interviews. Shinsei actually announced a strategy to improve shareholder value with stakeholders in the Shinsei vision and values.[64] The Shinsei vision is as follows:

> We are Japan's pre-eminent financial services firm, delivering trusted solutions to grow sustainable value with our customers, our employees and our shareholders.[65]

Shinsei Bank outlines its values thus:[66]

> Customer focus
> We provide unparalleled solutions with speed and ability based on our customers' evolving needs.
> Integrity
> We demand uncompromising levels of integrity and transparency in all of our activities.
> Accountability
> We are accountable for results, including the sound application of risk management, compliance, control and customer protection.
> Teamwork
> We connect people and resources to provide exceptional customer solutions and sustain a culture in which our employees' ideas are respected and valued.
> Community
> We are committed to the development of our employees, our customers and our shareholders, and will serve the communities in which they live.[67]

These values imply that Shinsei Bank focuses on the benefits to the customers, which is met through employee teamwork resulting in solid contributions to shareholders. In other words, the management must ensure that employees embrace and live the vision and values internally when meeting the needs of customers. However, staff appear to have dismissed this public claim as empty rhetoric. According to this interviewee (former Shinsei banker):

> I wanted to make profits through my continual focus on surpassing the expectations and needs of our customers. Yet the most important point for the management is not the customer but making quick profits. We work for now. Nobody thinks of the future of the firm (in five years).

The bank's management does not reinvest in its customers but operates a downsize and distribute model through which senior executives disregard employees and customers in favour of profits.[68] They are instructed to create short-term profits via a top-down system. Shinsei has rejected its predecessor's faithful customer service, which now seems to have taken a backseat to the pursuit of profit-making. The result of this reduction in customer care is reflected in the change in the savings balances of Shinsei's customers. The total balance of corporate customer accounts has actually decreased since Shinsei Bank began operating. The balance was ¥1.35 trillion in 1999 when LTCB went bankrupt, but it was only ¥598 billion in 2009 (see Table 5.3). The total balance of asset-building savings has also decreased since 1999. The balance was ¥449 billion in 1999 but subsequently declined to ¥254 billion in 2009.

Shinsei's public claims are dressed up as narratives about customer care, yet there is clealy a gap between saying and doing towards the bank's customers. This is again an undisclosed business model in terms of management's approach to its customers.

*Table 5.3* Total balance of corporate customer account and asset-building savings (1999–2009)[69]

| Year | Total balance of corporate customer accounts (¥) | Total balance of asset-building savings (¥) |
|------|---------------------------------------------------|---------------------------------------------|
| 1999 | 1.35 trillion | 449 billion |
| 2000 | 1.38 trillion | 375 billion |
| 2001 | 0.83 trillion | 352 billion |
| 2002 | 0.84 trillion | 337 billion |
| 2003 | 0.46 trillion | 318 billion |
| 2004 | 0.44 trillion | 300 billion |
| 2005 | 0.37 trillion | 289 billion |
| 2006 | 0.39 trillion | 281 billion |
| 2007 | 0.44 trillion | 272 billion |
| 2008 | 0.75 trillion | 263 billion |
| 2009 | 0.59 trillion | 254 billion |

According to the following interviewee, given the gap between saying and doing, staff are confused about what their priorities lie in their daily work:

> Which is the most important priority? It is important to satisfy our customers. The most important thing for the firm is to make profits, but there are many cases where this is not possible. So I think how to cover the gap between the firm's goal and mine. Satisfying our customers' needs does not often contribute to the growth of profits because the financial products I want to sell are sometimes different from those the customers want to buy.

Shinsei staff are faced with an acute dilemma. The bank's employees are confused by the management's pursuit of its own interests (value-skimming), which generates a conflict with the bank's own public policies (shareholder value and customer value). Many staff found this conflict insurmountable and eventually decided to move to another firm. These two interviewees chose to leave the bank:

> Although Shinsei Bank officially declares that it offers a customer-oriented service, they actually ask us to hit good numbers. Customer satisfaction is never valued. Top management never listened to us. The firm where I am working now respects customer satisfaction together with numbers. This is one of the reasons why I left Shinsei Bank.

> I wanted to make profits through continuing to focus on surpassing the expectations and needs of our customers. We had no choice but to prioritize our new customers who make quick profits, because the management never seemed to care about its existing customers. One of my bosses tried to adopt a long-term strategy for our customers while spreading costs, but it took a long time to produce an outcome. Then he was fired. We could not treat our existing customers kindly. This is one of reasons why I quit my job there.

The management does not give staff personal discretion in achieving numbers. This is against Shinsei Bank's vision ('we sustain a culture in which employee ideas are respected and valued'). Shinsei did not appear to have generated a sense of responsibility for saying and doing, which led to strong disappointment among staff about Shinsei's new approach. Many eventually decided to quit the firm. Shinsei totally neglected to focus on its internal audience, resulting in a widening of the gap between saying and doing to such an extent that many employees began to reconsider their futures at the firm. Internal PR might be one of the ways to reduce such a gap. As stated earlier, Nissan and BTMU publish internal newsletters every month. LTCB has published its newsletter since its inception in 1952. Similarly to Nissan and BTMU, LTCB had explained its vision, newly introduced business official statement and so on. However, this internal circulation was abolished when Shinsei started operating in 2000, according to former LTCB bankers. Shinsei's distinctive gap triggered further scepticism among staff, as well as dissatisfaction and distrust towards Shinsei's US-style restructuring plans.

Clearly the undisclosed business model aimed at all stakeholders and the gap between saying and doing caused a crisis among the bank's staff. Many of these staff eventually chose to leave Shinsei Bank. Staff at Shinsei are highly criticial of management's lack of care and responsibility towards its stakeholders. Many have moved to other organizations in order to work for what they consider to be more trustworthy management, suggesting a powerful role for individual agency, not only in refusing to take part in top management's reforms, but also taking the drastic measure of quitting the organization altogether.

This analysis reveals a totally different picture of Shinsei's new business strategy from that in earlier literature, which talked about Japan's slow change. The Japanese operating methods have been deinstitutionalized at Shinsei, in that a new employment system and greater focus on profit making based on short-term thinking have been introduced. It is probable that there is more dramatic change under foreign ownership.[70] However, Shinsei's methods of restructuring do not seem to be associated with SVA management, as the bank's actions do not tally with its public claims: increasing labor costs while enforcing regular lay-offs, poor customer care and prioritizing the creation of quick profits. It is unlikely that SVA was adopted as a main measure to improve shareholder value. As one of the values for Shinsei's shareholders, Shinsei's dividend has been consistently lower than other listed firms. Table 5.4 compares the dividends allocated by Shinsei and BTMU. Shinsei's dividend was 1 yen until 2004, approximately 2.5 yen until 2009 and 0 yen after 2010.

Shinsei's shareholders have received little from the company's profits. Also Shinsei Bank has not returned the public funds that the bank borrowed from

*Table 5.4* Shinsei Bank and BTMU's dividends

| Year | Shinsei Bank's dividend (¥) | BTMU's dividend (¥) |
| --- | --- | --- |
| 2002 | 1.11 | 6.00 |
| 2003 | 1.11 | 6.00 |
| 2004 | 1.11 | 4.00 |
| 2005 | 2.22 | 6.00 |
| 2006 | 2.58 | 6.00 |
| 2007 | 2.96 | 7.00 |
| 2008 | 2.66 | 11.00 |
| 2009 | 2.94 | 14.00 |
| 2010 | 0 | 12.00 |
| 2011 | 0 | 12.00 |

the government. In total the bank borrowed ¥336.9 billion; ¥96.9 billion when
LTCB went bankrupt in 1998 and ¥240 billion when Shinsei Bank started
operating as a new bank in 2000. Although the terms of repayment of ¥120
billion was 2007, the bank did not make this payment due to its –¥60.9 billion
net loss in 2007. The remainder of the funds were due to be repaid in 2008 and
2009, but Shinsei missed these repayments owing to further net losses, –¥143
billion in 2009 and –¥140 billion in 2010. In 2007, 2008 and 2009 the government converted some of the preferred shares that it received when it injected funds to common ones to collect debts. However, as explained above, the
top executive has continued to receive high salaries (even when the bank had
shown heavy losses since 2007; see Table 5.2). These facts go totally against
Shinsei's public message about SVA management: 'to achieve this goal, we are
now working on optimizing our operations including cost rationalization and
will introduce Shareholder Value Added (SVA) as one of the measures
designed better to allocate our capital. We will continue to focus on expanding
our quality customer base organically'.[71] Thus, behind SVA management there
seems to be an undisclosed business model towards employees, customers and
shareholders. Shinsei's SVA management seems to be a part of its narrative
management that is in many ways similar to US-style narrative strategy.[72]

This narrative management, however, far from helping to secure understanding, has actually caused a crisis at Shinsei. Neither Shinsei's narrative
nor its very ambiguous tactics have been tolerated and accepted by staff. One
of the reasons for this is the firm's inability to reduce the gap between saying
and doing internally. Given that SVA management has not worked within the
bank, the unsound management of Shinsei's new approach has hindered the
establishment of internal support. Under such circumstances, staff do not
trust the SVA management and have questioned it. Many staff eventually
choose to quit Shinsei. Shinsei's narrative is merely a superficial performance
aimed at short-term gain and value skimming, and does not consider the
majority of its stakeholders. There has been no actor to transmit Shinsei's
narrative onwards into the future given that three presidents have left the
company since the introduction of the reform plans, and the mass media,
customers and staff have basically turned against Shinsei. This represents a
total failure of narrative management to help staff to understand and come to
terms with US-style restructuring plans.

## 5.5 A lesson from Shinsei Bank

Following the takeover by Ripplewood, Shinsei Bank announced to the
investor community that it would undertake popular US-reform strategies,
through the adoption of SVA management. This case shows a very uncom-
promising Anglo-Saxon form of business practice in HR and management
structures designed to prioritize the chasing of short-term profits. At Shinsei
Bank much more drastic changes have occurred, rather than continuity; a
finding that supports existing studies on the scale of change in Japanese firms

under foreign ownership[73]. However, as with the other two cases above, Shinsei's publicized reform plans did not reflect what the bank actually did, according to the interview data. There is a gap between saying and doing in the reform plan as SVA Management acts as a smokescreen behind which there is an undisclosed business model. This case shows that Shinsei's SVA management was another element of false signalling, in that it was not really adopted. Shinsei's radical reform plans are, therefore, another example of narrative management being enacted in Japan. Unlike the other two cases above, however, Shinsei's narrative strategy is more financially driven and much more similar to the US-style narratives[74]. Shinsei Bank has attempted to integrate the US system of SVA management into its restructuring plans since 2000. Shinsei has publicly pledged to create shareholder value through SVA management. However, the bank's external audience did not understand this new approach. Shinsei appeared unable and unwilling to secure social understanding. Recent studies have suggested[75] that IR is becoming a more important part of Japanese firms' overall strategies. An announcement is not enough to get outsiders to understand a new strategy. This case shows that media reporting played a powerful role in the bank's failure to gain external support. How the firm manages to influence media reporting is an important factor in earning and sustaining external understanding. The mass media is one of the most influential actors and the effort by a company to get its new strategy accepted by media outlets is a key element of organizational reform.

Employment downsizing and customer treatment were closely scrutinized using interview data, and the analysis showed that Shinsei has not implemented its previously publicized employment downsizing. This is because Shinsei has instigated an unofficial lay-off system, the existence of which contradicts widespread agreement in the literature about the lack of a deinstitutionalization of traditional Japanese HR practices.[76] Having said that, labor costs have actually increased, despite announcements of reductions through lay-offs. It seems that shareholder value is unlikely to be improved by the regular use of employment downsizing. In the meantime, making quick profits has become the main task for staff. The focus on quick profits means that customer care is marginalized by Shinsei, in spite of the firm's comment that 'we believe we have made the right choices to position our business for future growth by strategically focusing our business around our customers'.[77] However, it seems that profits are not distributed to shareholders. Dividend has been consistently lower than at other Japanese listed banks while Shinsei's management continue to command high salaries. The stock price has reached the lowest ever level since 2007. More drastic changes have occurred within the bank, but they have not reflected what the bank has said it would do in the public realm. The actual ways of reform have been very different from the public announcements. This is similar to an undisclosed business model towards customers, employees and shareholders.[78] Financialized management is accompanied by the gap between saying and doing,[79] and Shinsei's SVA management shows strong similarity with this. The form of narrative management revealed in this case attempts to distract internal and external attention from the value-skimming carried out by Shinsei's top management. Interestingly, however, this shielding or smokescreening has not worked, and criticism from staff and outsiders remains severe. Staff have been confronted with Shinsei's undisclosed business model behind its new reform plans and have expressed dissatisfaction with Shinsei's official announcement; and many eventually choose to leave the company. It seems that Shinsei did not really consider how the new reform plans might be interpreted by staff. This widened the gap between saying and doing, which has caused internal rejection. SVA management ultimately emerges as a superficial performance in a (largely failed) attempt to conceal the undisclosed business model. Given that many employees have chosen to leave the firm, there is no continuing process to help Shinsei's narrative continue into the future; Shinsei staff therefore have served to terminate Shinsei's reform plans. There are no strong leaders continuing to build up the new system up within Shinsei Bank. As past studies[80] indicate, more changes are likely to happen at foreign-controlled firms in Japan than at Japanese-controlled firms. In particular, Vogel (2006), who also examined the case of Shinsei Bank, based on data gathered during early 2000 when Shinsei had just started operating, argued that Shinsei's new reforms had been introduced and worked well within the firm under foreign control. As far as the case of Shinsei shows, there is the evidence of real adoption of US-style practices in the bank as well as the existence of extremely unpopular forms of top management value-skimming. However, it seems that the US business model does not work well in this case. This case shows that the task of securing and sustaining understanding in a hostile environment is a long and profoundly difficult one.

Chapters 3–5 examined private firms. The next chapter looks at a public sector local government organization, Yokohama City Council. It is not a listed company, but it too has announced drastic restructuring plans based around the (largely US) principles of New Public Management. Again, the internal data gathered at Yokohama City Council explores how staff at the council have understood the new reforms and to what extent the council has implemented its plans. Similarly to Nissan and BTMU, the much vaunted public announcements are not reflected by significant changes within the organization. Moreover, like Shinsei, and unlike Nissan and BTMU, the narrative seems to have failed, as internal and external audiences have not fully accepted it. Chapter 6 will explain how and why this happened.

## Notes

1  See, for example, Jacoby (2005); Morgan and Takahashi (2002); Vogel (2006).
2  See, for example, those reported in Froud *et al.* (2000).
3  Consolidated number of employees as of March 2008.
4  J. C. Flowers is the chairman of J. C. Flowers & Co. LLC, a US hedge fund. (See http://jp.reuters.com/article/businessNews/idJPJAPAN-31934320080523). He took the helm at Shinsei Bank despite limited public discussion. Apart from economics

ones there have been few studies about private equity firms because they are not necessary for meeting the requirements of public disclosure (Kaplan and Schoar 2005). As a result we know little about how they work and how they are constructed. What is commonly known about J. C. Flowers is that he takes over firms that are in distress or facing bankruptcy using equity with other capital investors. For example, together with a Chinese hedge fund he considered taking over AIG and Lehman Brothers in 2008. (See http://jp.reuters.com/article/businessNews/idJP JAPAN-31934320080523). He gained control of IndyMac, which went bankrupt in 2008, and also purchased 24 per cent of the shares of a German financial group, Hypo Real Estate Holding AG, which was severely damaged by the sub-prime crisis (ibid).

5  According to interviews with former LTCB bankers.

6  Shinsei Bank annual report (2001). Available at http://www.shinseibank.com/corp orate/en/ir/arir/2000.html

7  HR departments have full responsibility for personnel management in Japanese organizations (e.g. Graham 2003; Jacoby 2005).

8  Shinsei Bank annual report (2000). Available at http://www.shinseibank.com/inves tors/en/ir/financial_info/arir_1999/pdf/ar00eng.pdf

9  Shinsei Bank annual report (2008). Available at http://www.shinseibank.com/corp orate/en/ir/arir/2007.html

10  The listing contains 776 firms, which is equivalent to 45 per cent (*Nikkei* newspaper, 26 November 2008).

11  http://www.shinseibank.com/investors/common/news/pdf/pdf1999/000302jyoto_j.pdf

12  http://www.shinseibank.com/investors/en/common/news/pdf/pdf2004/041202executi ve01_e.pdf and http://www.shinseibank.com/investors/common/news/pdf/pdf2004/ 041202executive01_j.pdf

13  Porté served as CEO of Shinsei Bank on behalf of J. C. Flowers, which took over Shinsei Bank in 2000. Flowers invited Porté to become CEO of Shinsei Bank in 2005 and oversee the day-to-day running of the bank. (See http://www.shinseibank. com/investors/en/common/news/pdf/pdf2004/041202executive01_e.pdf and http:// tlsb=-.02w?>www.shinseibank.com/investors/common/news/pdf/pdf2004/041202ex ecutive01_j.pdf). He was a president of Morgan Stanley Japan and both he and Flowers attended Harvard Business School (*Weekly Toyokeizai*, 28 June 2008: 88). Unlike Carlos Ghosn of Nissan, Porté has not published any books about himself or his business. Most of media portray these individuals as mysterious elites working behind the scenes. Past studies contain few public disclosures made by any of the private equity firms (Kaplan and Schoar 2005), and little information is available about Flowers or Porté.

14  http://www.shinseibank.com/investors/en/common/biography/biography_toma.html

15  Bloomberg Global Finance, 20 February 2009. See http://sv.business-i.jp/news/ bb-page/news/200902200078a.nwc

16  http://www.shinseibank.com/investors/en/common/news/pdf/pdf2009/090701merger _e.pdf

17  According to *Mainichi* newspaper, 25 April 2009. Available at http://mainichi.jp/ seibu/seikei/archive/news/2009/04/25/20090425ddg001020004000c.html

18  Shinsei Bank. Available at http://www.shinseibank.com/investors/en/common/ news/pdf/pdf2010/100514merger_e.pdf

19  Shinsei Bank annual report (Japanese edition) (2008: 8). Available at http://www. shinseibank.com/corporate/en/ir/arir/2007.html

20  Ibid. (English edition).

21  Dore (2000, 2004).

22  The introduction of new HR practices has divided all the staff into three different groups: former LTCB bankers; new graduates from Shinsei Bank; and mid-career workers from outside. Cultural barriers exist between the groups. There has been a

loss of trust between employees (Maguire and Phillips 2008). Accordingly, an equal number of interviews with staff from each group was carried out during the second half of 2008 and the first half of 2009 for this study.

23  See, for example, Dore (2000).
24  See, for example, Graham (2003).
25  Shinsei Bank annual report (2000: 14). Available at http://www.shinseibank.com/investors/en/ir/financial_info/arir_1999/pdf/ar00eng.pdf
26  See, for example, Jacoby (2005).
27  See, for example, Watanabe (2002); Nishihara (2002).
28  See, for example, Aoki (1996); Matanle (2003); Morgan and Takahashi (2002); Sato (1997); Vogel (2006).
29  See, for example, Morgan and Takahashi (2002).
30  *Forbes*, 1 December 2002: 78, 79.
31  Shinsei Bank annual report (2000: 5). Available at http://www.shinseibank.com/investors/en/ir/financial_info/arir_1999/pdf/ar00eng.pdf
32  Ibid.: 94.
33  Ibid.: 4.
34  Ibid.: 5.
35  Shinsei Bank. Available at http://www.shinseibank.com/investors/en/about/company/pdf/shinseihistory100331e.pdf
36  Ibid.
37  *Weekly Diamond* (2004b: 20).
38  According to Toyokeizai (2000).
39  http://www.shinseibank.com/investors/en/about/company/pdf/shinseihistory100331e.pdf
40  Shinsei Bank annual report (2006). http://www.shinseibank.com/corporate/en/ir/arir/2005.html
41  According to its annual report (2007). http://www.shinseibank.com/corporate/en/ir/arir/2006.html
42  Ibid.: 17.
43  Ibid.
44  Ibid.
45  *Weekly Diamond* (2008d: 14).
46  *Weekly Toyokeizai*, 28 June 2008: 86.
47  *Weekly Diamond* 2008d: 14, 16.
48  Toyokeizai online edition. Available at http://www.toyokeizai.net/business/strategy/detail/AC/dbce7c9e96f35c886e31ca8df2e32475/page/1/
49  Shinsei Bank annual report (2010). Available at http://www.shinseibank.com/corporate/en/ir/arir/2009.html
50  See, for example, Dore (2008).
51  See, for example, Maguire and Phillips (2008).
52  See, for example, Graham (2003); Okubayashi (2002).
53  Shinsei Bank annual report (2009: 3). Available at http://www.shinseibank.com/investors/en/ir/financial_info/quarterly_results_2008/pdf/4qfy08presentation090514e.pdf
54  Consolidated figures including Shinsei Bank and Shinsei Financial.
55  According to Vogel (2006).
56  See, for example, Matanle (2003).
57  as indicated by Littler (2006).
58  Olcott (2008)'s argument.
59  Froud (2006).
60  *Weekly Diamond* (2008a: 106).
61  Ibid.
62  Such as Engelen (2003) and Hassard *et al.* (2009).

63 On the contrary, Nissan, which is ranked in first position, does not receive staff complaints about a discrepancy in pay between average and top earners. Staff do not think that a massive payment for the top management represents exploitation by Ghosn. Instead, they seem to accept Ghosn's narrative.

64 Shinsei Bank annual report (2006). Available at http://www.shinseibank.com/corporate/en/ir/arir/2005.html

65 Shinsei Bank. Available at http://www.shinseibank.com/investors/en/common/visionvalue.html?p_blk=ir

66 Ibid.

67 Ibid.

68 See Lazonick and O'Sullivan (2000).

69 Annual reports 1999–2009.

70 As indicated by Jacoby (2005) and Vogel (2006).

71 Shinsei Bank annual report (2008). Available at http://www.shinseibank.com/corporate/en/ir/arir/2007.html. This public claim is introduced in section 5.2.

72 Indicated by Froud *et al.* (2000).

73 Such as Jacoby (2005).

74 Studied by Froud *et al.* (2000).

75 See, for example, Morgan and Kubo (2005) and Olcott (2009).

76 Aoki (1996); Morgan and Takahashi (2002); Olcott (2008).

77 Shinsei Bank annual report (2008). Available at http://www.shinseibank.com/corporate/en/ir/arir/2007.html

78 Similarly to Froud *et al.* (2000).

79 Ibid.

80 See, for example, Jacoby (2005); Morgan and Takahashi (2002); Vogel (2006).

# 6    Yokohama City Council

## Temporary and political form of narrative management with new public management

### 6.1 Introduction

This chapter looks at Yokohama City Council. Yokohama City is home to a large number of municipal organizations and workers, and its finances are currently in deficit. The VoC approach and the debate on restructuring in government organizations suggests that public administration in Japan has very limited impetus for administrative reform as it remains under very strong institutional restraints. Public bureaucracies worldwide have a reputation as being risk and change averse, and Japanese public sector organizations are thus even more unlikely to want to break with traditional administrative cultures.[1] Nevertheless, the case study presented here suggests that Yokohama City Council has employed private companies' business management strategies, often referred to as New Public Management (NPM) to reduce the city's extremely large municipal deficit. Yokohama named its particular reform plan the Yokohama Revival Plan in what appears to be direct mimicry of Nissan's Nissan Revival Plan (NRP). The council acts together with the mass media to deploy its reform plan. The strategy includes an invitation to Nissan to set up its head offices in Yokohama, in order to contain costs and effect downsizing, and reorganizing the internal system for municipal workers in order to increase their awareness of services available to local residents. Despite this new administrative reform plan, research interviews conducted at the council actually indicate very limited usage of NPM, which again indicates that the announcements made by the council about its proposed changes can be usefully thought of as a form of narrative management. The outcome of this case study is that while the publicly disclosed reform plans were popular among the public, they were not matched by drastic change within the workplace. The Yokohama Revival Plan is thus another example of narrative management as a form of concealment or a smokescreen.

### 6.2 Yokohama City Council's new reform plans: New Public Management

This section provides general information about Yokohama City Council prior to presenting the analysis in the ensuing sections. There follows an introduction to Yokohama City Council's Yokohama Revival Plan, whose underlying motives are closely aligned with the paradigm of NPM, which was originally developed in the USA and has been widely applied worldwide.

### 6.2.1 Yokohama City Council

Yokohama City Council is made up of a large number of municipal organizations and workers. The total number of staff is around 15,000. Yokohama City is located very near to Tokyo and at 2011 its population was 3.69 million.[2] The new mayor, former government minister Hiroshi Nakada,[3] has been in post since 2002. The council had expanded its projects in light of growing amounts of revenue under retired former civil service bureaucrats. It is common practice in Japan for retired bureaucrats to become city mayors. Indeed, the two former governors of Yokohama City Council were administrative vice ministers in the central government prior to taking up their positions as mayor, and remained in post at the council for 24 years.[4]

However, once the economy was faced with long-term stagnation from the early 1990s, city councils across Japan were required to cut costs. Local government bodies, that had up to this point never really needed to make financial efficiencies, met considerable opposition and anger from citizens, therefore practical efforts for restructuring were required. Indeed, Yokohama City Council is currently burdened by an enormous debt of approximately ¥6 trillion[5] as a result of major deficit financing owing to its dependence on the central government. In recent years many observers have argued that it is time for local governments to implement reforms. Yokohama City Council proposed to adopt a US-style reform plan. Its manifesto for the reform plan were based on the theories of New Public Management.[6] The plan was called the Yokohama City Revival Plan, and was very similar to the NRP. Yokohama City Council outlined the Yokohama Revival Plan in an internal newsletter: 'the goal of the municipal government is that "it is always for the citizen". For that we need to make constant efforts and innovative changes. Let's look at ways of rejuvenating Yokohama City Council.[7]

Yokohama's reform plan bears many strategies similar to those widely used in corporate business management, such as privatization, outsourcing, and total quality management. Under to the reform plan, Yokohama City will lay down a new underground line that will run to Tokyo in the hope of boosting industry in Yokohama City. It outsources some of its administrative functions, such as waste disposal, to private companies. In terms of internal organizational reform, the council declared that its traditional system should be changed in order to increase the awareness of city workers leading to the improvement of services for its citizens and increase communication between workers, both of which were restricted by an overly large and wasteful bureaucracy. Traditionally the government's operational culture did not encourage the council's staff to work hard and citizens were ignorant of the ways in which public administration was carried out. Yokohama also announced that the city would reorganize its administrative personnel and pay structure in order to encourage efficiency on the part of employees. It explains changes at the council thus:

> The reorganization of the internal system means introducing cooperation, a decentralized system, and efficient city management, which are basic principles for the new administrative management. Through this reorganization, we aim to improve further citizen satisfaction about our services and to build up a simple, efficient and effective system.[8]

Each department was reorganized internally in 2007 as part of the council's reforms.

Externally, Yokohama invited Nissan to relocate its head office to the city in 2004. The manufacturing company was offered the use of vacant land upon which to construct its offices, and Nissan moved to Yokohama in 2009. The naming rights to the facility that takes ¥800 million per year to manage it, were sold to Nissan at the price of ¥2.3 billion for five years. The media regularly reports on this joint venture with Nissan.

This wide acknowledgement further spread into other local governments, and Yokohama's administrative revolution started to generate fans, followers, and imitators. An increasing number of Japanese local governments began to employ similar NPM reforms (see below). According to council staff with whom interviews were conducted, foreign (including Chinese) local government bodies and universities came to Yokohama City Council to learn about the Yokohama Revival Plan. The next section will provide the background to the Yokohama Revival Plan.

### 6.2.2 New Public Management at Yokohama City Council

A part of its drastic restructuring plans Yokohama City Council introduced New Public Management (NPM)[9]. Administration under NPM conditions supposedly gives citizens better services as well as empowering them to assume more responsible action by taking part in services rather than being controlled by a traditionally bureaucratic elite. This idea was further developed through the approach of neo-liberal economic concepts based on rational choice economics. NPM is based on the following principles: (1) improving services for citizens on low incomes; (2) introducing market-based mechanisms such as outsourcing; (3) providing higher-quality services (4) decentralizng of system; (5) reforming the policy-making process; and (6) strengthening accountability.[10] All of these principles clearly relate to corporate restructuring ideas such as Total Quality Management (TQM) which are used to shake up public bureaucracies which have become undemocratic, unaccountable, and inefficient.

The council announced its reform of municipal government in an internal PR newsletter as follows:

The five principles for new city management are as follows:
First, we shall introduce positive disclosure and provision of information. The provision of information is a key element of our reforms and a fundamental principle of administrative management. Without trust between the council and its citizens we cannot hope for cooperation ...
Second, we shall introduce efficient and effective administrative management. We shall pursue cost-effective fiscal management ...
Third, we will establish sustainable finances ...
Fourth, we will seek to improve the environment and thereby stimulate the best in the private sector......
Fifth, we will seek to empower the individual by enhancing the citizens environment ...[11]

The concepts of efficiency and empowerment of citizens which were new to traditional Japanese public bureaucracies, were brought into its administration system by the council. For example, with respect to the fourth principle, under Nakada's leadership the council started a development strategy to ensure the development of the private sector. Furthermore, at the behest of Nakada, the council invited Nissan to set up its headquarters in the city, thus ensuring greater future tax as well as helping to reduce the deficit. As to the second principle the routine works have been cut as one of the costs through privatization, outsourcing and so on. The following target is outlined on the Yokohama City Council website:

1 Cutting labor costs: we will try to decrease personnel costs through reducing the number of employees and changing the pay system.
Personnel costs will be trimmed by ¥9 billion.
2 Cutting the cost of routine works: we will go ahead with the privatization, outsourcing, digitization and revision of administrative work in order to cut the costs from existing businesses.
Expenses incurred by administrative work will be reduced by 1 per cent per annum.
Expenses incurred by ordinary work will be reduced by 3 per cent per annum.[12]

In an attempt to reduce costs, the council reformed its personnel management and pay systems:

We have revised the seniority-based pay system and have provided staff with a more advanced workplace in which his or her motivation, ability and achievement will be valued. Given the staff's achievement, an additional ¥1 million will be offered as a bonus to those at the level of deputy manager and above
Other changes include the staff performance evaluation system, performance-based pay system and changes to the retirement allowance.[13]

The council adopted these new systems to encourage staff to help to improve way in which it functions. The council indicates that whether the reform plan is successful or not depends on the changed mindset of council employees. Staff need to be aware of any restructuring plans. The council emphasized this point in an article that appeared in a business magazine:

> The council considers that an integral part of the Yokohama Revival Plan is that each council employee needs to think how he or she can improve the council. Staff are encouraged to contribute their own ideas, to discuss them openly, and then to outline their vision for the way forward.[14]

Through the use of NPM, the council actually introduced the new concept of the value of the council, specifically the 'Yokohama brand value', a concept redolent of corporate practice and imagery. According to the messages from the council to insiders about the image value in its internal PR newsletter:

> It seems to outsiders that the pace of work at the council is slow. We have to change this perception. I am thinking that the council needs make the council more attractive to people so that they feel that they would like to work there. We need to make it like Sony and today's Nissan.[15]

Thus, the council declared its ambition to improve Yokohama City Council so that it becomes as well known as some of Japan's biggest firms, such as Sony and 'today's' Nissan (clearly a reference to the new, post-NRP Nissan). Presumably 'yesterday's Nissan' was representative of the now outdated Japanese traditions. The concept of a Yokohama City 'brand' is an excellent example of the penetration of US-style business 'best practice' in Japan, and represents a major departure from the traditions of Japanese public administration. According to the council's comment on this issue in a business journal:

> Yokohama City has always been ranked high on any list of the image of cities. Many people are attracted by the Yokohama brand and hope to live in Yokohama City. I think that it is important to increase the value of Yokohama City.[16]

The council has indicated that Yokohama city needs a brand value, the notion of which is unusual for a local government body. Thus, in adopting NPM Yokohama City Council was introducing a quite new reform strategy. Japan (and Germany) have been the least active in that NPM jurisdiction has been very limited and there is a low correlation between execution of NPM and macro-economic performance.[17] Internal data gathered at Yokohama City Council will be examined below to provide detail about its new plan.

## 6.3 External acceptance and internal distrust of the Yokohama Revival Plan

Yokohama City Council publicly demonstrates that it has adopted the currently fashionable 'best practice' of NPM. This section will show how external and internal audiences reacted to the much trumpeted Yokohama Revival Plan. News of its ambitious reform plan spread throughout Japanese society. This social acceptance was enhanced by a substantial PR offensive undertaken by the council. However, internal reactions to the plan appear to be quite different from those of outsiders. This section will explain how and why Yokohama's new plan received strong external acceptance but did not achieve internal acceptance.

### *6.3.1 External acceptance of the Yokohama Revival Plan*

The council's new reform plan was welcomed by Japanese society following the council's adoption of NPM. It quickly received public acceptance. The Japanese mass media reacted especially positively. For example, one of business magazines profiled Nakada thus;

> Three years have passed since Nakada, at the age of 37 years, became the youngest ever mayor of Yokohama City Council. Under this new vision of civil administration Nakada continues to frame his unique policies. There has been no relaxation in his efforts to reform Yokohama City Council.[18]

The Japanese news and business media set a high value on the young reformer's restructuring plan.[19] The council became a natural target for the media's interest. The Yokohama Revival Plan' came to be widely discussed among media in a similar way to that of the Nissan Revival Plan, in that outmoded, traditional Japanese ways of organizing were being overturned by ambitious new thinkers brought in from outside. The council's reform as a local government version of Nissan as both organizations try to change an enduring traditional system:

> It only took Yokohama City Council two months to draft its Yokohama Revival Plan. It has overthrown Japanese tradition. The council's reform plan is very similar to that carried out by Nissan, but in this case by a municipal government. Yokohama City Council's (3.5 million employees) reforms have had a huge impact on other local governments who have yet to carry out any reforms of their own.[20]

Discussions by the mass media mainly focused on the transition from a traditional system. The media regards the council's reform plan as an ideal restructuring plan that will in turn be additionally copied by other local and regional government bodies. Furthermore, the media claimed that its drastic reform plan is based on cutting-edge approaches. For instance, one business magazine stated that:

> The number of local governments who have tried to implement reform themselves has increased since Nakada started. All these governments are aiming to achieve efficient administrative finance, and a change of the awareness of staff members and disclosure of information, all of which have not been going well. However, only Yokohama City Council has made steady progress with their reform.[21]

The mass media praises Yokohama City's bold reform plan. This kind of support has spread to other local governments. A large number of local governments have claimed to have already or recently adopted NPM including Zushi City Council (Kanagawa Prefecture), Seto City Council (Aichi Prefecture), Tokai City Council (Ehime Prefecture), Sapporo City Council (Hokkaido government), Kaga City Council (Ishikawa Prefecture), Kuwana City Council (Mie Prefecture), Osaka prefectural government, Kurume City (Fukuoka Prefecture), and Munakata City (Fukuoka Prefecture). Yokohama's adoption of US-style NPM restructuring has contributed to the further development of institutional pressures for a similar convergence on these new organizational norms elsewhere in Japan. According to interview data, other local governments also come to Yokohama city council in order to ask about its reform plan.

> Thanks to the disclosures about the Yokohama Revival Plan, people took interest in our council. That looks good and raises our self-esteem. Other local government representatives often came to Yokohama City Council to ask about the details of the Yokohama Revival Plan. We began to charge them for this information. No other local governments have charged. In this way, we are creating value for Yokohama City Council.

While contributing to the spread of NPM, Yokohama City Council added value to the Yokohama Revival Plan by charging other local governments for the disclosure of details about the plan. Clearly the Revival Plan enjoys the advantage of strong social support that is referred to as the 'Yokohama brand value'. Although the council introduced the new concept of brand value (see below), staff members do not have a clear image about what the brand value is. Instead, insiders think that the mayor strongly influences the image and value of the council, which is evidenced by the following interviewee:

> How do you create Yokohama brand value? This has not been as clear as it might be in a private firm. In that there is competition among cities, we try to create a good community and environment so that citizens feel that they want to continue to live in Yokohama City and we can prevent them

from leaving. Moving from other cities to Yokohama City is also valuable. How we attract people is important for our brand value. Nakada leads to create the image of Yokohama City or its attraction and the value.

Interviews with employees at Yokohama City Council revealed that members of staff do not share its exact concept of brand and value of the council, but they appear to roughly stick to the council's image as directed by Nakada. Yokohama City Council staff appear willing to cling to the image of Nakada and his ground-breaking reforms. The following interviewee also indicates the relationship between the image of Yokohama City Council and Nakada.

> When I was sent on loan to the central government two years ago, and asked other people who also worked there about Yokohama City Council, they said that Nakada's image is strong. It is rare that the mayor of a city is more famous compared with mayors of other local governments. At every mayor's meeting, the mass media always asks Nakada or the governor of Tokyo, Ishihara, for an interview. When he became the mayor, his reform plan impacted on the public and on the image of Yokohama City Council. I think that anyone would find him a great influence.

This evidence shows a close relationship between the mayor and the image of the city council. Nakada has come to personify the image of a city council undergoing radical restructuring: a young, dynamic leader with many new ideas. The council certainly succeeded in building on this image in order to radically reform its own image and brand value. Thus, the council seems to enjoy strong benefits as a result of this.

This strong external understanding is considerably enhanced by the council-led story, especially by using verbal and visual narrative forms. The very high degree of Yokohama's media coverage has contributed to strong support from the public. For example, Yokohama citizens have emphasized that they strongly accept the reform plan and pin their hopes for change in the council, as embodied by the image of Nakada. The next interviewee indicates that expectations of the council grew rapidly:

> People often repeat what Nakada says on the TV or in the media. I think that he sets the stage up so that the public are interested in Yokohama City Council. His TV appearances have a huge impact on society. When I get calls from people, they often said that "why did you do differently from what the mayor said." I have never experienced this kind of reaction from people prior to the arrival of Nakada. I feel that through his disclosures, people's expectations of us increase.

There has been a significant dissemination of Nakada's NPM reform plan due to his frequent media appearances. People get information about the reforms through the media, which helps to shape their expectations about the reform plan. People start looking forward to change. The council's media announcements construct a set of expectations for the council to play, much as we have seen in prior research on US 'celebrity CEOs' and their corporations[22]. The amount of disclosures by Yokohama could influence public reaction. Indeed, staff indicated significant differences between current and previous media attention towards Yokohama City Council. The following interviewee explained this point as follows;

> What has been the biggest change as a result of the Yokohama Revival Plan? The public announcements by the mayor are highly influential. We appreciate that Yokohama City Council receives much more attention from the media than before, which is very helpful. This is the biggest change from the past. I think that the mayor has attracted the audience. Although the former mayor also gave information, the media did not show much interest. Whether the media is attracted or not may depend on the character of the mayor.

This interviewee recognizes that the media's interest in the mayor is a major change. The number of magazine reports about Nakada is reported as being three times that of the former mayor[23]. Articles about Yokohama City Council appeared regularly in television, newspaper, radio, and business journal reports. The mayor usually appears on television twice a month and radio three times per week on behalf of the council. According to a press secretary who deals with media requests,

> how many times has he been in the news? He has received high degree of media coverage comprising television, radio, magazines and conferences. Total coverage number has been 100–150 during one year. Just after he became mayor in 2002, he received 150 interview requests by the media because he was very young to be a mayor. Now the number has declined to 100, but we have still too many offers from them to be able to handle them all.

Despite the fact that Nakada left office in 2009, he still continues to receive numerous interview requests,[24] far more than the incumbent mayor of Yokohama City Council, Fumiko Hayashi.[25] The high degree of media coverage contributed to securing strong external support for the council. Thus, strong social understanding was fundamentally boosted by the proactive PR strategy.

The effect of PR is enhanced further by its public information strategy with the help of the media. This public information strategy was verbally and visually designed by the council itself just like Nissan's. It was fortunate enough to interview the mayor, Nakada on 10 December 2008, and to be able to ask him direct about the intended purposes of his media strategy:

If society is interested in the information directly transmitted by our council, it is helpful for us. However, in reality the public's interest in our council is created by the media because people get a lot of information from the media. They hear something via the media and contact us for confirmation, which often happens. While the impact of disclosing information through the media is effective, the media is not interested in routine information, which make us cater to the media's taste by offering exciting information.

(Hiroshi Nakada[26])

It seems that the very person who rouses the media's interest in the council and encourages it to comment positively on the reforms is Nakada himself. As a commercially oriented organization Yokohama City Council feeds information to the media, which might eventually boost social understanding of the reform plan. The council dresses the story up for the media, and thus that external understanding is originated by Yokohama City Council, which emerges as a clever narrator.[27]

In addition, the council has adopted a visual as well as a verbal information strategy. For example, a photograph showing Ghosn and Nakada together was published by the council in 2005.[28] Yokohama imitates Nissan's narrative method of visually attracting society. This is a strong example of how Nakada follows Ghosn's public communications strategy. Through this image the council demonstrates that it is sharing in Nissan's cutting-edge US-style restructuring scheme. Thus, Yokohama actively provides verbal and visual information that meet the demand of current social pressures towards reforming moribund Japanese organizations. The council's sophisticated verbal- and visual-led discourses enhance its PR offensive.

External support was led by Yokohama's PR offensive which joins forces with its partner, the mass media.[29] Yokohama's considerable and sophisticated efforts to attract outsiders results in external understanding.

Yokohama City Council employs a similar strategy to Nissan in its search for external understanding. As Chapter 3 discussed, the way in which the council manages its PR and influences media reports are important elements of organizational restructuring. The difference between the reforms effected by Yokohama and Nissan is that external understanding of the council's reforms has not been sustained in quite the same way as previously. Indeed, the story has not been publicized as often as before to the public. There seems to be far less attention paid to the reform plan today, as a result of Nakada leaving office in 2009. Neither the city council nor its mayor currently receive much media attention.[30]

This section showed that social support for the NPM is secured by the council. Along with NPM, it has changed PR activity; it has adopted the council's proactive PR which is enhanced by sophisticated verbal and visual strategies. In particular, the mass media is closely involved in the public communication under Yokohama control. However, the change process was embodied by the well-known mayor Nakada, and since he left the council in 2009, there have been fewer actors to sustain this publicly accepted story. Yokohama thus emerges in the final analysis as a short-term performer that temporarily secured the necessary social acceptance. Thus, it is clearly not easy to sustain the effect of PR in the long term.

### 6.3.2 Internal scepticism and rejection

Although external audiences supported Yokohama's revival plan (at least at the outset), how did internal audiences interpret the new plan? This section will show how the council managed to get its staff to understand its new reform plan.

First, this section reveals that staff are rather sceptical about the PR offensive launched by the council. Some insiders claimed that they viewed the mayor's popularity dubiously owing to his manner of disclosing information to the public:

> I feel that the mayor appears on television or magazine for his own purposes. It means that Yokohama City has become famous nationally, but I wonder if the mayor's work might be for the benefit of his future career. I would not be surprised if he were to leave suddenly and run for election to the Lower House election now.

This insider wonders if Nakada's frequent appearances on media are not for the benefit of the council employees but for himself. This is because the mayor had been actually a member of the Lower House from 1993–2002 prior to becoming mayor. Another interviewee again complains about Nakada taking advantage of the media, which incurs a certain distrust:

> What is the impact of the mayor's disclosing information through the mass media about insiders? It depends on how we are received. I feel that 70 per cent of insiders respond negatively. This is because we suspect that he uses media for his own benefit. He has not been understood by us. We distrust him. We think that he wants to become well known because it will make it easier for him to rejoin the central government in the future.

By this point some distance has opened up between the mayor and staff. Insiders feel that the audience for insiders is different from the audience for the mayor. The two interviewees doubt that Nakada really has the council's best interests at heart, and are sceptical about his PR crusade. As the charismatic leader of the council Nakada was feted by outsiders; however, he has not been welcomed by insiders. Charismatic leaders are not necessarily preferred by insiders.[31] Nakada himself has not been understood, trusted and legitimized by the staff.

Furthermore, such internal scepticism about him affects the internal credibility of the reform plan. This interviewee indicates that staff came to reject the popular term 'restructuring'.

> We feel that the term 'restructuring' denies our pasts, and mistrust has grown every time Nakada uses the term. My colleagues in my department do not like the term, 'Yokohama Revival Plan' because they are proud of their past achievements. Last year we decided that we would not use the term. If we do use it, we try to rephrase it thus: 'restructuring does not mean that our past work was not good'. The term Yokohama Revival Plan suggests that we are superfluous to requirements.

This staff member showed scepticism and some degree of resentment about the council's new language. While that term has become popular within society, it has weighed heavily on staff. Insiders have eventually become tired of the term, which is further evidenced by the following interview:

> The mayor always repeats the term 'Yokohama Revival Plan' in public. The fact that he does so has won social trust for it. On the other hand, we are tired of that term and are not comfortable with it. I feel that insiders are wondering who is to blame for this mess? We tend to blame the mayor now. I think that Nakada stresses the term 'reform' too much.

Staff feel alienated from the supposedly radical reform plans and eventually begin to deny and tacitly resist them. Although Yokohama won social acceptance for the Yokohama Revival Plan, it did not manage to secure acceptance from staff. The council was faced with a tougher process of securing internal understanding than external understanding. Given this situation, how has the Yokohama Revival Plan been implemented within the council? This will be examined in the following section.

## 6.4 Yokohama City Council's narrative management

Yokohama City Council has not been able to get staff to understand and support the Yokohama Revival Plan that had been so strongly welcomed by wider Japanese society. This section will examine the extent to which the Yokohama Revival Plan has been carried out by the council in practice and how the council failed to manage internal acceptance of the plan. Among its restructuring plans, this research focuses on its attempts to reform the awareness of insiders and to transform HR practices within the council. The following section provides further details about the ways in which insiders' involvement in the reform process becomes increasingly limited as they disengage from it. This section will show how the failure to gain internal support caused further scepticism about the popular reform plan as the external PR machine became undermined by the neglect of focus on internal perception.

### *6.4.1 Yokohama's narrative management: employment downsizing*

Under the Yokohama Revival Plan the city council announced a sharp reduction in traditional Japanese HR practices. Given the fact that insiders have become less motivated to accept change within the council, how were the new HR practices deployed and enacted within the council? In official documents, the council claims that a considerable number of internal posts had been cut as part of the Yokohama Revival Plan organizational restructuring. During the period 2002–09 6.926 internal employees were laid off (20.5 per cent). As a result of this, labor costs were expected to be reduced by ¥19.3 billion (8.6 per cent) by 2010.[32]

These lay-offs took effect from 2006 onwards. Yet the council did not disclose how these lay-offs were made. During 2005–2006 (during H16-H17 in the above figure), it reduced by 3,606 staff. Yet that number includes 2,633 staff who were cut by Yokohama city university which is technically independent of the city council.[33] Furthermore, the council has included in its total of staff reductions a number of staff who have belonged to not only the council but to also other administrative groups including city universities, junior and high schools, the board of education, the waterworks bureau, and the fire authorities. The council itself comprises approximately 15,000 staff. Given this wider picture, the number has hardly changed; the overall number has fluctuated between 15,414 in 2006, 15,089 in 2007, 14,899 in 2008, 14,625 in 2009, and 14,489 in 2010 (see Table 6.1).[34]

One of member of the council staff[35] talked about the lay-offs:

> As public servants we are guaranteed employment until 60 years of age according to the law of Yokohama City Council. There have been no layoffs as a large number of staff born during the baby boom continues to retire every year. Staff numbers have been reduced naturally without any need for employment downsizing.

Born soon after the Second World War,[36] the baby boom generation numbered 8.05 million persons.[37] During 2007–09 a large number of these baby boomers retired every year in Japan. In 2007, 60 per cent of staff who left the council were due for retirement;[38] thus 168 of 278 staff retired; 28 left owing to sickness or injury, and 82 departed for personal reasons. Yokohama City Human Affairs Committee said that it had gradually extended the retirement age from 60 to 65 years owing to the large number of retired officials from this baby boom generation.[39] From 2003 the council adopted a reappointment system for retired officials. While 50–60 per cent had been reappointed by the council in 2003, the current number stands at 70 per cent.[40] Reappointed staff now amount to about 5 per cent of the total number of officials in the council.[41]

The announcement about the Yokohama Revival Plan neglected to mention the reappointment system. Instead, the council emphasized how much it had reduced a (very vaguely calculated) total number of staff. This is similar to Vogel (2006)'s 'over-announcement' about lay-offs. As we saw in Chapter 3 similar methods have also been used by Nissan. This is an example of downsizing fraud[42] in that the narrative deliberately misleads the public understanding through its rather vague and often tendentious messages. The council's public statements form part of its overall strategy of narrative management. The extensive use of Japanese firms' employment downsizing[43] seems to be true only if one takes Japanese companies' public statements literally, rather than actually closely exploring companies' actual (often very limited) downsizing practices.

Moreover, a gap between saying and doing is also visible in terms of the 'non-change' represented in the council's supposedly new pay system. The council has made several public comments about the need for a new personnel and pay system. It has indicated that 'staff can earn rewards and eventually improve his or her motivation under this new system'.[44] The following interview data, however, shows that the seniority-based pay system remains in place (as it does at Nissan and BTMU) and that the new evaluation system has only been very superficially introduced.

> Under the employee evaluation system, we are required to plan each goal and report whether we achieve it or not at the end of each year. The bosses rate our performance on a scale of one to five. However, we do not think that this system works. The top 5 per cent of employees get an increase of 5 per cent in bonuses. This works out at ¥10,000 each, which is not very much.
>
> The seniority-based pay system has been maintained here, so older staff who are just at general officer level earn higher wages than the younger staff who are above deputy manager level. In other words, not higher titled staff but older staff generally have the authority to control the workplace. In the worst workplace, the staff do not respect even deputy managers as his or her boss. Maybe this is one of the biggest reasons why some employees are not prepared to work hard.

*Table 6.1* Total staff headcount: Yokohama City Council (2003–10)

| Year | Total staff headcount |
| --- | --- |
| 2006 | 15,414 |
| 2007 | 15,089 |
| 2008 | 14,899 |
| 2009 | 14,625 |
| 2010 | 14,489 |
| 2011 | 14,509 |

The traditional (arguably semi-dysfunctional) Japanese seniority-based pay system seems to remain in place at the council. Under the existing seniority-based pay system, older employees tend to control the workplace. If the seniority-based pay system has been maintained (which is contrary to the public assertions made by the council), it seems to be incompatible with the new job evaluation system that was supposed to have modernized employment practices in the organization. It seems that new pay system has been superficially introduced. This point is highlighted by the following interviewee:

> Actually, only a very small number of employees aspire to reach deputy manager level or above, even under the new evaluation system. The council's staff generally choose to go out to work because they value their personal lives. Many women work here, and they do not really expect or plan to be promoted. When they reach their late twenties staff have the right to take the exam for deputy manager level. However, only about 10 per cent of those who have this right take the exam. If someone take the exam, their colleagues will ask them why they are taking the exam. This situation has not changed so far.

This interview data also shows that the evaluation system does not motivate staff to work towards promotion along the lines of a modernized employment relationship as part of archetypal NPM reforms. Indeed, less than 10 per cent of staff qualified to do so take the exam.[45] In fact, the number of staff who take the exam for deputy manager positions has been decreasing since the new system was introduced in 2006; 182 staff in 2006 and 164 staff in 2007.[46] Despite the apparently low levels of staff motivation within the workplace, the council nevertheless announced positive outcomes for its new NPM-style evaluation system. For example, the council announced in 2009 that its new system has had a 100 per cent success rate.[47] Its public claims do not mirror what is happening within the council under the new HR practices, and instead serve to create a smokescreen effect with its public narrative of change and modernization. Unlike its public message, it seems that employee motivation and reward remain thorny issues that have changed little within Yokohama City Council.

### 6.4.2 *Yokohama's narrative management: levels of internal consciousness*

Through its Yokohama Revival Plan, the council primarily focuses on changes in the awareness of its staff (see below). These business magazines emphasized that council staff motivation had been considerably enhanced as a result of the reforms.

> Internally a greater number of workers start speaking out about their own visions, which were promoted by their own free will. Furthermore, 79 per

cent of staff have worked with a sense of mission and have felt more need to reform within their organizations.[48]

Contrary to such announcements by the council, the interview data drawn from within the council seems to show that staff are not really buying into this supposedly new approach. When the council first announced the Yokohama Revival Plan, the NPM-style approach was generally welcomed by younger staff but not by older staff. The older staff basically did not have the desire for change in the council. In this example, this member of staff explained that older staff completely rejected change within the council;

> We have the impression that the Yokohama Revival Plan means cutting the number of staff. Some of them are union activists, so this reform plan can cause bigger problems. As part of the plans a reform committee was set up so that staff can bring up a reform proposal and discuss what the council needs to change. One representative from each department has to be a member of the reform committee. I was a member last year, but it was very difficult to discuss the issue within my department because there are many older staff in my department. If I were to tell the older staff about what was discussed within the committee, I wonder if they might bully me.

The response of older staff to the organizational reform was never favourable. The following interviewee also pointed out the older staff's negative reaction to the reform plan:

> I have gained the impression from within the workplace that older staff are hostile to the term 'restructuring'. How successful is the Yokohama Revival Plan? To be honest, we have not shared the purpose of that plan though we know that popular term. There is a gap between the term and our everyday work.
>
> Every time he [Nakada] uses the term 'reform', I feel a heaviness within me. I regard our efforts to make advances in our daily work as 'reform', but that term suggests that we should change. I do not feel that we need to change. The term 'reform' does not explain what we need to do or change. It is a vague term.

The older staff feels uneasy about organizational change as prior research[49] indicates that Japanese organizations and employees are reluctant to change traditional styles. In this case, it seems that it is not easy for older staff to welcome a new reform plan.

On the contrary, some younger staff seemed to have higher hopes of Nakada's change program and appeared to be highly motivated by the prospect of reform and change. One of the reasons is the strong external support secured by the reform plan. The positive social reaction to the plan helped to awaken expectations of staff. The younger staff came to support the council's reform plan because they were influenced by the mayor's substantial levels of public disclosure, according to the following interviewee:

> Ever since the new mayor took office, he has used the term 'reform'. The younger staff expect some changes to occur through his reform plan. They hear about his reform plan through the mass media, so their viewpoints are not from insiders but outsiders. The younger staff bring up some issues that staff should reform together at a reform committee which is composed of younger staff from each unit.

When society had a good understanding of Nakada's reform plan younger staff reacted more positively to the media's reports about the council, accepted it, and came to have expectations as to what the reform would do for them as newer council employees. Media coverage can increase the credibility of a restructuring plan, and it could lead to the boosting of insiders' expectations for the new reform plan.[50] Indeed, much like the general public which is influenced by the council's media performances, staff also express an interest in what the mayor says about the Yokohama Revival Plan according to the following interviewee:

> Every Monday staff discussed what the mayor said about the Yokohama Revival Plan on television programs that had been broadcast at the weekend. He often appears in the mass media. We are interested in his comments. I think that this is the biggest change. In addition, new officers took pictures of the mayor at the welcoming party when Nakada took office. They asked to have their picture taken with him. This did not happen before. He is a charismatic person.

Some employees pay more attention to Nakada's public comments about the reform plan. In particular, it seems that younger staff who have just started work after graduating from university tend to support Nakada, who is now popular among society. He came to be treated as a hero of Yokohama City Council just like Nissan's Ghosn, with staff wanting to meet him and take photographs of him. Despite the past argument by academics in Japanese organizational studies[51] that it is not easy for staff to absorb totally different management styles, Yokohama younger staff appeared not to be put off by the reform plan.

However, this internal motivation did not seem to last very long. Young staff who had relatively higher expectations of the reform plan began to show feelings of discontent with the reform plan. The following interviewee explained this point thus:

> We actually tried to improve the communications system, but while we did not believe that the current system would improve, we do not want to

return to the former system. That is, we have not found the current situation to be satisfactory. Given the stringent fiscal situation, our ideas and views have not been put to practical use. Although communication among the internal employees has improved, we have not been able to do anything owing to a lack of financial resources. The budget is reduced every year. The Yokohama Revival Plan is not functioning well now. We will refuse these continuous reforms and his [Nakada's] frequent use of term 'restructuring'.

The younger staff had great expectations of the reform plan, but soon realized that severe difficulties had ensued once the reforms started. Considerable pressure was exerted on younger staff to change and engage in tough reform measures, and as a result many staff became reluctant and resistant. One younger member of staff complained about the difficulties caused by the radical changes at the council:

> Whether insiders support the mayor's reform plan or not depends on the insider's sense of value and level of consciousness. To put it bluntly: it depends on whether they like the mayor or not. It is difficult to fundamentally change those points. On the negative side, they have become brainwashed by the mayor. However, the language which he often uses implies that there is a need for change. Then they gradually reject the mayor's comments because he stresses the term 'reform' too much.

Younger insiders' high motivation that was provided by the council's reforms was allowed to rapidly dissipate. The interview data related to this area indicate two important points. First, the council publicly keeps promoting the Yokohama Revival Plan which is popular externally but increasingly unpopular among the staff. Insiders have eventually become tired of the name. This implies that Yokohama might not pay attention to how staff understands its new reform plan. The council appears to lack genuine consideration for the feelings of its staff when it is explaining the council's reform plan. Public communication has been changed,[52] but it is not, by itself, sufficient to sustain genuine organizational reform. It also requires serious and committed work to encourage insiders to join the restructuring plan. Second, productivity and efficiency are notoriously difficult to assess in public sector service environments.[53] As we can see below, the total amount of the council's debts has actually increased in recent years, despite the repeated pronouncements about restructuring to clear the council's deficits (see Table 6.2). The debt was ¥2.33 trillion in 2003 but this had risen to ¥2.41 trillion in 2011.[54]

Various reasons have been suggested for the failure of the reforms within the council, including inadequate budgets, and the fact that it has proved more difficult than originally envisaged to deinstitutionalize the existing system than it might have been within a private firm. A wide range of research indicates that it is especially difficult for local governments to adopt private firms' management strategies.[55]

The reforms may involve a much more difficult set of tasks than many employees expected. Both the older and younger staff started to resist the supposedly drastic organizational reforms in certain ways. Whether or not they increased their awareness of Yokohama's reform plan hugely depended on their understanding of what its practical implications might mean for them. Past arguments about Japanese restructuring tend to place greatest emphasis on the perspective of outsiders and does not see the daily pragmatic forms of resistance or indifference that take place at the level of insiders' behaviour. This case sheds light on the importance of internal interpretation when considering organizational change, which articulates that insiders often also act out of self-interest. It seems that it is more difficult to encourage insiders to join the new reform plan than the council planned.

This section showed that the council introduced its new HR system through the Yokohama Revival Plan but did not endeavour to make it work for its staff. After a promising start, Yokohama's plan never really managed to achieve substantial organizational reform in both insiders' consciousness levels and HR practices. The reform plan focused more on saying than doing. Thus, the Yokohama Revival Plan is another example of Japanese corporate narrative management, in this case enacted in a public sector setting. It appears that the acceptance and resistance of organizational change are extremely delicate processes.

Insiders' ambivalence and even hostility towards reform is perhaps partly a result of Yokohama City Council's low levels of care and attention towards communicating with its staff. The process of organizational change could be managed better by if greater effort was expended on internal action to avoid the trend towards rejection by employees. The council expended much more energy and effort on trying to create external understanding, and gave insufficient attention to internal factors. The council did not recognize how its staff began to experience and interpret its narrative. Its narrative was always aimed

*Table 6.2* Total amount of debts

| Year | Yokohama's amount of debts |
|------|----------------------------|
| 2003 | ¥2.33 trillion |
| 2004 | ¥2.41 trillion |
| 2005 | ¥2.42 trillion |
| 2006 | ¥2.41 trillion |
| 2007 | ¥2.39 trillion |
| 2008 | ¥2.38 trillion |
| 2009 | ¥2.37 trillion |
| 2010 | ¥2.38 trillion |
| 2011 | ¥2.41 trillion |

more at external audiences, which means that it was mostly made up of an external social performance. Due to its inadequate focus on staff, employees began to deny and resist the council's reform plan and their distrust of it increased. Eventually most employees refused to associate themselves with the new reform plan. This is one aspect of insider's behaviour in organizational change that could have probably have been better shaped if the council had been more attentive and sustained its internal narrative management.

As of today, Yokohama's PR is no longer working; the media attention on the Revival Plan has dissipated and none of the staff are willing to sustain Yokohama's narrative, especially following the departure of the iconic Nakada. With internal instability, nobody has taken over the Nakada narrative to maintain the focus on external support. Skilfully handled PR activity has not been backed up by insiders joining in and supporting the PR over a longer time period. In the end, it appears that the internal rejection eventually impacts negatively on the effectiveness of Yokohama City Council's new reform plans and PR activity.

## 6.5 A lesson from Yokohama City Council

In Japan great pressure has recently been brought to bear even on local government organizations to reform. Yokohama city council embarked on a dramatic and nationally famous restructuring strategy, embodied by Nakata and influenced by US-style NPM ideas. The Yokohama Revival Plan came to be widely supported by Japanese society. However, the interview data gathered at the council shows that its NPM – especially in terms of its new HR practices and internal level of consciousness – does not reflect the actual reforms undertaken with Yokohama City Council. The finding of this case study is that there is a gap between its saying and doing, as manifested in the very limited real uptake of NPM. Unlike external acceptance, internal acceptance has been particularly weak. Yokohama's public announcements are another example of Japanese narrative management used as a smokescreen.

Japanese local government reforms have received very little academic attention, and it is widely believed that there has been barely any meaningful change in Japanese public administration.[56] However, the case of Yokohama City Council demonstrates significant novelty in the new restructuring plan based around NPM. In particular, this chapter focused on the council's active PR for its reform plan. It seems that Japanese organizations have started restructuring their traditional ways of operating.[57] US-style restructuring becomes diffused even into highly conservative public sector organizations. The council became a high-profile example of a public bureaucracy undergoing change and embarking on a significant and sophisticated PR offensive which had a national impact, the effects of which were further enhanced by sophisticated verbal and visual-led messages. Among the past literature on Japan little attention has been paid to organizations' public activity.[58] Morgan and Kubo (2005), and Dore (2011) suggest that IR is being given greater priority by Japanese firms than ever before. The present case suggests that this is indeed true, even in a local government of which public activity, and demonstrating change and modernization, is becoming a much more important part of its strategy.

This case further shows that the council joined forces with the mass media in order to transmit its reform plan in the same manner as Nissan.[59] Its message can be adjusted to suit the media. In this sense, the target of the council's PR strategy is therefore the media rather than internal stakeholders. Through its proactive use of PR via media outlets, the Yokohama Revival Plan came to be highly recognized by Japanese society. How to establish connections with the mass media is an issue of vital importance in the securing of acceptance as the case of Nissan shows. How the council affects the reactions of the mass media to the reform plan is an important process of organizational change. The media is an important tool to transmit organizations' restructuring in US and UK firms.[60] Although past studies about Japan have typically shown little focus on the relationship between organizations and media, it is demonstrated here that the media is playing an increasingly important role in the ongoing restructuring of Japanese organizations.

Unlike external interpretations, interview data gathered within the council articulates a different picture. Under the changed conditions of the supposed introduction of NPM, the extent to which internal levels of consciousness and HR practices have changed, is examined. The interview data actually shows that these new practices have not changed very much, and that the change measures have not really worked among staff. It is quite difficult for a local government to deal with these issues. The fundamental reason is that insiders do not really value the reforms and fundamentally are resisting them. Nevertheless, Nakada and Yokohama City Council still felt the need to press on with their public messages of change. It is argued that this is a clear case of a gap between saying and doing and thus the Yokohama Revival Plan is another pertinent example of Japanese corporate narrative management.

This finding indicates that the development of US-style restructuring is becoming accepted among Japanese firms,[61] which is only true in terms of the public statements by top management level. Similarly, recent work[62] has suggested that further changes are taking place in Japanese organizations. However, these arguments are not based on internal perspectives. This earlier work did not fully consider the deeper aspects of insiders' reactions to top-level management strategies and actions. This analysis, through consideration of more in-depth side of insiders' behaviour under new reform plans, demonstrates that change within Japanese organizations is still limited, which supports the argument about slow change indicated by Dore's earlier writings[63] and other classic works on Japan.[64]

The analysis further shows that the gap between saying and doing has not really been reduced at the council. Staff have found it irritating that the council has continued to advertise and promote what is essentially empty rhetoric in public arenas. As a result of its very limited consideration of insiders' mental conflict, the council lost internal support. Yokohama failed to recognize how staff understands its new organizational change. The majority of the council employees have rejected the Yokohama Revival Plan and distrust it. Thus they refuse to be involved in the council's narrative management and PR activity. This outcome could perhaps have been lessened or avoided if the organization had been more attentive and sustained in its communication processes towards insiders.

Although this chapter demonstrated that the Yokohama Revival Plan is a form of narrative management, it also shows how the council reformed its PR activity. Its PR strategy bears many similarities to Nissan's, but the fundamental difference is that Yokohama City Council's PR strategy has not really worked well over the long term. Few actors remain at the council who might be willing publicly to sustain this externally supported project of transformation. As this has not happened, media attention in the council seems to have decreased recently. This seems to be a result of Nakada's departure from the organization and the increase in internal distrust, and this eventually influences public discussions about the effect of organizational change. Internal processes of accepting or rejecting change and narratives of change are very delicate issues. There are many complex reasons why even subtle changes in PR activity can be difficult to sustain.

Bearing in mind this issue of complexity, and the ease with which change – and narratives of change – can fail, the next chapter provides theoretical consideration of the findings of this study. The chapter will also go on to discuss potential prospects for the ongoing debates on 'continuity and change' and narrative management theory, especially as they apply to the highly complex Japanese environment.

## Notes

1  See, for example, Amable (2003); Osborne and Gaebler (1992); Pollitt (2003).
2  See Yokohama City Council's website. Available at http://www.city.yokohama.lg.jp/ex/stat/index-e.html (accessed 30 August 2012).
3  The mayor of Yokohama City Council, Hiroshi Nakada is widely recognized as a successful reformer within Japanese society. Nakada found it easier to gain external acceptance for Yokohama's reform measures as he was following the proven, now legitimized path taken by Ghosn at Nissan. Nakada ran as a candidate for mayor in 2002, when the council just started to consider plans to break away from a dependence on deficit-financing bonds. At that time, Nakada was a member of the House of Representatives. When he announced his candidacy in 2002, he also outlined plans for reforms; restructuring the bureaucratic system that sought to dramatically reduce the deficit and improve services for citizens. Nakada, who is young, dynamic, media-friendly and motivated about effecting reform, easily won over the hearts of his audience. Local and national media reacted particularly positively towards him. With the strong support of the media he became the youngest ever mayor of a major Japanese city at the age of 37 years.
4  See *Ajino-techo* (2006) 'Nakada Hiroshi; Seicho Kakudai no Jidai, Sonokotowo Ninshiki Sitemoraitai'. *Ajino-techo:* 5–19.
5  As of 2006.

6  See, for example, Osborne and Gaebler (1992).

7  Yokohama City Council internal PR newsletter (June 2004: 5).

8  Yokohama City Council (2007) 'The Reorganization of the Internal System'. Available at http://www.city.yokohama.lg.jp/somu/org/jinji/soshikiteisu/kishahapp you/041202.pdf (accessed 11 September 2010).

9  Osborne and Gaebler (1992).

10  According to Kettl (2000).

11  Yokohama City Council internal newsletter (June 2004: 5).

12  Yokohama City Council website. Available at http://www.city.yokohama.jp/me/ keiei/seisaku/newplan/zaisei02.html

13  Yokohama City Council mid-term report (2006: 56).

14  *Weekly Diamond* (2004: 135).

15  Yokohama City Council (May 2004: 5).

16  *Fooga,*May 2007: 23.

17  See, for example, Pollitt (2003).

18  According to *Weekly Diamond*, 21 May 2005: 94.

19  The young mayor immediately began to attract media attention, with multiple requests for interviews and TV appearances coming his way. In addition, the media follows the history of his life, his profile, and his guru-like tips on how to reform companies successfully in books. The mass media views Nakada as a successful reformer like Nissan's Ghosn. His extraordinary success story is told in many Japanese 'pop business' books. Like Carlos Ghosn, who published his account of the Nissan Revival Plan, Nakada has also written 11 books about his experiences and the road to successful leadership. According to one of his books, 'Whether you succeed or not depends entirely on how hard you try ... When I was a high school student, I dropped behind in class and therefore failed to get into any of the universities. I spent two whole years preparing for the entrance examinations after I left high school. I finally succeeded in the examination for Aoyama Gakuin University. For other things, I keep challenging anything I am interested in and can now enjoy and have a full life. We can break new ground if we try our hardest. In 2002 I was elected as the mayor of Yokohama City Council and I am now striving to reform it'. (Nakada 2005: 7–11). He claims that he has had to work hard for his career success, implying that dreams can come true for those prepared to work hard. This book has been purchased by more than 50,000 people, most of who are businessmen and university or high school students. He has come to be recognized as a hard worker, and a successful new leader by Japanese society. He was selected as an example of a new, young global leader by the World Economic Forum in 2005. He was later elected again in the secondary stage of a mayor in 2006. Thus, Nakada quickly came to be recognized as a new, young and global political high-flier.

20  Minami and Kamiyama (2004).

21  According to *Weekly Diamond*, 19 June 2004: 133. This magazine devoted six pages to Nakada's reform plans.

22  See, for example, Khurana (2002).

23  See, for example, Aikawa *et al.* (2005).

24  Yokohama City Council. Available at http://www.city.yokohama.jp/se/mayor/log/ (accessed 11 September 2010).

25  Ibid.

26  Interview with the mayor on 10 December 2008 at his office at Yokohama City Council.

27  See, for example, Stark (2003); Froud *et al.* (2000); Boje (2001).

28  See *Hamagin Sogo Kenkyusho*, March 2005: 18.

29  See, for example, Froud et al. (2000); Khurana (2002).

30  Yokohama City Council. Available at http://www.city.yokohama.jp/se/mayor/log/ (accessed 11 September 2010).

31  See, for example, Collins (2001).
32  Yokohama City Council (2006: 9). Available at http://www.city.yokohama.lg.jp/za isei/ir/mayor2104.pdf
33  Yokohama city university. Available at http://www.yokohama-cu.ac.jp/ (accessed March 2012).
34  According to Yokohama City Council. Available at http://www.city.yokohama.lg. jp/ex/stat/index2.html#20
35  According to interview data from deputy manager (21 November 2008).
36  Sakaiya (1976).
37  Ministry of Health, Labour and Welfare (2009). See http://www.mhlw.go.jp/toukei/ saikin/hw/jinkou/kakutei09/dl/2-1hyo.pdf
38  Yokohama City Council Statistics Department. Available at http://www.city.yoko hama.lg.jp/jinji/kankoku/h22bessi3.pdf
39  Yokohama City Council Human Affairs Committee (2009). See http://www.city. yokohama.lg.jp/jinji/kankoku/20honbun.pdf
40  Yokohama City Council, Statistics Department (2011: 44, 45). See http://www.city. yokohama.lg.jp/jinji/kankoku/h22bessi3.pdf
41  Ibid.
42  As indicated by Littler (2006).
43  Ahmadjian and Robinson (2001)'s view.
44  Yokohama City Council mid-term report (2006: 56).
45  Yokohama City Council Human Affairs Department (2009: 5, 6).
46  Ibid. (2006–08). See http://www.city.yokohama.lg.jp/jinji/houdou/syounin-061207. pdf and http://www.city.yokohama.lg.jp/somu/org/jinji/kentou/040223/shiryo-jyosei. pdf
47  Yokohama Middle Plan (2009: 4).
48  PHP (2005).
49  See, for example, Matanle (2003).
50  See, for example, Higgins and Dzjkzbach (1989).
51  See, for example, Graham (2005); Okubayashi (2002).
52  Dore (2008).
53  Pollitt (2003).
54  According to Yokohama City Council Financial Affairs Bureau. Available at http://www.city.yokohama.lg.jp/zaisei/org/zaisei/daidokoro/ (accessed 30 March 2012).
55  See, for example, Pollitt (2003), (2007); Brunsson (1993).
56  Pollitt (2003).
57  Ahmadjian and Robinson (2001)'s suggestions.
58  With the recent exception of Olcott (2009).
59  See Fligstein (1990); Froud et al. (2000); Khurana (2002).
60  See, for example, Froud et al. (2000).
61  Ahmadjian and Robinson (2001)'s suggestion.
62  See, for example, Dore (2008); Olcott (2009); Morgan and Kubo (2005).
63  See Dore (2000).
64  See Sato (1997).

# 7 Explaining narrative management in Japan

## 7.1 Introduction

This chapter provides the final conclusions of this research, explaining the theoretical contributions it makes in the field of 'continuity and change' within Japanese organizations and the theory of narrative management amid wider debates on Japanese organizational restructuring.

The book discussed the official use of US-style reform measures within Japanese organizations, focusing in particular on what they might mean for staff, in a context whereby most of them are widely understood to maintain traditional ways of operating and restructuring. The book demonstrated that interview data drawn from within four organizations identifies a significant gap between saying and doing, in that there is a very limited use of US-style reform plans, despite these organizations making widespread and often bold public statements about their adoption of such reform measures (see Table 7.1 for a simple overview). This means that all four organizations engaged in varied forms of narrative management, and clearly demonstrate false signalling. This use of narrative as a shield or a smokescreen was common to the four cases, even though the specific details and contexts differed in subtle ways.

## 7.2 'Continuity and change' in the Japanese economy and organizations

The evidence of Chapters 3–6 has captured important facets of Japan's progressive but awkward movement towards new business models. In particular, the case of Shinsei Bank shows a rather different facet of movement that does seem to represent genuine movement towards attempting to establish a US-style business model in Japan. The Japanese government seeks to follow the example of the US economic model and transform the nature of the Japanese economic system as it tries to tackle the long-term deterioration of the macro economy. Japanese organizations have formally and publicly gone along with these reform measures but, when explored in detail, Nissan Motor, BTMU and Yokohama City Council (but not Shinsei Bank) appear to show limited concern with transformation. What has changed is that Japanese organizations have engaged much more widely and deeply in processes of IR (as a form of PR). Narrative management within Japanese organizations articulates one particular form of the complex mixture of continuity and change in Japan.

Alongside this rather contradictory situation, great pressure has been increasingly brought to bear on Japanese organizations (even local governments which have suffered from huge deficits and been asked to be independent of the central government) to see that macro- and microeconomic performance recover from prolonged recession and that Japanese organizations match their strides to global corporations. After the depressing 1990s, the Japanese people appeared to have no answer to the breakdown of the Japanese economy and this period was notoriously called 'the lost decade'. Japanese firms searched for specific antidotes while the government believed that the Japanese business model had become exhausted and that the US business model was most appropriate solution to rescue the distressed Japanese economy. The Japanese government has strongly advocated a sustained and concerted push toward US-style systems, first in 1996 when it introduced its version of the Big Bang reforms, which effected a significant liberalization of the Japanese insurance and banking industries. Since then, a great deal of knowledge about US systems has been officially brought into Japan. The US business model has been imported via foreign-affiliated firms. They are represented by Nissan, which formed its famous alliance with Renault in 1998; Shinsei Bank's highly symbolic takeover by US firm Ripplewood in 2000 following its bankruptcy in 1998; and Aozora Bank which was also taken over by a US hedge fund, Cerberus Capital Management, also following its bankruptcy in 1998.

In 2001 the then prime minister, Junichiro Koizumi,[1] and the Minister of State for Economic and Fiscal Policy (and Minister of State for Financial Services), Takenaka Heizo, (who had experience as a visiting professor at US universities including Harvard and Columbia) instigated structural reform that encouraged corporate management to change its ways of thinking, to rearrange their financial goals and to develop, reconfigure and modernize the corporate system. The Japanese government has modified its corporate laws since the 1990s, including removing the ban on the purchase and redemption by employees of their firm's stocks in 1994, on stock options in 1997, on the stock exchange system that allows firms to pay using their own stock in merger and acquisitions with other firms in 1999, and on staff dispatched for temporary work in the manufacturing sector and the extension of period to work for three years in 2004. The government has attempted to create a neo-liberal environment for Japanese firms, to encourage and enable them to be ready to shift towards the US-style liberal market model of capitalism. Similarly to the government, the Japanese mass media has altered its tone, and has increasingly adopted a more US language, attacking exhausted and moribund traditional Japanese systems, praising innovators and advocating liberal corporate reforms. Chapters 3–6 explored this change in the external

*Table 7.1* Comparative organizational restructuring by the four organizations: continuity and change

|  | Nissan Motor | Bank of Tokyo-Mitsubishi UFJ (BTMU) | Shinsei Bank | Yokohama City Council |
|---|---|---|---|---|
| New reform plan | US-style reform plans | US-style reform plans | US-style reform plans | New Public Management |
| Change | Investor Relations Active PR via media (less change) | Investor Relations with Mitsubishi brand (less change) | Investor Relations US methods of operating; new employment system; short-term basis for profit-making (more changes) | Investor Relations Proactive PR via media (less change) |
| Continuity | Limited reform in employment downsizing; VBM (more continuity) | Limited reform in employment downsizing; Shareholder value creation (more continuity) | Limited reform in SVA management (less continuity) | Limited reform in employment downsizing; insiders' consciousness level (more continuity) |
| New kinds of reform | Ongoing and sophisticated narrative management | Mitsubishi brand-led narrative management | Financialized, Anglo-Saxon-style narrative management | Temporary and political (NPM) narrative management |

environment, and noted the ways in which firms had to adapt their messages in order to meet new pressure for legitimization; the media taken a great interest in restructuring by Japanese organizations and welcomes organizational change.[2] Business experts, government officials, economists and financial analysts have increasingly started to make public comments on the justification and definition of the US model as a global standard, and Japanese organizations had to show that they were up to the task of meeting this new standard.

Thus, the government and the media are exerting ever more pressure on Japanese organizations. Japanese organizations (apart from Shinsei Bank), however, have been rather slow to react to this external pressure. Their response has been mostly to react by putting much more intense focus on their development of public communication. For example, this research found that they have chosen to appeal to the public by claiming that many of the company's established business systems, practices and organizational norms have been swept aside in the new reform plans. (Shinsei Bank has been less slow to react to pressure but similarly put more focus on public communications.) Such pronouncements have been well received by society, even if there is often evidence of initial hostility to change by the public. Companies' new strategies for restructuring have been highly recognized by the public as representing a significant shift towards stock market capitalism. The recent debate on continuity and change in Japan views corporate change as becoming more drastic and profound in recent years.[3] This book has shown that Japanese organizations make good use of public activity and some of them manipulate the interests of mass media. However, this research has demonstrated that we must look at both macro and micro activities under the process of institutional evolution. This brings us to the main issue examined here – that of continuity and change and narrative management.

## 7.3 'Continuity and change' revisited

Thus far this book has explored the facets of how the management of four Japanese organizations have reacted to external pressure from economic, social and political changes that have forced them to abandon traditional methods. The evidence of Chapters 3–6 has shown two aspects of organizational reform that coexist in the notion of continuity and change within each organization and across the four organizations. Overall this research supports Jacoby and Vogel,[4] who discuss a wide range of restructuring styles across the Japanese firms, as the case of Shinsei Bank shows more aspects of change than other three cases (which show more aspects of continuity). At company level, this study agrees with Olcott,[5] who suggests a mixed strategy of 'convergence and divergence' within Japanese firms.

With regard to change at local level, the case studies have presented interesting pictures about new organizational behaviour, with the four studies all showing that corporate PR strategies appear to have become much more developed than previously when corporations and bureaucracies could get away with being much more inward-looking. They have significantly changed the messages presented in their annual reports, which are increasingly published with the notion of an investor community in mind (or towards external stakeholders such as taxpayers and the central government in the case of Yokohama City Council). While corporate restructuring has been facilitated, Japanese organizations have been inspired by external pressure to a make great play of the changes they claim to have carried out. Their public claims emphasize that many of the company's established business systems, practices and organizational norms were swept aside in the new reform plans, claiming a state of great change which contradictions the widely held view of past literature about slow change in Japan. Among the academics who update the discussion, Dore indicates that Japanese firms have at last come to regard IR as important, even claiming that investor capitalism has reached Japan.[6] Similarly, Olcott suggests that CEOs of Japanese firms are placing much greater emphasis on IR than ever before.[7]

IR refers to management's overall approach towards its relationship with shareholders, investors and those who might be interested in a firm's stock. The US National Investor Relations Institute defines IR as follows: 'Investor relations is a strategic management responsibility that integrates finance, communication, marketing and securities law compliance to enable the most effective two-way communication between a company, the financial community, and other constituencies, which ultimately contributes to a company's securities achieving fair valuation'.[8] How, what and when firms disclose the information depends on a firm's own attitude towards the capital markets;[9] there is plenty of scope for firms to improve their image through IR.

Although there is evidence of the diverse ways in which the IR announcements were made (especially as they refer to restructuring plans) by the four case studies, the conversation with the media is becoming a more central part of the purpose of IR for all the cases. One of the reasons is because Japanese organizations' IR is judged by the media. According to an interview with a reporter for *Yomiuri* newspaper,[10] 'market capitalism style has been justified by the former US President, George W. Bush, and the former Japanese prime minister, Junichiro Koizumi, and Japanese firms have to adjust to the current social standards that have suddenly been set up by both of these key persons. As journalists we report positively about firms which improve shareholder value'. As the case studies have shown, since the early 2000s the corporate messages about reform plans have won acceptance by the media. Likewise, the Securities Analysts Association of Japan has implemented a corporate disclosure evaluation and award system. According to its website,[11] 'the group has attached greater importance to voluntary and positive disclosure rather than mandatory disclosure when formulating its corporate disclosure review criteria. Evaluations of emerging market companies and also of disclosure to retail investors were introduced in 2005'. The group selects companies exhibiting 'superior' (for which read US-style) disclosure in each industry. BTMU was awarded in 2011 and Nissan in 2007, 2008, 2009, 2010 and 2011. The way that a firm establishes an effective relationship with the media is becoming an ever more important part of top-level strategy. Kondo and the Japan Investor Relations Association suggest that firms which have improved IR have enjoyed higher stock prices than those which have not.[12] Although this research has not discussed the link between them, it found that the organizations that have managed their PR well (Nissan, BTMU and Yokohama City Council) appear to have enjoyed higher social status (including higher stock prices, external support and external expectations). There does indeed seem to be a dividend accruing to firms which invest seriously in PR/IR. This emergent finding may be applied to other Japanese organizations and indeed, it appears that IR activities have proliferated and improved in Japan. The Japan Investor Relations Association,[13] the privately run not-for-profit organization that was established in 1993 to share information on IR activities among the listed Japanese firms, has seen its membership soar; from 117 firms in 1993 to 669 firms as of 2011, including Nissan, BTMU and Shinsei Bank. An increasing number of organizations have engaged in the modification of their behaviour in terms of IR towards a US-style form of stock market capitalism.

However, it is crucial to note that contrary to the assertions made in firms' IR activities towards the public, there is no clear link between the announced restructuring plans and actual changes to practices.

This book argues that in practice most of the organizations' existing business systems, practices and norms have not been swept aside. Japanese organizations have not changed their practices and have been relatively cautious to move towards a shareholder model. The Organisation for Economic Co-operation and Development reported in 2006 that Japan was still conservative in its HR practices, with strictly imposed restrictions on lay-offs, which discourages Japanese organizations from adopting employment downsizing. This research backs up most literature about Japan in suggesting that there is little real movement in Japanese firms towards shareholder value logic.[14] Using the concept of institutional restraint, the VoC school speculates that the US-style management approach is unlikely to take root or to work effectively in Japanese firms. This seems logically correct, but it seems from the evidence presented in this book that the lack of genuine change is not so much to do with institutional restraint, because institutional change has been generated by external stakeholders such as the government and the media, who have actively attempted to modernize and reinvent Japan's institutions through deregulation and the encouragement of a new economic environment. Yet the firms' timid execution of their reform plans is shaped by existing institutions, and fundamentally the Japanese traditional system seem to remain largely intact. Where there is solid evidence available (especially at Nissan, BTMU and Yokohama City Council), Japanese organizations have not changed in line with their high-profile proposed reforms plans. Even Shinsei Bank, which has enacted drastic changes, still has not reformed in a way that is true to its announced plans. The IR or PR of the four cases appears as a form of downsizing fraud.[15] It still seems clear that other Japanese firms do not prioritize shareholder value, and corporate governance scandals have occurred, for example at Olympus, Daio Paper Corporation and Toyota Motor, all of which claimed to have grand plans for the reform of financial performance for their shareholders. Olympus had concealed massive losses for over twenty years, amounting to one of Japan's biggest ever corporate scandals; Toyota suffered terrible PR damage owing to the 'sticky' pedals scandal and recall in October 2009; Daio Paper Corporation (the fourth biggest paper corporation in Japan and listed on the Tokyo Stock Exchange), had hidden borrowings and diverted ¥8 billion for the president's personal use, and this became public in September 2011. All of these scandals caused big losses to stock prices on the Tokyo Stock Exchange.[16] Current external pressures have been very powerful in reformatting organizations' public messages, largely against the will of the organizations themselves and their employees. However, the pressure was not very powerful in forcing organizations to actually carry out their reform plans in practice. Thus, this research clearly indicates continuity and change within each of the four organizations, and it seems likely that similar forms of continuity and change are common across Japan.

Thus far this book has largely supported the idea of continuity and change as regards Japan, but it has also articulated something different from the previous literature about continuity and change. The main original point that this book makes is that narrative management has been used to cover up firms' limited change. (The case of Shinsei Bank is somewhat different from other three cases in that narrative management has been used more like a signal to the financial community that Shinsei aims to improve its shareholder value, but even here there are clearly noticeable smokescreen effects.) The more recent studies about continuity and change have suggested that there more drastic changes are taking place in Japanese firms than previously. For example, Dore indicates that progressive revisions in the law are clearly shifting the Japanese corporate system towards the US system as new laws encourage Japanese firms' management to change their ways of thinking, to rearrange their financial goals and to develop modern, transparent corporate governance systems.[17] Indeed Olcott[18] indicates more change than continuity, which is to a large degree reflected in the case of (US-owned) Shinsei Bank. Yet the past debate on continuity and change is mostly based on research on the views of top management and on official corporate and government documents and statements. By introducing a range of individual voices in the interview research, especially by focusing on the lesser-heard voices of middle managers, this research has demonstrated what US-style reform plans have meant on a personal level to middle-level employees working in Japanese organizations. The research found that previous arguments about change only reflect the official messages issued by Japanese organizations, since only the surface-level of the recent situation in Japanese organizations has been looked at; a lack of change is observed when one looks at deeper, less high-profile levels within the organizations. What is new – and very real – however, is the much greater emphasis on IR, which usually makes particular use of American language and tone. Japanese organizations have now begun to apply – with some skill – new strategies of narrative management to provide a smokescreen behind which they can largely continue their traditional ways of operating and restructuring. Of the four organizations under study, Shinsei Bank stands out because it has changed the Japanese ways of operating and has broadly introduced US ways of restructuring under American ownership, although not without its own form of obfuscation associated with narrative management. Japanese organizations have chosen the form of narrative management to satisfy the demand from the rapidly increasing pressure from outside. Changes have taken place but these have, in a curious way, helped to reinforce continuity.

Organizations' official claims offer limited real knowledge about themselves and we must look to the employees in order to get a real sense of the extent, or absence, of organizational change in Japan. This book has explored in depth how four large Japanese organizations react to financialization, globalization and economic slowdown, and especially at how staff within these organizations react to the new restructuring plans in different ways. Through an in-depth exploration of the processes of organizational change, this book offers a richer understanding of how staff have accepted, challenged or resisted these change programs. This study found that the ways in which employees at organizations perceive new reform programs differ across the four organizations. Many insiders in Shinsei Bank and Yokohama City Council are very sceptical about the new reform programs and this increases their distrust of the organization they work in. Yet many employees at Nissan and BTMU understand what their organizations have publicly said about new reform plans, while at the same time struggling to see real evidence of change at their level. Understandably, insiders tend to be cautious of any changes that affect their working lives and there is evidence that some of them have tacitly resisted or at least distanced themselves from organizational changes, especially at Shinsei Bank and Yokohama City Council, where the narratives appear to have been less convincing. Adaptation to new corporate narratives and organizational restructuring simultaneously involves aspects of resistance and cooperation and there is inconsistency in insiders' handling of restructuring. This research revealed some connection to the traditional concepts of *honne* and *tatemae* in the way that firms' handled restructuring. At C-Life (one of the biggest Japanese life insurance companies, which went bankrupt in 2000 and was taken over by Prudential Financial) staff manage both the new system and the old system through resorting to *honne* (one's stated purpose/ private intention) and *tatemae* (one's anticipated end/ public principle).[19] This study shows that staff have cooperated with narrative management at Nissan and BTMU, thus helping to transmit their firms' IR. It is difficult for qualitative research in the Japanese context to understand internal perceptions and read underlying motives without examining the deeper side of the organization or *honne*, and a large portion of the research available on Japan analyzes only at a superficial or *tatemae* level.

## 7.4 Narrative management in Japan

The previous section showed that Japanese organizations have been engaged in the developing narrative management which can be linked to the concept of *honne* and *tatemae*, in that corporate public messages are skilled forms of communication designed to act as cover for the very limited real changes that firms are actually willing and able to make. While there is certainly a novelty in Japanese firms having to engage in such corporate communication as a response to changed external norms, pressures and conditions, in practice firms' new forms of narrative management are used to reinforce stability, rather than to trigger real change. The development of public communication through US-style reform programs at four Japanese organizations illuminates narrative management in the context of Japan. The theory of narrative management has implicitly assumed that a firm is given the incentive to form narratives through stock market capitalism. As there has been general agreement about little movement towards shareholder value logic in Japan, the concept of narrative management has not, so far, been applied to the case of Japan. In this respect, this study provides an initial insight into the development of Japanese narrative management. What this research found is that Japanese firms have been under significant and growing pressure from the financial community (i.e. financial analysts and economists) and the government, which creates a strong impetus to create official narratives to respond to the pressure. In this respect, they are indeed under pressure from shareholder value logic, moving towards stock market capitalism as indicated by Dore's most recent works.[20] Japanese IR or PR activity, however, is mostly highly rhetorical and somewhat empty, and designed for circulation within the investor community arena. Froud *et al.* (2000), who are among the originators of the field of narrative management, have stated that corporate narrative management is accompanied by a gap between saying and doing. The interview findings in this study clearly indicate that there is a significant gap between saying and doing between such public announcements and their (often limited) translation on the ground. This is clearly a form of false signalling.[21] Moreover, this research has found evidence of narrative management in the context of Japan including not only listed public firms but also local government.

Narrative management is closely modelled on US or UK notions of financialized best practice such as shareholder value. In Japan this narrative is currently highly ritualized and is developed to meet the needs of the times. As the fundamental assumptions of narrative management theory, the methods, texts and audiences for Japanese narrative management are similar to those of US narratives. The aim of US firms' narratives is fundamentally about boosting stock prices and the audience is the investor community, and while this research cannot show evidence as to whether or not the purpose of Japanese narrative management is improvement of stock prices, Japanese organizations' messages are setting the tone for what is considered a new norm of US-style governance in Japanese business, and transmitted more towards the investor community than before. They use the language and trappings of US-style restructuring measures, and indeed Froud et al. (2006)[22] show that the media is an important medium for narrative management. The media has been increasingly used by Japanese firms for delivering information to the public. Thus, one can see that Japanese narrative management is constituted by similar sets of messages, signals, and tools to US corporate narrative management, which has been studied by many authors.[23] This Western sense of narrative management was most closely (but not fully) reflected in Shinsei Bank's narrative that focused so closely on measurable financial targets. Yet one could also argue that Japanese narrative management (represented by the other three cases) is still different from that in the USA, in that Japanese organizations are under less direct pressure from shareholders to quickly improve shareholder value and are under more indirect pressure from the wider financial community (including the media and the government).

This study has also revealed another angle of narrative management. It enriches narrative management theory by making organizational members' perceptions more central to the discussion. Narrative management theory highlights the impact of narrative-making only really by reference to outsiders' perceptions, especially the financial community (shareholders, financial analysts, and the mass media), hence the focus on financial elements such as false signalling, firms' announcements about lay-offs and subsequent increases in their stock prices.[24] General Electric, Ford and P&G are examples of firms which have had positive reactions from shareholders to announcements about their restructuring goals.[25] Khurana[26] indicates that CEOs' narratives encourage the financial community to form certain expectations of firms' future successes. Announcements are delivered by the mass media which welcomes organizational reform as and indication of future improvements in financial value.[27] Yet when organizations earn externally positive reactions through narrative-making, a legitimacy gap can open up among organizational insiders. This can be explained by scandals such as that of Olympus. in this case the former CEO, Michael Woodford, asked questions about accounting practices at the firm. He raised 'specific concerns about Olympus' payment of $687 million to financial advisers during the acquisition of UK medical equipment company Gyrus'.[28] This study advances this theoretical stream by highlighting internal legitimacy perceptions as one determinant of long-term effective narrative management, alongside the more short-term focus of external announcements. Insiders are not only recipients of narratives but also, over time, they can become narrative-makers.

Furthermore, this research demonstrates the often exceedingly tough processes of narrative management. Indeed, a commonality in this study's findings is that all forms of narrative management are untidy and their outcomes highly uncertain. This research also argues that it is considerably harder for organizations to reap positive reactions from their own members than from external audiences. A lot of previous research pays attention to the consequences of narrative management at the level of the investor community, but this research helps to provide greater insight from internal perspectives into the way in which the four organizations conducted narrative management, and explores the multiple processes involved in narrative management by demonstrating its complex nature. The findings show some successes and failures. Narrative management is riddled with unexpected consequences; it can result in at least as many unsuccessful outcomes as successful ones. Based on the findings presented here, it would appear that its success or failure depends, to a significant extent, on how it is backed up by insider validation. Narrative management that is perceived to be exclusively about external narrative performance can easily generate negative reactions from staff; it requires huge efforts on the part of organizations and their leaders, and its success is far from certain. These findings imply that if narrative management is to succeed in convincing its audiences, it probably requires a repeated, ongoing series of narrative events and, crucially, genuine support from all stakeholders within the organization is essential. In the context of the Japanese 'convoy system' (whereby other organizations are said to emulate closely what their competitors are doing) its use requires considerable tactical delicacy. Another implication of this analysis is that narrative management is easy to start but hard to sustain. If organizations really seek change, they must initiate a program of long-term narrative management towards both external and internal audiences. Further research is necessary to determine whether narrative management is similarly contingent in other, non-Japanese, contexts.

## Notes

1 Junichiro Koizumi was prime minister from 2001–06.
2 Since the early 2000 the media has welcomed new reforms introduced by Japanese organizations. However, the media reacted negatively to Shinsei because the perceived abuse of public funds by the top management caused public dissatisfaction.
3 See, for example, Dore (2009); Olcott (2009).
4 Jacoby (2005) and Vogel (2006).
5 Olcott (2008).
6 Dore (2011).
7 Olcott (2009).
8 http://www.niri.org/
9 Kondo (2007).
10 Interviews held on 22 August 2008 and 17 December 2008.
11 http://www.saa.or.jp/disclosure/selection.html
12 Kondo (2007).
13 https://www.jira.or.jp/
14 Morgan and Takahashi (2002).
15 Littler (2006).
16 Olympus's value on the Tokyo Stock Exchange was depressed by 83.5 per cent following the scandal; ¥2,787 as of June 2011 and ¥460 as of November 2011. Toyota's value on the Tokyo Stock Exchange was depressed by 42 per cent following the scandal; ¥4,150 as of August 2009 and ¥2,413 as of November 2011. Daio Paper Corporation's value on the Tokyo Stock Exchange was depressed by 42 following the scandal; ¥740 as of October 2011 and ¥433 as of November 2011. See http://www.tse.or.jp/market/index.html
17 Dore (2006, 2008).
18 Olcott (2009).
19 Graham (2005).
20 Dore (2006, 2008, 2011).
21 Littler (2006).
22 Froud *et al.* (2000).
23 See, for example, Froud *et al.* (2000); Martin (2002); Clark *et al.* (2004); de Goede (2004); Thrift (2001).
24 Lazonick and O'Sullivan (2000).
25 Froud *et al.* (2000).
26 Khurana (2002).
27 Engelen (2003).
28 See http://www.bbc.co.uk/news/business-17281837http://www.bbc.co.uk/news/business-16901110http://www.ft.com/indepth/olympus

# 8 Conclusion

## Lessons for the future

### 8.1 Introduction

This section presents a summary of the book and simultaneously addresses the research questions. It goes on to explore the managerial implications arising from this book, and lessons for the wider audience (including companies, investors and regulators) are addressed. The chapter makes comparisons with narrative management and false signalling in other nations (such as in the Anglo-Saxon context), drawing out the peculiarities and commonalities of the Japanese experience. In doing so, the book aims to make a lasting contribution to the literature, both on Japanese organizational reform and on narrative management more generally.

### 8.2 Summary of the findings and research questions

This research set out to examine qualitatively the meaning of Japanese organizations' new restructuring proposals. To achieve this, forty-three interviews with staff (mostly middle managers) involved in organizational restructuring were conducted. Based on the analysis of the interview data, the research found that, as noted at the beginning of this book, we would expect that the recent public claims by large Japanese organizations about US-style restructuring plans are indeed a form of image restructuring. It is perhaps surprising that Japanese organizations, which are widely recognized as being risk- and change-averse, currently announce extremely different forms of restructuring in the public realm. This research found substantial evidence to suggest that firms are claiming to conform to US-style methods of restructuring, yet an in-depth examination shows that limited conformity actually occurs. In particular, this research found little adoption of employment downsizing and shareholder value creation. Exceptionally, Shinsei Bank has adopted US methods of operating (such as new HR practices and a greater focus on profit based on short-term thinking) but even this does not fully demonstrate a full implementation of US ways of restructuring despite the bank's public messages. Differences in financial performance are convincing explanations for these profound gaps between saying and doing. For example, BTMU has reported a very stable financial performance yet it has also publicly announced US-style restructuring measures. However, the research cannot explain why Nissan and Yokohama City Council, which reported less stable financial performances, have not reformed as drastically as they pledged they would. This case study does not find consistent evidence that foreign-owned firms reform more aggressively and restructure as much as they promise to do. This study addressed the first research question, that public claims made by Japanese organizations are indeed a form of narrative management. All four organizations have commonly developed their own forms of narrative management. It appears that they deploy narrative management in order to preserve their original business model (Shinsei Bank's deployment of narrative management is perhaps backed up by greater evidence of real change, but even here there are important discrepancies).

The development of narrative management implies a rather intense and profound development of PR activities by Japanese organizations. They are shown to focus more on public activity than on actual restructuring. This book has shown that IR/PR has grown rapidly among Japanese organizations, and the four case studies' annual reports (council reports in the case of Yokohama City Council) consistently appeal for change. Each of them have announced substantial reform programs. This leads to the second research question about how Japanese organizations have developed new forms of public messaging, with the ways in which they announce IR information becoming more diversified and strategic. Corporate PR strategies appear to be developed in differing ways according to their differing historical contexts, and the differing demands and audiences that organizations face. The analysis shows that Nissan and Yokohama City Council outwardly appear to undertake major PR offensives and try to manage and influence media outlets. However, in the case of BTMU public communication is constituted by a rather different set of processes than the other three case studies. The bank does not appear in public to make major PR announcements about its reform plans, or not as often as Nissan and Yokohama City Council. BTMU maintains public interest in the bank through the strong credibility of the Mitsubishi brand value. This is a rather different situation from the one pertaining to Nissan and Yokohama. Public communication is nevertheless a very important process in all four cases. It is important to note, therefore, that public communications may be managed through a wide variety of strategies that suit each firm's various interests and cultures. Differences in levels of PR activity help to explain, for example, the much higher levels of external acceptance extended to the new strategy for restructuring by Nissan, BTMU and Yokohama City Council than for Shinsei Bank.

Moreover, one of the central questions in this research is to understand the extent to which employees of Japanese organizations are involved in the firms' new reform strategies and narrative management as shown in the third research question. The effects of IR on Japanese organizations are determined to a significant degree by internal acceptance. Employees can have a powerful impact on this new change in IR. We can view this effect most clearly by comparing Yokohama City Council, Shinsei Bank, BTMU and Nissan. Such comparisons allow us to understand how important it is for the process of organizational change to gain acceptance not only from external stakeholders but also from internal stakeholders. Fundamentally employees tolerate IR in the longer term if organizations make the effort to earn internal support for new reforms, focusing on internal justification and validation as well as external support. The book can confirm this pattern by comparing two organizations that show evidence of significant internal focus with two which seem to show only an external focus. Both Nissan and BTMU have taken extra care to gain internal understanding for their new reform programs through internal discourse and internal actions, and these firms seem to have successfully encouraged their staff to take part in the IR activity and in turn this has helped to sustain public support for their new programs. Shinsei Bank and Yokohama City Council, both of which focus mostly on external performance about their reform plans and have neglected to develop an internal focus, have had to confront less external acceptance and far less internal support. Shinsei Bank and Yokohama City Council's PR strategies have not really worked in public in the longer term as they have suffered from a lack of internal acceptance. (This suggests that PR activity by itself is not enough to change even subtle practices.) This research proposes that internal acceptance is important for the process of organizational change. How to maintain and advance the existing institutions rests to a large extent on their internal strategies. The effect of organizational changes in IR (public activity) differs across the four organizations depending on how they have weighed up the everyday work of internal stakeholders as well as external shareholders.

This book has explored the way in which Japanese organizations change or choose to not to effect change. It achieved this by exploring in detail the more human and internal aspects of perceptions, focusing on the often confused and pragmatic levels of action and interpretation for internal members faced with what they actually do behind the scenes, as compared to officially proposed reform programs. From a narrative management perspective, it argued that Japanese organizations are exposed to the difficult processes of organizational change in order to satisfy external demand.

This research sheds light on the facets of new and subtle changes (in IR) made by Japanese organizations, but it cannot highlight all of them. Yet the study's findings are important because new and original findings have emerged through the application of the concept of narrative management to the context of Japan. Moving Japanese organizations' performance into 'recovery mode' is a continuous process of trial and error with organizations faced with near constant pressure from the outside to demonstrate change. As the main 'choice' of models of reform, the US business model has been promoted through the government's institutional deregulation. The US model, however, appears not to have been greatly preferred or valued by Japanese organizations. They have refused to conform to increasing pressure. The findings indicate that the four organizations' publicized reform programs are also a form of 'window-dressing'. In order to continue to use their original business model, they have selectively adopted forms of sophisticated narrative management to provide a smokescreen effect. Narrative management appears to have been used intensively and has rapidly taken root in the wider Japanese economy.

The fourth and final research question addressed the issue of what narrative management means for Japanese organizations. Japanese narrative management is essentially an articulation of Japan's large organizations' ways of making tentative steps towards economic evolution, financialization and globalization. The Japanese business model has not undergone a fundamental shift away from tried and tested Japanese models. Japanese organizations, while showing considerable change as regards the need for, and the direction of, their public pronouncements, remain cautious and change-resistant internally. If the Japanese government is to have any real traction with its stated goals of pushing the Japanese economy down an Anglo-Saxon route, then it needs to recognize the intensely pragmatic and cautious behaviours of Japanese corporations, and the smokescreen effect of their narrative management.

## 8.3 Implications, recommendations and further research

This section makes suggestions for future research in the area of narrative management in Japan, and explores the managerial implications arising from the research.

This study helps to identify four possible further directions for future research. The first is to examine the staff views and then to engage in further forms of qualitative research in order to probe deeper into the human elements of Japanese organizations. Interestingly, this interview-based case study revealed broadly two types of behaviour of organizational insiders. Insiders at Nissan and BTMU mostly supported their firms' reform programs and narrative management, while those at Shinsei Bank and Yokohama City Council generally did not support them. Although these four cases cannot represent all Japanese organizations, this difference does enable me to make some speculations. The reasons why internal audiences come to accept or reject narratives and organizational change are complex and unclear. In this study some emphasis has been placed on the failure of senior leadership to provide coherent and convincing narratives as the reason for staff rejection of narratives. This may be partially true in this study but equally it may not be the case elsewhere, and the current study lacks a truly deep investigation into working cultures and individual responses to change and narrative management. In other words, future research on Japan should be based on interviews that have been conducted over a longer time frame, carefully analyzed and deeply probed in order to understand the data provided by insiders. This could avoid any misunderstanding of what is said and provide fresh insights into Japanese firms. As mentioned above, insiders may manipulate *honne* and *tatemae* when responding to interview questions.

The second is to examine much deeper perspectives of a particular industry or organization, which may give us different levels of understanding of organizational change and narrative management. This research has analyzed two banks, one automobile company and a local government, which has helped me to make generalizations to a certain degree. At the same time, each case study has shown subtly different and complex backgrounds to the enactment of narrative management and continuity and change. Future research targeting one or more specific case study analyses, for example, can explore more precise levels of continuity and change. How different versions of narrative management play out within different industries and sectors could also be explored in more detail.

The third is to analyze small and medium-sized organizations, as this study only covered large organizations. Previous studies about narrative management have a strong bias towards exploring giant firms, because narratives made by big firms are more influential and are thus the main target for researchers. An examination of smaller organizations might provide us with new perspectives on organizational change and narrative management that have not previously been recognized.

The fourth is to examine the meaning and role of narrative management strategy as it pertains to outcomes of continuity and change in other countries and industries. The context of this research is only on Japan. Clearly there is room for further examination of similar questions in other research settings that may provide different insights. Further research is necessary to determine whether narrative management plays a similar role in other non-Japanese contexts, especially in other non-liberal or 'coordinated' economic environments (such as Germany or France, for example). Assumptions and concepts about narrative management may need to be redeveloped following research into different geographic settings. Moreover, there are some managerial implications that can be identified from the findings of the current research.

It is widely accepted that US firms consciously deliver narratives to quickly boost share prices. Yet potentially much broader effects of narrative management strategies should not be underestimated. From a managerial perspective, narrative management strategies can have significant effects on external and internal business relationships. Narrative management was found positively and negatively to influence the long-term orientations of external and internal audiences. The narrative management of Shinsei Bank and Yokohama City Council seems eventually to have damaged those organizations' image, both from the perspective of external and especially internal audiences, eventually bring a significant credibility gap into relief. The four case studies have commonly shown some important suggestions for managers, especially the importance of harnessing external and internal support. Narrative management seems almost always to include a gap between saying and doing but its messages can be of fundamental importance in terms of communication between organizations and their various stakeholders. Given the importance of attempting to manage relationships and media coverage, a high level of managerial discretion is required to build long-term and successful relationships. While this may entail large costs and efforts, organizations may achieve sustainable benefits if relationships are successfully managed over time. This research particularly shows the importance for senior management not to neglect the importance of communicating effectively to staff, whose support for (or rejection of) narratives and change measures can be critical to their success or failure. An appreciation of these issues may result in benefits accruing to firms' strategic competitiveness as they attempt to develop long-term goals.

## 8.4 Conclusion

This chapter summarizes the findings derived from the qualitative interviews in this study in order to address the research questions described in Chapter 2. Given the findings, this section discussed the limitations of this research and provided some basic suggestions for the possible future direction of similar work in the field. This book indicated four main directions that further research might reasonably take. It also showed the implications of this research for organizations' managers.

Viewing the findings in comparison with others shows that they may become more significant in the future. This is because, in today's highly information-oriented society, more public stories from a more complex management culture in Japan will probably evolve. What Japanese organizations should not forget is to pay more attention to their narrative style, and to make genuine efforts to make these narratives convincing and credible, bearing in mind the sometimes serious side effects that can come into play if internal staff or external audiences reject these narratives. Japanese organizations should analyze the strengths and weakness of Japanese approaches to corporate narrative-making if they are to survive in a globalizing world that is increasingly characterized by competing, high-profile, and often confusing narratives. The same is true for organizational researchers, who have to pick their way through an ever more complex, and ever more information-rich, environment, increasingly filled as it is with strident and clashing narratives. It is hoped that this book contributes a useful early step on this road.

# Appendix

## Research methodology

This section presents research methodology.

## Research design

This research theme is how and why Japanese organizations have engaged in the process of Investor Relations (IR) and Public Relations (PR), as well as how and why insiders at organizations have come to understand and interpret these new activities, drawing on the debate on continuity and change and the theory of narrative management. As a review of the previous literature shows (see Chapter 2), the concept of narrative management has not been yet applied to the case of Japan and the debate on continuity and change has continued to develop. This kind of new research area needs new empirical data. In such situations, where there is not much data available in the preceding literature, exploratory field studies can be especially beneficial (Stone 1978). Qualitative rather than quantitative research was used to provide us with deeper and richer descriptions (Holland 1997), especially because research on Japan lacks a focus on the level of everyday agency. Qualitative research used by organizational studies scholars clarifies the reasons and the significances of interviewees' activities (Stone 1978).

Qualitative research methods are ideal in that there has been a lack of detail on the internal, company-level aspects in the three kinds of literature explored in Chapter 2 (i.e. literature on Japanese organizational restructuring, narrative management and continuity and change). The existing studies on corporate narrative management have tended to focus on external rather than internal interpretations of narratives. The debate on continuity and change has also paid somewhat limited attention to internal understandings of organizational change. In addition, a significant part of the past debate on Japanese organizational restructuring has been basically occupied by the VoC approach that tends not to consider the role of agency. As the VoC concept often relies on stereotyped and abstract models, the past argument missed various diversified actions of agency that seem to take place within firms but have little purchase on the model. It is necessary, therefore, to examine internal perspectives that provide deeper human aspects of organizational restructuring. Quantitative research is ill-suited to such a task. According to Matanle,

> quantitative surveys fail to alert us to the multiple and layered understandings that people possess regarding the complex nexus between self, family, institution, and society that unavoidably must inform the route that an individual follows from needs, desires, and values through to decisions and, thence, actions.

> (2003: 144)

Quantitative research methods are not designed to shed light on the complicated backgrounds to people's decisions, actions, values, and so on. Quantitative methods cannot provide us with a micro view of interviewees' behaviour (Stone 1978). Nor do they give us rich contexts about how people feel, think and behave. By contrast qualitative data can provide us with detailed descriptions of the interactions between people and events (Patton 1980). Creswell indicates that 'qualitative research is an inquiry process of understanding based on distinct methodological traditions of inquiry that explore a social or human problem' (1998:15). Qualitative methodology clarifies 'a complex picture and detailed views of informants' (ibid.). To this extent, qualitative research methods are appropriate for the research which focuses on social, cultural and human contexts.

Among the variety of qualitative methods available, interview-based case studies can articulate more humanized aspects of the empirical world and contribute to an in-depth exploration of the multiple processes of institutional enterprise. It can help to reveal the complexities of change and continuity within workplaces. Insiders are closest to reality as they know about, enact, support, ignore and resist the processes of organizational reforms. Case study analysis has been widely used to examine the processes of changes within organizations (Yin 1982). Creswell suggests that 'a case study explores a "bounded system" or a case (or multiple cases) over time through detailed, in-depth data collection involving multiple sources of information rich in context' (1998: 6l). For example, the past debate on Japanese organizational restructuring mainly comprises simple case studies (for example those used by Graham 2005 and Mehri 2005) and comparative case studies with interviews (used by many academics such as Hassard *et al.* 2009; Jacoby 2005; McCann *et al.* 2004, 2006; Morris *et al.* 2006 and Vogel 2006)[1]. A simple case study is used to show that interested phenomena are logically connected (Yin 1982). Simple case studies give us specified characteristics that can be applied to one case. The wider meaning of such simple case studies may change according to subsequent case research. This is one of the problems associated with simple case studies. On the contrary, comparative case studies with interviews could provide us with broader knowledge about interested phenomenon than a simple case study. Therefore, this research used qualitative data derived from research interviews conducted within four Japanese organizations, using a comparative case study design based on the methodology of in-depth interviewing.

## Data sources and data collections

### *Interviews with four major Japanese organizations*

Personal interviews were conducted in Japan. Before that, pilot interviews were conducted with some interviewees from each organization during July–August 2008 in order to check whether or not the interview questions were adequate for the research. Letters inviting staff to take part in interviews and all the questions were written first in English and then a Japanese translation was sent to each interviewee by the author beforehand. As the author is a native Japanese speaker, there were no language restrictions when interviewing Japanese employees. All interviews were conducted in Japanese.

It was managed to schedule a roughly even number of interviews across each organization. Around ten people in each organization, and forty-three people were interviewed in total. These were in-depth, one-on-one interviews, and each interviewee talked to me for between one and a half to two hours. (In a few cases the interview took more than three hours). It was chosen to conduct interviews in cafés or restaurants to enable interviewees to speak freely. The interviewees worked in a variety of positions; mostly they were general employees, or had reached deputy manager and general manager level. However, the majority of interviewees were at line management level or above because they deal with organizational restructuring on a daily basis.

Although the author is Japanese, it was not easy to access Japanese organizations (especially public firms) on an official basis. For this reason, the author personally contacted all of the interviewees.

Moreover, a reporter from *Yomiuri* (Japan's biggest newspaper) was interviewed twice to understand about current social trends in Japan and how they affect large Japanese organizations which are more exposed to social demand.

Questions were open-ended in order to encourage the interviewees to respond freely. The contents of the questions were changed from individual to individual. Interview questions were all generally connected to issues of corporate value, the aims and progress of organizational restructuring, the extent to which organizations have genuinely changed, the authority of corporate brands, the importance of corporate names (based on *zaibatsu* and *keiretsu*), the role of the mass media and the significance of shareholder value. The interview question is reproduced in the appendix.

### *Documentation*

While the interview data provided us with an insight into the human perspective, documents were also used as another source of data to see how organizations publicize their official adoption of US-style restructuring plans.

Documents included (1) organizations' official documents such as annual reports, corporate websites and presentations, which were given by some interviewees; (2) internal newsletters that were obtained from some interviewees; and (3) government reports, newspapers and business magazines which had included reports on firms' restructuring plans. Such documents describe organizations' positions, views, values, principles, audiences, and so on. Among a large number of secondary documents, only well-known sources were chosen because they are more influential, trustworthy and objective. The biggest and most widely read newspapers such as *Yomiuri, Asashi*, and *Nikkei*. In addition, some of the most well-known business magazines, e.g. *Weekly Diamond* (best-selling publication), *Toyokeizai* (second best-selling), and *President* (third best-selling) were perused. *Weekly Diamond* and *Toyokeizai* include objective accounts of companies' official data. Also, the listed company information volume known as *Shikiho* published by Toyokeizai were used so as to gain more objective data than that found in companies' publicized data. This book is published quarterly and covers general information about all listed firms.

These official documents were collected both before and after interviews were conducted. General information was obtained prior to each interview in order to provide me with background information on the nature of an organization and the challenges facing it. In particular, the author tried to collect any information that firms had officially disclosed about their restructuring plans. More detailed documents obtained after the interviews had taken place helped the author to highlight the gap between what insiders do or think and what firms officially say to the public.

## Data analysis

The analysis of the collected data takes the form of a theoretically driven empirical analysis. After the data collection, findings from case studies were carefully built into a case-by-case analysis process.

Data analysis in case studies can be the most difficult part of the research (Yin 1994). It involves various techniques such as arranging information chronologically, categorizing, using diagrams, examining and so on (ibid.). Researchers must set aside their personal prejudices when analysing and producing persuasive conclusions (ibid.). This research follows Yin's suggestions regarding the analysis of interview data. First, taped interview data were reviewed multiple times and data relevant to the key themes of the book were identified as important segments. These data segments were then displayed thematically in a new, large document for each case study. The segments covered the categories of US-style restructuring measures in their public claims, external and internal acceptance. This process was ongoing during the course of data collection. When there are contradiction and ambiguity, clarification was sought through comparison with other interview data from the same organization.

After the process of data reduction, interview data from each of the four case studies were analyzed using the following steps: (1) what does each piece of data say or what can the researcher discover from that data?; (2) what can the researcher interpret from that finding?; and (3) is there any other possible interpretation of that finding? This step made it possible for the author to analyze such primary data from as an objective a viewpoint as possible. In addition, not only interview data but also secondary data such as official documents from four organizations, business magazine reports and the government analysis reports were used. Documentary sources were analyzed when interview data were analyzed, and then findings in each case were confirmed. This helped the author to clarify a gap between the organizations' saying and doing, i.e. their own forms of narrative and to what extent they implemented their publicized reform plans.

During the final stage, the findings, conclusion and interview data were translated into English because all interviews were conducted in Japanese. When each case had been analyzed, the author tried to understand the characteristics of each case and to look for similarities and differences among the four cases. These were tabulated when the author drew conclusions. Given this, the outcome and argument are deducted by the empirical analysis. The continuity and change debate and the theory of narrative management were confirmed and revised. Research questions based on the findings of each case study were answered.

## Credibility, strengths and limitations of the study

Interview-based case studies have a number of limitations that must to be acknowledged and addressed as far as possible. There are three main limitations to the research method.

First, it was not easy to gain personal access to large organizations. This can result in the researcher managing to arrange only a small number of interviews. The author was able in the end to conduct interviews with forty-three insiders from four large Japanese organizations (including three public firms). This dataset was large enough to make an in-depth examination of the process of organizational changes and has, the author feels, led to the development of richer findings that could not otherwise be developed using other methods, and they contribute to deepening and widening our current knowledge about the internal perceptions of organizational studies into narrative and restructuring.

Second, when international research is conducted, interviews often require the use of interpreters. The author did not need an interpreter to conduct interviews in Japan. All interviews were conducted in the same way using the same interview schedule. Also, interviewing without an interpreter allowed the author to manipulate different ways of interviewing based on mood, distance between the researcher and the interviewee and time constraint without diluting the possibility to encourage them to answer.

Third, given that examining the role of organizational narrative based on interview data, was examined, there was the possibility that the author actually made a narrative herself. Obviously, interviewers can influence respondents' answers in multiple ways. For their part, interviewees do not necessarily provide accurate answers to especially sensitive questions. In particular, Japanese salarymen are widely known to prefer tactful, conservative and diplomatic conversations, especially with outsiders. Dore (2000) indicates that Japanese people have the tendency to talk ambiguously in order to conceal what they really think. It is not easy to bring out and distinguish between what they might really think and what they say superficially. Japanese salarymen work for the same company under a system of lifetime employment that is virtually guaranteed. Through long-lasting relationships among insiders, they can share the same organizational codes that make it possible to converse efficiently. In other words, they can, in the Japanese phrase, 'hear one, understand ten' (Kopp 2001). There are many modes of communication and include non-word sounds and gestures (ibid.). They can interpret what others want to say or are thinking through the environment or feeling without using words. Given such characteristics that are unique to Japanese salarymen, it is not easy to establish the validity and reliability of primary data from interviews carried out within Japanese organizations. Therefore, the author tried to analyze each piece of interview data, comparing it with other interview data from the same organization in order to check its accuracy. At times the author also asked interviewees for clarification and asked follow-up research questions. Also external locations in which to conduct interviews so that interviewees could express their personal viewpoints were chosen. In this sense, mindful of the above limitations, the author is confident of the value of the gathered data.

## Note

1  These have been divided into three methodologies: simple case studies, comparative case studies, and questionnaires which some scholars use (e.g. Robinson and Shimizu 2006; Okubayashi 2002; and Yoshikawa 2005; Ahmadjian and Robinson 2001).

# Bibliography

Abe, T. (2003) *Carlos Ghosn's Way: Leadership and Coaching Skills*. Tokyo: Asa Syuppan.

Abegglen, J. C. (1958) *The Japanese Factory: Aspects of its Social Organization*. Glencoe: Free Press.

Aglietta, M. (2000) 'Shareholder Value and Corporate Governance: Some Tricky Questions'. *Economy and Society* 29(1): 14–59.

Ahmadjian, C. and Robinson, P. (2001) 'Safety in Numbers: Downsizing and the Deinstitutionalization of Permanent Employment in Japan'. *Administrative Science Quarterly* 46(4): 622–654.

Aikawa, T. and Yokohama Kaikaku Tokubetsu Shuzaihan (2005) *Yokohama Kaikaku Nakada Shicho 1000 nichi no tatakai*. Tokyo: Bookman sha.

Aitken, R. (2005) 'A Direct Personal Stake: Cultural Economy, Mass Investment and the New York Stock Exchange'. *Review of International Political Economy* 12(2): 334–363.

*Ajino-techo* (2006) 'Nakada Hiroshi; Seicho Kakudai no Jidai, Sonokotowo Ninshiki Sitemoraitai'. *Ajino-techo*: 5–19.

Amable, B. (2003) *The Diversity of Modern Capitalism*. Oxford: Oxford University Press.

Amin, A. and Thrift, N. (2004) *The Blackwell Cultural Economy Reader*. Oxford: Blackwell.

Aoki, M. (1986) *The Co-Operative Game Theory of the Firm*. Oxford: Clarendon.

Aoki, M. (1988) *Information, Incentives and Bargaining in the Japanese Economy*. Cambridge: Cambridge University Press.

Aoki, M. (1996) *New Approaches to Macroeconomic Modelling: Evolutionary Stochastic Dynamics, Multiple Equilibria and Externalities as Field Effects*. Cambridge: Cambridge University Press.

Aoki, M. and Dore, R. (1996) *The Japanese Firm: The Sources of Competitive Strength*. Oxford: Clarendon Press.

Aoki, M., Jackson, G. and Miyajima, H. (2007) *Corporate Governance in Japan: Institutional Change and Organizational Diversity*. Oxford: Oxford University Press.

Arrighi, G. (1994) *The Long Twentieth Century: Money, Power and the Origins of our Time*. London: Verso.

Auerbach, A. J. (1988) *Corporate Takeovers: Causes and Consequences*. Chicago: University of Chicago Press.

Ball, K. and Woytiuk, M. (2007) 'Introduction: Cultures of Finance: When the Crisis, which Was a Certainty, Becomes a Contingency'. *Cultural Critique* 65: 1–5.

Bamber, G., Lansbury, R. D. and Wailes, N. (2004) *International and Comparative Employment Relations: Globalization and the Developed Market Economies.* London: Sage.

Bank of Tokyo-Mitsubishi UFJ (2000–08) BTM and BTMU's internal PR newsletters. Bank of Tokyo-Mitsubishi UFJ :Tokyo.

Barley, S. R. and Kunda G. (2004) *Gurus, Hired Guns, and Warm Bodies: Itinerant Experts in a Knowledge Economy.* Princeton, NJ: Princeton University Press.

Baumol, W. J., Blinder, A. S. and Wolff, E. N. (2003) *Downsizing in America: Reality, Causes, andnd Consequences.* New York: Russell Sage.

BBC News, 'Olympus Scandal'. Available at http://www.bbc.co.uk/news/business-17281837, http://www.bbc.co.uk/news/business-16901110, (accessed 30 March 2012).

*Bloomberg Business Week* (2009) 'Toyoda on Toyota: Grasping for Salvation'. Available at http://www.businessweek.com/blogs/eyeonasia/archives/2009/10/toyoda_on_toyot.html, (accessed 10 September 2010).

*Bloomberg Global Finance* (2009) 'Largest Shareholder of Shinsei Bank'. 20 February. Available at http://sv.business-i.jp/news/bb-page/news/200902200078a.nwc, (accessed 10 August 2009).

Boje, D. (2001) *Narrative Method for Organizational and Communications Research.* London: Sage.

Brunsson, N. and J. P. Olsen (1993) *The Reforming Organization.* London: Routledge.

Buchanan, J. (2007) 'Japanese Corporate Governance and the Principle of "Internalism"'. *Corporate Governance* 15(1): 27–35.

Buchanan, J. and Deakin, S. (2009) 'In the Shadow of Corporate Governance Reform: Change and Continuity in Managerial Practice at Listed Companies in Japan', in D. H Whittaker and S. F. Deakin (eds) *Corporate Governance and Managerial Reform in Japan.* Oxford: Oxford University Press.

Cabinet Office, Government of Japan. 'Japan's Nominal Gross Domestic Product: 1980–2008'. Available at http://www.doyukai.or.jp/policyproposals/articles/2011/pdf/110602a.pdf, (accessed 11 September 2011).

Cabinet Office, Government of Japan (1949) *Economic White Papers.* Tokyo. Available at http://www5.cao.go.jp/keizai3/keizaiwp/wp-je65/wp-je65-0000i1.html (accessed 30 March 2012).

Cabinet Office, Government of Japan (1953) *Economic White Papers.* Tokyo. Available at http://www5.cao.go.jp/keizai3/keizaiwp/wp-je65/wp-je65-0000i1.html (accessed 30 March 2012).

Cabinet Office, Government of Japan (1958) *Economic White Papers.* Tokyo. Available at http://www5.cao.go.jp/keizai3/keizaiwp/wp-je65/wp-je65-0000i1.html (accessed 30 March 2012).

Cabinet Office, Government of Japan (1965) *Economic White Papers.* Tokyo. Available at http://www5.cao.go.jp/keizai3/keizaiwp/wp-je65/wp-je65-0000i1.html (accessed 30 March 2012).

Cabinet Office, Government of Japan (1969) *Economic White Papers.* Tokyo. Available at http://www5.cao.go.jp/keizai3/keizaiwp/wp-je65/wp-je65-0000i1.html (accessed 30 March 2012).

Cabinet Office, Government of Japan (2003) *Economic White Papers.* Tokyo. Available at http://www5.cao.go.jp/keizai3/keizaiwp/wp-je65/wp-je65-0000i1.html (accessed 30 March 2012).

Cabinet Office, Government of Japan (2005) *Economic White Papers.* Tokyo. Available at http://www5.cao.go.jp/keizai3/keizaiwp/wp-je65/wp-je65-0000i1.html (accessed 30 March 2012).

Cabinet Office, Government of Japan (2009) *White Paper on the National Lifestyle.* Cabinet Office, Government of Japan:Tokyo.

Cabinet Office, Government of Japan (2011). Available at http://www.doyukai.or.jp/p olicyproposals/articles/2011/pdf/110602a.pdf

Callon, M. (1998) *The Laws of the Markets.* Oxford: Blackwell.

Cappelli, P., Bassi, L., Katz, H., Knoke, D., Osterman, P., and Useem, M. (1997) *Change at Work.* New York: Oxford University Press.

Cascio, F. W. (2002) 'Strategies for Responsible Restructuring'. *Academy of Management Executive* 16(3): 80–91.

Cascio, W. F. (1993) 'Downsizing: What Do We Know? What Have We Learned?' *The Executive* 7(1): 95–105.

Cascio, W. F. (1998) 'Learning from Outcomes: Financial Experiences of 311 Firms that Have Downsized', in M. K. Gowing, J. D. Kraft and J. C. Quick (eds) *The New Organizational Reality: Downsizing, Restructuring, and Revitalization.* Washington, DC: American Psychological Association.

Clark, G. L., Thrift, N. and Tickell, A. (2004) 'Performing Finance: The Industry, the Media and its Image'. *Review of International Political Economy* 11(2): 289–310.

Collins, D. (2008) Has Tom Peters Lost the Plot? A Timely Review of a Celebrated Management Guru. *Journal of Organizational Change Management* 21(3): 315–334.

Collins, J. C. (2001) *Good to Great: Why some Companies Make the Leap – and Others Don't.* New York: Harper Business.

Collins, J. C. (2009). *How the Mighty Fall: And Why Some Companies Never Give In.* New York: HarperCollins.

Collins, J. C. and Porras, J. I (2000) *Built to Last: Successful Habits of Visionary Companies.* New York: Harper Business.

Collins, T. C. (2003) 'Hagetak wo Minaoso-Kigyo Saisei ni Mitsu no Gokai'. *Nikkei Business*: 44.

Creswell, J. W. (1998) *Qualitative Inquiry and Research Design: Choosing among Five Traditions.* Thousand Oaks, CA: Sage.

de Gay, P. and Pryke, M. (2002) *Cultural Economy: Cultural Analysis and Commercial Life.* London: Sage.

de Goede, M. (2003) 'Beyond Economism in International Political Economy'. *Review of International Studies* 29(1): 79–97.

de Goede, M. (2004) 'Repoliticizing Financial Risk'. *Economy and Society* 33(2): 197–217.

Dore, R. (1973) *British Factory, Japanese Factory: The Origins of National Diversity in Industrial Relations.* London: Allen & Unwin.

Dore, R. (2000) *Stock Market Capitalism: Welfare Capitalism: Japan and Germany versus the Anglo-Saxons.* Oxford: Oxford University Press.

Dore, R. (2002) 'Stock Market Capitalism vs. Welfare Capitalism'. *New Political Economy* 7(1): 115–127.

Dore, R. (2003) 'Nihonga Yoi Shakaini Narutameno Shohosen towa'. Available at http://www.rieti.go.jp/jp/special/af/011.html (accessed 31 August 2008).

Dore, R. (2005) 'Deviand or Different? Corporate Governance in Japan and Germany'. *Corporate Governance* 13(3): 437–446.

Dore, R. (2006) *Darenotameno Kaishani Suruka.* Tokyo: Iwanami Shinsho.

Dore, R. (2008) 'Imawanaki "Nihongata Shihonsyugi" wo Itamu'. *Weekly Economist*: 49.
Dore, R. (2009) 'Japan's Conversion to Investor Capitalism', in D. H. Whittaker and S. F. Deakin (eds) *Corporate Governance and Managerial Reform in Japan*. Oxford: Oxford University Press.
Dore, R. (2011) *Kinyu ga Notoru Sekaikeizai*. Tokyo: Cyuo Koron Shinsha.
Drucker, P. F. (2004) *Peter F. Drucker on Management*. Harvard, MA: Harvard Business School Press.
Druckman, D. Singer, J. and Van Cott, H. (eds) (1997) *Enhancing Organizational Performance*. Washington, DC: National Academy Press.
Dumenil, G. and Levy, D. (2004) 'Neoliberal Income Trends: Wealth, Class and Ownership in the USA'. *New Left Review* 30: 105–133.
Ebikawa, Y. and Miyajima, H. (2005) 'Naze M&A wa zoukashitaka?' Available at http://www.rieti.go.jp/jp/papers/journal/0606/rr01.html (accessed 10 August 2009).
Elasbach, K. D. (2003) 'Organizational Perception Management', in R. M. Kramer and B. M. Staw (eds) *Research in Organizational Behavior*. Stanford, CA: JAI Press, 297–332.
Engelen, E. (2003) 'The False Necessities of State Retreat'. *Environment and Planning* 35(8): 1377–1380.
Engelen, E. (2003) 'The Logic of Funding European Pension Restructuring and the Dangers of Financialization'. *Environment and Planning* 35(8): 1357–1372.
Erturk, I. (2008) *Financialization at Work: Key Texts and Commentary*. London and New York: Routledge.
Feldman, M. (2003) 'A Performative Perspective on Stability and Change in Organizational Routines'. *Industrial and Corporate Change* 12(4): 727–752.
Feldman, M. S. and Pentland, B. T. (2003) 'Reconceptualizing Organizational Routines as a Source of Flexibility and Change.' *Administrative Science Quarterly* 48(1): 94–118.
Feng, H. J. and Froud, J. (2001) 'A New Business Model? The Capital Market and the New Economy'. *Economy and Society* 30(4): 467–503.
Fligstein, N. (1990) *The Transformation of Corporate Control*. Cambridge, MA: Harvard University Press.
Fligstein, N. (1997) 'Social Skill and Institutional Theory'. *American Behavioral Scientist* 40: 397–405.
Folkman, P., Froud, J., Johal, S. and Williams, K. (2007) 'Working for Themselves: Capital Market Intermediaries and Present-day Capitalism'. *Business History* 49(4): 552–572.
Fombrun, C. J. and Shanley, M. (1990) 'What's in a Name? Reputation Building and Corporate Strategy'. *Academy of Management Journal* 33(2): 233–258.
Forbes (2002) 'A Concession Hunter or a Vulture Has Caused further Recession in Japan'. *Forbes* (October): 78–79.
Froud, J. (2006) *Financialization and Strategy: Narrative and Numbers*. London: Routledge.
Froud, J., Haslam, C., Johal, S. and Williams, K. (2000) 'Restructuring for Shareholder Value and its Implications for Labour'. *Cambridge Journal of Economics* 24(6): 771–798.
Fuji Xerox (2012) 'Nissan Value-up: Nissan's COO, Toshiyuki Shiga'. Available athttp://www.fujixerox.co.jp/support/xdirect/magazine/rp0701/07011a.html#pageTop (accessed 30 March 2012).
Gabriel, Y. (2000) *Storytelling in Organizations: Facts, Fictions and Fantasies*. Oxford: Oxford University Press.

Gabriel, Y. (2004) 'Narratives, Stories and Texts', in D. Grant, C. Hardy, C. Oswick and L. Putnam (eds) *The Sage Handbook of Organizational Discourse*. London: Sage.

Gedajlovic, E. and Shapiro, D. (2002) 'Ownership and Firm Profitability in Japan'. *Academy of Management Journal* 45(3): 565–575.

Gedajlovic, E. and Yoshikawa, T. (2005) 'Ownership Structure, Investment Behaviour and Firm Performance in Japanese Manufacturing Industries'. *Organization Studies* 26(1): 7–36.

Gerlach, M. L. (1992) *Alliance Capitalism: The Social Organization of Japanese Business*. Berkeley, CA: University of California Press.

Ghosn, C. (2001) *Carlos Ghosn no Kotae ha Kaishanonakaniaru: Kaisha wo kaeta rida no saisei to fukkatsu no goroku*. Tokyo: Asa Syuppan.

Ghosn, C. (2001) *Renaissance: Challenge to Reform*. Tokyo: Diamond sha.

Ghosn, C. (2006) *Ghosn Text: Business Textbook*. Tokyo: Bungei Syunjyu.

Ghosn, C. (2008) *Ghosn Dojyo*. Tokyo: Asahi Shinbun Syupan.

Ghosn, C. and Ries, P. (2003) *Carlos Ghosn Talks about his Management Style*. Tokyo: Nihon Keizai Shinbun Sha.

Ghosn, R. (2006) *Ghosn Family's Precept*. Tokyo: Syueisha.

GM Inside News (2009) 'Toyota Head: Toyota Is on the Brink of Capitulation to Irrelevance or Death'. Available at http://www.gminsidenews.com/forums/f37/toyota-head-toyota-brink-capitulation-irrelevance-death-84691/ (accessed 2 October 2009).

Goede, M. D. (2005) *Virtue, Fortune and Faith: A Genealogy of Finance*. Minneapolis, MN: University of Minnesota Press.

Goffee, R. and Jones, G. (2006) *Why Should Anyone Be Led by You?: What It Takes To Be An Authentic Leader*. Harvard, MA: Harvard Business School Press.

Goto, A. (1982) 'Business Groups in a Market Economy'. *European Economic Review* 19(1): 53–70.

Graham, F. (2003) *Inside the Japanese Company*. London: RoutledgeCurzon.

Graham, F. (2004) *A Japanese Company in Crisis: Ideology, Strategy and Narrative*. London: RoutledgeCurzon.

Grant, D., Hardy, C., Oswick, C., and. Putnam, L. (eds) *The Sage Handbook of Organizational Discourse*. London: Sage.

Hakuno, T. (2007) *Requiem: Japanese Bankers Sacrificed by Japanese-type Financial Philosophy*. Tokyo: NHK.

Hall, P. A and Soskice, D. W. (2001) *Varieties of Capitalism: The Institutional Foundations of Comparative Advantage*. Oxford: Oxford University Press.

Hamada, K. (2004) *Hagetaka ga Warata Hi*. Tokyo: Syueisha International.

Hamagin Sogo Kenkyusho (2005) 'Syuku Nissan Honsha Iten'. *Best Partner*. Yokohama: Hamagin Research Institute, 18–22.

Hasegawa, H. (2002) 'Japanese Global Strategies in Europe and the Formation of Regional Markets', in H. Hasegawa and D. H. Glenn (eds) *Japanese Business Management: Restructuring for Low Growth and Globalization*. London: Routledge, 38.

Hasegawa, Y. (2011) *Ghosn-san Learned Japanese Business Management*. Tokyo: Nihon Keizai Shinbun Syuppansha.

Hasegawa, H. and Glenn, D. H. (eds) *Japanese Business Management: Restructuring for Low Growth and Globalization*. London: Routledge.

Hassard, J., McCann, L. and Morris, J. (2009) *Managing in the Modern Corporation: The Intensification of Managerial Work in the USA, UK and Japan*. Cambridge: Cambridge University Press.

Higgins, B. R. and Bannister, D. B. (1992) 'How Corporate Communication of Strategy Affects Share Price'. *Long Range Planning* 25(3): 27–35.

Higgins, B. R. and Dzjkzbach, J. (1989) 'Communicating Corporate Strategy: The Payoffs and the Risks'. *Long Range Planning* 22(3): 133–139.

Hiroshi Nakada Official Website (2011) 'Nakada Hiroshi's Profile'. Available at http://www.nakada.net/profile.shtml (accessed 10 September 2010).

Holland, J. (1997) 'The Use of Qualitative Survey Material to Inform the Design of the Core Welfare Indicators Questionnaire'. *Report for the Social Development and Poverty Elimination Division of UNDP*. Swansea: University of Wales (May).

Ikeda, M. (2002) 'Globalization's Impact upon the Subcontracting System', in H. Hasegawa and G. D. Hook (eds) *Japanese Business Management: Restructuring for Low Growth and Globalization*. London: Routledge: 109–127.

Interbrand (2003) 'Interbrand's Methodology'. Available at http://www.interbrand.com/ja/best-global-brands/best-global-brands-methodology/Overview.aspx and http://www.interbrand.com/ja/best-global-brands/best-global-brands-methodology/Brand-Strength.aspx (accessed10 October 2010).

Interbrand (2003) Interbrand's Lists of Ranking for 2003, 2004, 2005, 2006, 2007. Available at http://www.interbrand.com/ja/best-global-brands/best-global-brands-2008/best-global-brands-2003.aspx, http://www.interbrand.com/ja/best-global-brands/best-global-brands-2008/best-global-brands-2004.aspx, http://www.interbrand.com/ja/best-global-brands/best-global-brands-2008/best-global-brands-2005.aspx, http://www.interbrand.com/ja/best-global-brands/best-global-brands-2008/best-global-brands-2006.aspx, http://www.interbrand.com/ja/best-global-brands/best-global-brands-2008/best-global-brands-2007.aspx (accessed 10 October 2010).

Isomura, H. (2003) *Why Can't the Japanese Understand the Global World? The Secret of Carlos Ghosn's Success*. Tokyo: Asashi Syuppansha.

Itagaki, E. (2006) *Carlos Ghosn's Language*. Tokyo: Asa Syuppan.

Ito, K. (2000) *Corporate Brand Management: Competitive Advantages*. Tokyo: Nihon Keizai Shinbunsha.

Jacoby, S. M. (2005) *The Embedded Corporation: Corporate Governance and Employment Relations*. Princeton, NJ: Princeton University Press.

Jameson, A. C. (2000) 'Telling the Investment Story: A Narrative Analysis of Shareholder Reports'. *Journal of Communication* 37(7).

Japan Investor Relations Association. Available at https://www.jira.or.jp/ (accessed 30 March 2012).

*Japanist* (2007) 'Yokohama Shicho Nakada hiroshi Rebosyushon'. *Fooga*: 23.

Kamiyama, S. (2002) *Gyousei no Keiei Kaikaku Kanrikara Keiei*. Tokyo: Daiichihouki Syuppan.

Kanda, H. (2009) *Kaisha-ho*. Tokyo: Kobundo.

Kanter, R. M. (1992) *When Giants Learn to Dance: Mastering the Challenges of Strategy, Management, and Careers in the 1990s*. New York: Simon & Shuster.

Kaplan, S. N. and Schoar, A. (2005) 'Private Equity Performance: Returns, Persistence, and Capital Flows'. *Journal of Finance, American Finance Association* 60(4): 1791–1823.

Katayama, O. (2002) *Toyota ha Ikanishite Saikyo no Shain wo Tsukkutak*. Tokyo: Shodensha.

Katzenbach, J. R. (2001) *Commitment Management*. Tokyo: Diamond sha.

Katz, R. (2003) *Japanese Phoenix: The Long Road to Economic Revival*. London: M. E. Sharpe.

Kawai, A. (2010) *Iwasaki Yataro and Four Generations*. Tokyo: Gentosha.

*Keizaikai* (2004) 'Nakada Hiroshi'. *Keizaikai*: 52–54.

Kettl, D. F. (2000) *The Global Public Management Revolution: A Report on the Transformation of Governance.* Washington, DC: Brookings Institution Press.

Khurana, R. (2002) *Searching for a Corporate Savior: The Irrational Quest for Charismatic CEOs.* Princeton, NJ: Princeton University Press.

Kim, S. C. (1994) 'Guest Editor's Note: Investigating Organizational Downsizing – Fundamental Issues'. *Human Resource Management* 33(2): 183–188.

Knights, D. and Willmott, H. (2000) *The Reengineering Revolution?: Critical Studies of Corporate Change.* London: Sage.

Koike, K. (1983) 'Internal Labor Markets', in T. Shirai (ed.) *Contemporary Industrial Relations in Japan.* Madison, WI: University of Wisconsin Press.

Koller, T., Goedhart, M. H., Wessels, D., Copeland, T. E. and McKinsey and Company (2010) *Valuation: Measuring and Managing the Value of Companies.* Hoboken, NJ: John Wiley & Sons, Inc.

Kondo, K. (2007) *Kigyo Kachi Kojyo no tameno Keiei Senryaku – IR no Honshitsu nitsuite.* Tokyo: Cyuo-Keizaisha.

Kopp, R. (2001) 'Why It Is So Difficult to Tell What a Japanese Person Is Thinking'. *Japan Close-up* November: 20–31.

Krippner, G. R. (2005) 'The Financialization of the American Economy'. *Socio-Economic Review* 3(2): 173–208.

Kuronuma, E. (2009) *Kinyu-shotorihiki-ho-nyumon.* Nihonkeizai-Syuppansha: Tokyo

Kyodo Tsushinsha Shakaibu (1999) *Hokai Rensa-Chogin, Nissaigin Funshoku Kettusan Jiken.* Tokyo: Kyodo Tsushinsha Shakaibu.

Langley, P. (2004) 'In the Eye of the "Perfect Storm": The Final Salary Pensions Crisis and the Financialization of Anglo-American Capitalism'. *New Political Economy* 9(4): 539–558.

Lash, S. and J. Urry (1994) *Economies of Signs and Space.* London and Thousand Oaks, CA: Sage.

Lazonick, W. and O'Sullivan, M. (2000) 'Maximizing Shareholder Value: A New Ideology for Corporate Governance'. *Economy and Society* 29(1): 13–35.

Lazonick, W. and O'Sullivan, M. (2002) *Corporate Governance and Sustainable Prosperity.* Basingstoke: Palgrave Macmillan.

Lincoln, James R. and Gerlach, Michael L. (2004) *Japan's Network Economy: Structure, Persistence, and Change.* Cambridge: Cambridge University Press.

Littler, C. R. (2003) 'Downsizing and Deknowledging the Firm'. *Work, Employment and Society* 17: 73–100.

Littler, C. R. (2006) 'Corporate Comets or Typical Trajectories? Corporate Dynamics in the 1990s', *Critical Perspective on Accounting* 17(5): 627–655.

McCann, L., Hassard, J. and Morris, J. (2004) 'Middle Managers, the New Organizational Ideology and Corporate Restructuring: Comparing Japanese and Anglo-American Management Systems'. *Competition and Change: The Journal of Global Business and Political Economy* 8(1): 27–44.

McCann, L., Hassard, J. and Morris, J. (2006) 'Hard Times for the Salaryman: Corporate Restructuring and Middle Managers' Working Lives', in W. P. L. Matanle (ed.) *Perspectives on Work, Employment and Society in Japan.* London: Palgrave Macmillan, 99–116.

McCann, L., Hassard, J. and Morris, J. (2010) 'Restructuring Managerial Labour in the USA, the UK and Japan: Challenging the Salience of "Varieties of Capitalism"'. *British Journal of Industrial Relations* 48(2): 347–374.

MacKenzie, D. and Millo, Y. (2003) 'Constructing a Market Performing Theory: The Historical Sociology of a Financial Derivatives Exchange', *American Journal of Sociology* 109: 107–145.

MacKenzie, D. A. (2006) *An Engine, No a Camera: How Financial Models Shape Markets.* Cambridge, MA: MIT Press.

Magee, D. (2003) *Turnaround: How Did Ghosn Rescue Nissan?* Tokyo: Toyo Keizai Shinposha.

Maguire, S. and Phillips, N. (2008) 'Citibankers at Citigroup: A Study of the Loss of Institutional Trust after a Merger. *Journal of Management Studies* 45(2): 372–401.

*Mainichi* (1999) 'Public Fund into 15 Major Banks'. Available at http://www.mainichi.co.jp/life/money/invest/030129-1.html. 4 (accessed 30 March 2012).

*Mainichi* (2009) 'Consolidated Assets of Domestic Big Financial Groups in Japan', 26 April. Available at http://mainichi.jp/select/biz/news/20090426ddm002020164000c.html.

Martin, J. D. and Petty, J. W. (2000) *Value Based Management: The Corporate Response to the Shareholder Revolution.* New York: Oxford University Press.

Martin, R. (2002) *The Financialization of Daily Life.* Philadelphia, PA: Temple University Press.

Matanle, P. C. D. (2003) *Japanese Capitalism and Modernity in a Global Era: Refabricating Lifetime Employment Relations.* London: RoutledgeCurzon.

Matanle, P. C. D. and Lunsing, W. (2006) *Perspectives on Work, Employment and Society in Japan.* New York: Palgrave Macmillan.

Matanle, P., McCann, L. and Ashmore, D.-J. (2008) 'Men Under Pressure: Representations of the "Salaryman" and his Organization in Japanese Manga'. *Organization* 15(5): 639–664.

Mehri, D. (2005) *Notes from Toyota-land: An American Engineer in Japan.* New York: Cornell University Press.

Meyer, J. W. and Rowan, B. (1977) 'Institutionalized Organizations: Formal Structure as Myth and Ceremony'. *American Journal of Sociology* 83: 340–363.

Miller, P. and Rose, N. (2008) *Governing the Present: Administering Economic, Social and Personal Life.* Cambridge: Polity Press.

Minami, M. and Kamiyama, S. (2004) *Yokohama shi kaikaku enjin furukado Nakada shisei no senryaku to hasso.* Tokyo: Toyokeizai Shinposha.

Ministry of Health, Labour and Welfare (2009) 'The Baby Boom Generation'. Available at http://www.mhlw.go.jp/toukei/saikin/hw/jinkou/kakutei09/dl/2-1hyo.pdf (accessed 30 March 2012).

Mitsubishi Public Affairs Committee. Mitsubishi Committee Members. Available at http://www.mitsubishi.com/mpac/j/companies/index.html (accessed 30 March 2012).

Mitsubishi-Tokyo Financial Group (2001–05) Annual reports. Tokyo. Available at http://www.mufg.jp/english/ir/annualreport/backnumber/ (accessed 30 March 2012).

Mitsubishi UFG (English edition) *Outside Directors.* Available at http://www.mufg.jp/english/profile/governance/ (accessed 11 September 2010).

Mitsubishi UFG (Japanese edition) *Outside Directors.* Available at http://www.mufg.jp/profile/governance/ (accessed 11 September 2010).

Mitsubishi UFJ Financial Group (2006–11) Annual reports. Tokyo.

Miwa, Y. (1990) *Kabuka Model to Nihon no Kabuka in Nihon no Kabuka.* Tokyo: Tokyo University Press.

Miwa, Y. (1996) *Firms and Industrial Organization in Japan.* Basingstoke: Macmillan.

Morgan, G. and Takahashi, Y. (2002) 'Shareholder Value in the Japanese Context'. *Competition and Change: The Journal of Global Business and Political Economy* 6(2): 169–192.

Morgan, G. and Kubo, I. (2005) 'Beyond Path Dependency? Constructing New Models for Institutional Change: The Case of Capital Markets in Japan', *Socio-Economic Review* 5: 55–82.

Morris, J., Hassard, J. and McCann, L. (2006) 'New Organizational Forms, Human Resource Management and Structural Convergence? A Study of Japanese Organizations'. *Organization Studies* 27(10): 1485–1511.

Motomiya, H. (2004) *Takeki Ogonnokuni Iwasaki Yataro* [Golden Country]. Tokyo: Syueisha.

Munakata, M. (2002) 'The End of the "Mass Production System" and Changes in Work Practices', in H. Hasegawa and G. D. Hook (ed.) *Japanese Business Management: Restructuring for Low Growth and Globalization*. New York: Routledge, 181–194.

Nakada, H. (2005) *Naseba Naru*. Tokyo: Kodansha.

Nakano, A. (2010) *Iwasaki Yataro: Mitsubishi's Corporate Policy*. Tokyo: Asahi Shinbun Syupan.

News, J. (2008) 'Toyota and Nissan's Layoffs in 2008'. Available at http://www.j-cast.com/2008/11/04029658.html (accessed 8 July 2011).

Nicolai, A., Schulz, A.-C. and Thomas, T. W. (2010) 'What Wall Street Wants: Exploring the Role of Security Analysts in the Evolution and Spread of Management Concepts'. *Journal of Management Studies* 47(1): 162–189.

*Nikkei Business* (2007) 'Haisuino Nissan Monotsukuri Dokohe'. Available at http://business.nikkeibp.co.jp/article/topics/20070510/124461/?P=1 (accessed 10 August 2008).

*Nikkei Asian Review* (2008) 'BTMU Returns Public Funds'. Available at http://www.nikkei.co.jp/sp1/nt32/20030818AS1F1800718082003.htm (accessed 30 March 2012).

Nishihara, M. (2002) 'Ownership and Control of Large Corporations in Contemporary Japan', in H. Hasegawa and D. H. Glenn (eds) *Japanese Business Management: Restructuring for Low Growth and Globalization*. London: Routledge, 128.

Nissan Motor. Number of Employees. Available at http://www.nissan-global.com/EN/COMPANY/PROFILE/ (accessed 10 August 2010).

Nissan Motor (1996–2011) Nissan Annual Reports. Available at http://www.nissan-global.com/JP/IR/LIBRARY/AR/index.html (accessed 10 September 2011).

Nissan Motor (2006) *Guiding Principles: The Nissan Way*. Yokohama: Nissan Motor.

Noguchi, Y. (1995) *The 1940 System*. Tokyo: Toyokeizai Shiposha.

Noguchi, Y. (2002) *The 1940 System*. 2nd edn. Tokyo: Toyokeizai Shinpo Sha.

OECD (2006) *OECD Employment Outlook 2006*. Available at: http://www.oecd.org/document/38/0,3746,en_2649_33927_36261286_1_1_1_1,00.html#table (accessed 30 March 2012).

Okubayashi, K. (2002) 'Small Headquarters and the Reorganization of Management', in H. Hasegawa and G. D. Hook (eds) *Japanese Business Management: Restructuring for Low Growth and Globalization*. London: Routledge, 143–162.

Okumura, H. (1999) *Daikigyou Kaitai: Kabushikigaisya ga kawaru*. Tokyo: Diamond.

Olcott, G. (2008) 'The Politics of Institutionalization: The Impact of Foreign Ownership and Control on Japanese Organizations'. *International Journal of Human Resource Management* 19(9): 1569–1587.

Olcott, G. (2009a) 'Whose Company Is It? Changing CEO Ideology in Japan', in D. H. Whittaker and S. F. Deakin (eds) *Corporate Governance and Managerial Reform in Japan*. Oxford: Oxford University Press.

Olcott, G. (2009b) *Conflict and Change: Foreign Ownership and the Japanese Firm*. Cambridge: Cambridge University Press.

Oliver, C. (1990) 'Determinants of Interorganizational Relationships: Integration and Future Direction'. *Academy of Management Review* 15(2): 241–265.

Oliver, C. (1991) 'Strategic Response to Institutional Processes'. *Academy of Management Review* 16: 145–179.

Oliver, C. (1992) 'The Antecedents of Deinstitutionalization'. *Organization Studies* 13: 563–588.

Omori, T. (2000) *The Economic Policy after the Bubble and Industrialized Economy*. Tokyo: Nihhonkeizai-shinbunsha.

Ono, T. (1978) *Toyota Seisan Hoshiki*. Tokyo: Diamond-sha.

Osano, H. and Tsutsui, Y. (1986) 'Credit Rationing and Implicit Contract Theory'. *International Journal of Industrial Organization* 4: 419–438.

Osborne, D. and Gaebler, T. (1992) *Reinventing Government: How the Entrepreneurial Spirit Is Transforming the Public Sector*. Reading, MA: Addison-Wesley.

O'Sullivan, M. (2000) *Contests for Corporate Control: Corporate Governance and Economic Performance in the United States and Germany*. Oxford: Oxford University Press.

Patton, M. Q. (1980) *Qualitative Evaluation Methods*. Beverly Hills, CA: Sage.

PHP (2005) 'Yokohama Revival No Syukku'. *Voice*: 148–161.

Pollitt, C. (2003) *The New Public Management in International Perspective: An Analysis of Impacts and Effects*. London: Routledge.

Pollitt, C., Thiel, S. V. and Homburg, V. (2007) *New Public Management in Europe: Adaptation and Alternatives*. New York: Palgrave Macmillan.

Pollock, G. T. and Rindova, P. V. (2003) 'Media Legitimation Effects in the Market for Initial Public Offerings'. *Academy of Management Journal* 46(5): 631–642.

*President* (2003) 'Kinyu/Kashitanpo kigengire de Shinsei Ginko no Keiei wa'. *President*: 38.

Ray, L. and Sayer, A. (1999) 'Introduction', in L. Ray and A. Sayer *Culture and Economy after the Cultural Turn*. London: Sage.

RIETI (2005) 'M&A in Japan'. *RIETI Discussion Papers*. Available at http://www.rieti.go.jp/jp/publications/act_dp2005.html (accessed 30 March 2012).

*World Investment Report* (2006) 'Nominal Gross Domestic Product – Japan (during 1980–2008)'. Available at http://www.meti.go.jp/report/tsuhaku2007/2007honbun/html/i3120000.html (accessed 11 August 2011).

Redding, G. (2005) 'The Thick Description and Comparison of Societal Sysems of Capitalism'. *Journal of International Business Studies* 36: 123–155.

Rivas, M. and Carvell. K. (2007) *The Carlos Ghosn Story*. Tokyo: IBC Publishing.

Robinson, P. and Shimizu, N. (2006) 'Japanese Corporate Restructuring: CEO Priorities as a Window on Environmental and Organizational Change'. *Academy of Management Perspectives* 20(3): 44–75.

Rumelt, R. P. (1974) *Strategy, Structure, and Economic Performance*. Boston, MA: Harvard University Press.

Sakamoto, F. (1996) *Iwasaki Yataro no Dokusoukeiei: Mitsubishi wo Okoshita Karisuma* [Unique Management by Iwasaki Yataro: Mitsubishi's Charismatic Leader]. Tokyo: Kodansha.

Sakaiya, T. (1976) *Dankai no Sedai*. Tokyo: Bungeisyunjyu.

Sako, M. and Sato, H. (eds) *Japanese Labour and Management in Transition: Diversity, Flexibility And Participation*. New York: Routledge.

Sankei Shinbun Syuzaihan (2002) *Brand ha naze ochitaka*. Tokyo: Kadokawa shoten.

Sato, H. (1997) 'Human Resource Management Systems in Large Firms. The Case of White-Collar Graduate Employees', in M. Sako and H. Sato. (eds) *Japanese Labour and Management in Transition: Diversity, Flexibility And Participation*. New York: Routledge, 104–130.

Sato, H. (2001) 'Atypical Employment: A Source of Flexible Work Opportunities?' *Social Science Japan Journal* 4(2): 161–181.

Sato, K. (1999). *The Transformation of the Japanese Economy*. An East Gate Book. Armonk, NY: M. E. Sharpe.

Sekiguchi, K. (1996) *Syushin Koyo*. Tokyo: Bunshindo.

Sennett, R. (1998). *The Corrosion of Character: The Personal Consequences of Work in the New Capitalism*. London: Norton.

Sheard, P. (1986) 'Main Banks and Internal Capital Markets in Japan'. *Shoken Keizai*:157.

Shigeki, K., Ogaki, F., Takeda, H., Yakabe, K., Kawahara, R., Miyazaki, T. and Hyodo, D. (1990) *Keiei rida no Showa Romushi*. Tokyo: Nihon Keieisha Dantai Renmei Kohobu.

Shiller, R. J. (2005) *Irrational Exuberance*. Princeton, NJ: Princeton University Press.

Shimaoka, S. (2010) *Iwasaki Yataro: The Founder of Mitsubishi*. Tokyo: Kawade Shobo Shinsha.

Shinsei Bank, 'Shinsei Timeline 2000–10'. Available at http://www.shinseibank.com/investors/en/about/company/pdf/shinseihistory100331e.pdf (accessed 10 August 2010).

Shinsei Bank (2004) 'Personal Profile about Thierry Porte'. Available at http://www.shinseibank.com/investors/en/common/news/pdf/pdf2004/041202executive01_e.pdf (accessed 10 August 2010).

Shinsei Bank (2009) 'Alliance Agreement with Aozora Bank'. Available at http://www.shinseibank.com/investors/en/common/news/pdf/pdf2010/100514merger_e.pdf (accessed 10 August 2010).

Shinsei Bank (2009) Shinsei Bank Presentation Document. Available at http://www.shinseibank.com/investors/en/ir/financial_info/quarterly_results_2008/pdf/4qfy08presentation090514e.pdf (accessed 10 August 2010).

Shinsei Bank (2010) Shinsei Bank Annual Report 1998–2011. Available at http://www.shinseibank.com/investors/en/ir/financial_info/arir_2010/arir_index_2010.html (accessed 10 August 2011).

Shleifer, A. and Summers, L. (1988) 'Breach of Trust in Hostile Takeovers Corporate Takeovers: Causes and Consequences'. *National Bureau of Economic Research*: 33–68.

Sloan, A. (1996) 'The Hit Men'. *Newsweek* 127(9).

Stewart, G. B. (1991) *The Quest for Value: The EVA(TM) Management Guide*. New York: Harper Business.

Stockhammer, E. (2004) 'Financialization and the Slowdown of Accumulation'. *Cambridge Journal of Economics* 28(5): 719–741.

Stone, E. F. (1978) *Research Methods in Organizational Behavior*. Santa Monica, CA: Goodyear.

Strange, S. (1986) *Casino Capitalism*. New York: Basil Blackwell.

Strauss, A. and Corbin, J. (1990) *Basics of Qualitative Research: Grounded Theory Procedures and Techniques*. London: Sage.

Streeck, W. and Yamamura, K. (2001) *The Origins of Nonliberal Capitalism: Germany and Japan in Comparison*. London: Cornell University Press.

Takarabe, S. (2002) *How Did Carlos Ghosn Change Nissan?* Tokyo: PHP Kenkyusho.

Tamura, T. (2002) *Corporate Governance: Kigyo saisei heno michi*. Tokyo: Cyuo Koron Shinsha.

Tateishi, Y. (2009) *Iwasaki Yataro*. Tokyo: PHP Kenkyusho.

Tett, G. (2003) *Saving the Sun: A Wall Street Gamble to Rescue Japan from Its Trillion-Dollar Meltdown*. New York: Harper Business.

*The Economist* (2009) 'Struggling Giants, Toyota Slips Up: What the World's Biggest Carmaker Can Learn from Other Corporate Turnarounds'. Available at http://www.economist.com/node/15065913 (accessed 10 December 2009).

*The Economist* (2005) 'The Sun also Rises'. 8 October. Available at http://www.economist.com/node/4454244 (accessed 30 March 2012).

Thrift, N. (2001) 'It's the Romance Not the Finance That Makes the Business Worth Pursuing: Disclosing a New Market Culture'. *Economy and Society* 30(4): 412–432.

Togashima, Y. and Toda, H. (2002) *Carlos Ghosn's Success Story*. Tokyo: Shogakukan.

Tokyo Stock Exchange. 'Nissan Motor, BTMU and Shinsei Bank's Net Incomes'. Available at http://www.tse.or.jp/market/index.html (accessed 30 March 2012).

Toporowski, J. (1999) *The End of Finance: Capital Market Inflation, Financial Derivatives and Pension Fund Capitalism*. London: Routledge.

*Toyokeizai* (2000–12) *Kaisha-Shikiho*. Tokyo: Toyokeizai syuppansha.

Trends in Japan (2005) 'Keiretsu Comeback'. Available at http://web-japan.org/trends/business/bus050905.html#pagetop (accessed 10 August 2009).

UFJ-Holdings (2001–05) Annual Reports. Tokyo. Available at http://www.mufg.jp/english/ir/annualreport/backnumber/

*Ushio Syuppansha* (2004) 'Riritsu 0.5% no saiken de yokohama ha kawaruka'. *Ushio Syuppansha*: 144–149.

Vogel, S. K. (2006) *Japan Remodelled: How Government and Industry Are Reforming Japanese Capitalism*. Ithaca, NY: Cornell University Press.

Watanabe, T. (2002) 'The Rise of Flexible and Individual Ability-oriented Management', in H. Hasegawa and D. H. Glenn (eds) *Japanese Business Management: Restructuring for Low Growth and Globalization*. London: Routledge, 163–178.

*Weekly Toyokeizai* (1996–2011) *Kaisha-Shikiho*. Tokyo:Toyokeizai.

*Weekly Toyokeizai* (1999) 'Dissolution of Keiretsu, Ghosn and Nissan'. *Weekly Toyokeizai*: 12–13.

*Weekly Diamond* (1999a) 'Carlos Ghosn Talks about the Nissan Revival Plan. "Nissan Will Be Bankrupt if it Cannot Be Reformed"'. *Weekly Diamond*: 52–54.

*Weekly Diamond* (1999b) 'Dissolution of Nissan's Keiretsu Has Started'. *Weekly Diamond*: 138–144.

*Weekly Diamond* (1999c) 'Nissan Revival Plan: Cutting the "Keiretsu" System'. *Weekly Diamond*: 17–19.

*Weekly Diamond* (2001a) 'Carlos Ghosn'. *Weekly Diamond*: 144–146.

*Weekly Diamond* (2001b) 'Current Ghosn's Nissan I'. *Weekly Diamond*: 122–124.

*Weekly Diamond* (2001c) 'Current Ghosn's Nissan II'. *Weekly Diamond*: 140–142.

*Weekly Diamond* (2003a) 'Carlos Ghosn's Management Seminar'. *Weekly Diamond*: 32–34.

*Weekly Diamond* (2003b) 'Tokyo-Mitsubishi Bank: Aiming to Be the Best Bank in the World'. *Weekly Diamond*: 52–55.

*Weekly Diamond* (2004a) 'BTMU's Goals. *Weekly Diamond*: 18.

*Weekly Diamond* (2004b). 'Public Expectations of Shinsei Bank'. *Weekly Diamond*: 20.

*Weekly Diamond* (2004c) 'Yokohama; Toshi Keiei Senryaku no Zenbo'. *Weekly Diamond*: 130–135.

*Weekly Diamond* (2005) 'Nakada Hiroshi'. *Weekly Diamond*: 94–97.

*Weekly Diamond* (2007) 'Ghosn's Counterargument'. *Weekly Diamond*: 30–55.

*Weekly Diamond* (2008) 'CEO's Annual Incomes'. *Weekly Diamond: Weekly Diamond*: 106 (155).

*Weekly Diamond* (2008a) 'Shinsei and Aozora Bank: Both Have Shown Losses'. *Weekly Diamond*: 70–71.

*Weekly Diamond* (2008b) 'Shinsei Bank: It Is Difficult to Achieve the Plan for Sound Finance'. *Weekly Diamond*: 23.

*Weekly Diamond* (2008c) 'Shinsei Bank's Amazing Reality'. *Weekly Diamond*: 14–146.

*Weekly Diamond* (2008d) 'Shinsei's Scandalized Reality', *Weekly Diamond*: 14–16.

*Weekly Toyokeizai* (2008e) 'With Financial Difficulties even in Retail Sections, Shinsei Bank Has Been Quite at a Loss'. *Weekly Toyokeizai*: 86–89.

*Weekly Toyokeizai* (2008f) 'Shinsei's Retail Banking Has Showed Net Losses'. *Weekly Toyokeizai*: 86–89.

*Weekly Toyokeizai* (2010) 'Shinsei's Lost Decade'. Available at http://www.toyokeizai.net/business/strategy/detail/AC/dbce7c9e96f35c886e31ca8df2e32475/page/1/ (accessed 20 December 2010).

Westphal, J. D. and Zajac, E. J. (1994) 'Substance and Symbolism in CEO's Long-term Incentive Plans'. *Administrative Science Quarterly* 39: 367–390.

Westphal, J. D. and Zajac, E. J. (2001) 'Decoupling Policy from Practice: The Case of Stock Repurchase Programs'. *Administrative Science Quarterly* 46: 202–228.

Whitley, R. (1999) *Divergent Capitalisms: The Social Structuring and Change Of Business Systems*. Oxford: Oxford University Press.

Whittaker, D. H. and Deakin, S. F. (eds) *Corporate Governance and Managerial Reform in Japan*. Oxford: Oxford University Press.

Williams, K. (2000) 'From Shareholder Value to Present-day Capitalism'. *Economy and Society* 29: 1–12.

Witt, M. A. (2006) *Changing Japanese Capitalism: Societal Coordination and Institutional Adjustment*. Cambridge: Cambridge University Press.

Wolfe, D. A. (1994) 'The Wealth of Regions: Rethinking Industrial Policy'. Working paper no. 10 (May). Toronto, ON: Canadian Institute for Advanced Research.

Wolfe, R. A. (1994) 'Organizational Innovation: Review, Critique and Suggested Research'. *Journal of Management Studies* 31(3): 405–431.

Womack, J. P., Jones, D. T. and Roos, D. (1990). *The Machine that Changed the World*. New York: Rawson Associates.

Worrall, L. and Cooper, G. L. (1998) *The Quality of Working Life: The 1998 Survey of Managers' Experiences*. London: Institute of Management.

Worrall, L., Parkes, C. and Cooper, C. (2004) 'The Impact of Organizational Change on the Perceptions of UK Managers'. *European Journal of Work and Organizational Psychology* 13(2): 139–163.

Yamano, K. (2004) 'Ghosn, Rita: Success of Rita's Restaurant'. Available at http://www.globe-walkers.com/ohno/interview/ritaghosn.htm (accessed 11 September 2011).

Yashiro, N. (2006) *Rodo Keizai Kaikaku no Keizaigaku*. Tokyo: Toyo Keizai Shinposha.

Yin, R. K. (1982) 'Studying the Implementation of Public Programs', in W. Williams*et al.* (eds) *Studying Implementation: Methodological and Administrative Issues*. Chatham, NJ: Chatham House, 36–72.

Yin, R. K. (1994) *Case Study Research: Design and Methods*. Thousand Oaks, CA: Sage.

Yin, R. K. (2011) *Qualitative Research From Start to Finish*. New York: Guilford Press.

Yin, R. K. (2012) *Applications of Case Study Research*. Thousand Oaks, CA: Sage.

Yokohama City Council (1997–2008) Yokohama City Council internal PR newsletters. Yokohama: Yokohama City Council.

Yokohama City Council (2006) *Yokohama City Council Mid-term Report*. Yokohama: Yokohama City Council.

Yokohama City Council (2006) *Yokohama Revival Plan*. Available at http://www.city. yokohama.lg.jp/zaisei/ir/mayor2104.pdf (accessed 11 September 2010).

Yokohama City Council (2009) *Yokohama Middle Plan 2009*. Yokohama: Yokohama City Council.

Yokohama City Council (2010) *Kyoudo niyoru Atarashi Toshi Keiei*. Available at http://www.city.yokohama.lg.jp/shimin/tishin/kyoudou/forum/2003indexhtml/2kicho u.pdf (accessed 11 September 2010).

Yokohama City Council (2010) *Yokohama City Budget*. Available at http://www.city. yokohama.lg.jp/zaisei/org/zaisei/daidokoro/20mikata (accessed 11 September 2010).

Yokohama City Council Finance Affairs Bureau (2008–12) *Total Amount of Debt*. Available at http://www.city.yokohama.lg.jp/zaisei/org/zaisei/daidokoro/ (accessed 30 March 2012).

Yokohama City Council General Affairs Division (2008–12) *Number of Staff at Yokohama City Council*. Available at http://www.city.yokohama.lg.jp/ex/stat/index2. html#20 (accessed 30 March 2012).

Yokohama City Council Human Affairs Committee (2009) *Extension of the Retirement Age*. Available at http://www.city.yokohama.lg.jp/jinji/kankoku/20honbun.pdf (accessed 30 March 2012).

Yokohama City Council Human Affairs Committee (2009) *The Reappointment of Retired Officials*. Available at http://www.city.yokohama.lg.jp/jinji/kankoku/h22be ssi3.pdf (accessed 30 March 2012).

Yokohama City Council Human Affairs Committee (2009) *Deputy Manager Positions*. Available at http://www.city.yokohama.lg.jp/jinji/houdou/syounin-061207.pdf and http://www.city.yokohama.lg.jp/somu/org/jinji/kentou/040223/shiryo-jyosei.pdf (accessed 30 March 2012).

Yokohama City Council Public Announcements Department (2006) 'Zaigen wa Mizukara Kasegu: Yokohamashi Koukoku jigyo no challenge'. Yokohama: Yokohama City Council.

Yokohama City Council Statistics Department (2007) *Reasons for Retirement*. Yokohama: Yokohama City Council.

Yokohama City University (2005) *Yokohama City University Is Independent of the City Council*. Available at http://www.yokohama-cu.ac.jp/ (accessed 30 March 2012).

*Yomiuri* (2004) 'Mitsubishi Fuso'(12 March). Available at http://www.yomiuri.co.jp/a tcars/news/20040312ve03.htm (accessed 11 March 2011).

Zaikai Kenkyusho (2004) 'Yokohama wo Kigyoka no Machi ni'. *Zaikai*: 63–65.

Zysman, J. (1983) *Governments, Markets and Growth*. Ithaca, NY: Cornell University Press.

# Index

Abegglen, J.C. 9, 34
Alliance capitalism 7, 11–12, 16
Anglo-Saxon economies 7, 10; capitalism 10; form of business practice 103; form of employment system 96; forms of financial narrative management strategy 84; style of narrative management 84
Amable, B. 9, 33–4, 130
Asset downsizing 15–16, 42

Bank of Tokyo-Mitsubishi UFJ (BTMU) 3, 5–7, 9, 12, 16, 32–4, 57, 60–84, 91, 101–2, 105, 122, 133, 135, 137–8, 140, 144–7
Big Bang 3, 14, 16, 27, 86, 134
Bubble burst 13–14, 62

Continuity and change 3, 9, 17, 20, 28–32, 130, 133–6, 139, 148
Corporate communication 4, 20, 50, 57, 140
Corporate governance 10, 15, 28, 30–1, 57, 63–4, 138–9
Convergence 10, 29, 31, 64, 115, 136
Cross-shareholdings 1, 12
Cultural economy 26; theory 24; theories 8

Deinstitutionalization 17, 19, 88, 104
Delayering 22
Divergence 29, 136
Dore, R. 9, 12, 19, 28, 30–1, 33–6, 59, 81–3, 106–7, 128–9, 132, 136, 139, 141, 143, 155
Downsizing 6, 15–16, 19, 21–5, 35, 37, 42, 46–8, 50, 52, 55–6, 63, 66–7, 71–3, 79–80, 88, 95–7, 104, 109, 121–2, 135, 138, 144

Early retirement 15, 48, 71–2, 79, 95–6
Embeddedness 10, 19
Employment downsizing 6, 15–16, 19, 21–3, 25, 35, 46–8, 50, 52, 55–6, 63, 66–7, 71–3, 79–80, 95, 97, 104, 121–2, 135, 138, 145
External acceptance 42, 46–7, 69, 91, 94, 114, 128, 130, 145–6
External narrative 54–5, 142

False signalling 25, 55, 72–3, 95, 104, 133, 141–2, 144
Financialization 8, 16, 21–2, 25–8, 39, 139, 147
Froud, J. 7, 9, 24–7, 35–6, 58–9, 97, 105, 107–8, 131–2, 141, 143

Gap between saying and doing 25–7, 48, 52, 55, 60, 73, 78–9, 84, 95, 97, 100–5, 122, 129, 133, 141, 148
General Electric (GE) 22, 24, 142
Globalization 2, 10, 13–14, 16–18, 62, 140, 147
Growth in the practice of crafting official corporate announcements 20; in the spinning of official messages 4; of public communication 19; of shareholder activism 11; of the Japanese economy 12, 85

Hall, P.A. and Soskice, D.W. 9, 33, 81
Hedge fund 3, 6, 22, 81, 85–6, 89, 92, 94, 105–6, 134
*Honne* and *tatemae* 140, 148
HR 14–15, 18, 29, 42, 56, 59, 71, 85, 87–8, 96, 103–4, 106, 120–1, 123, 127–9, 138, 144; departments 15, 87, 106; system 14, 18, 56, 71, 88, 127

Institutional adjustment 14, 28; arrangement 14–15, 18–19, 31; change 14, 28, 138; complementarity 11, 13; deregulation 146; differences 30; economics 2; evolution 136; norms 17; pressures 72, 115; relationships 10, 13, 16, 62; restrictions 16, 60; structure 17, 37; theory 10, 17, 19; trust 94

Internal acceptance 41, 44, 54–5, 57, 66, 70, 95, 98, 114, 120, 128, 145–6, 153; distrust 114, 130; legitimacy 4, 142; narrative 4, 52–3, 128

Investor relations (IR) 4, 8–9, 19–20, 31–2, 56, 65–6, 70, 79–80, 94, 104, 128, 134–141, 145–6, 150

Jack Welch 22, 25

Jacoby, S.M. 15, 28–9, 33, 36, 59, 105–8, 136, 143, 151

Japanese business model 1–2, 8, 10–13, 30–1, 134, 147; system 2, 27–8, 80

Jim Collins 4

Keiretsu 1, 3, 7, 12–13, 16–18, 38, 42, 47, 57, 60–2, 68–9, 72, 74–83, 152

Lazonick and O'Sullivan 26, 31, 33, 35–6, 108, 143

Legitimacy gap 4, 142

Lifetime employment 11–2, 14, 16, 18, 29, 48, 56, 74–5, 80–1, 88, 155

Limited change 28, 139

Littler, C.R. 24, 25, 35, 59, 83, 107, 132, 143

Long-term credit bank (LTCB) 2, 3, 29, 66, 84–6, 88–95, 99–103, 106

Mass media 25–8, 41–2, 47–8, 50, 53, 56, 68, 88, 90, 92, 94, 103–4, 110, 114–6, 118–9, 125, 129, 131, 134, 136, 142, 152

Merit based pay system 56, 88

Middle manager 32, 37, 42, 46, 48, 51, 54–5, 139, 144

Mitsubishi brand 60, 63, 66, 68–71, 73–9, 81, 83, 135, 145; keiretsu 3, 7, 12, 16, 57, 60–2, 69, 72, 74–5, 78–83; zaibatsu 61, 68, 74

Narrative construction 24–5, 48, 55; maker 5, 25, 57, 142; making 4, 17, 18, 60, 142, 149; management 4–5, 7–10, 20–21, 24, 26–8, 32, 37, 46–8,

50, 52–7, 60, 71, 73, 79–80, 84, 95, 97–8, 103–4, 109, 120–3, 127–130, 133–6, 139–148, 150, 154; strategy 103–4; work 25, 55

Neo-institutional theory 19

1940 system 12, 14

New Public Management (NPM) 105, 109–111, 113–116, 118, 123–4, 128–9, 135

Nissan 3, 5–6, 9, 16–17, 28–9, 32–4, 37–60, 68–71, 73, 75, 79–81, 84–5, 88–90, 93, 96, 98, 101, 105–6, 108–9, 111–4, 117–8, 122, 125, 129–131, 133–5, 137–8, 140, 145–7; Revival Plan (NRP) 6, 37, 40–3, 47, 49–50, 56, 58, 90, 109–10, 113–4, 131

Organizational change 3, 7, 14, 17, 19, 24, 32, 47, 50, 52, 60, 70–1, 78–80, 88, 124, 127–130, 135, 139–140, 146–8, 150, 154; reform 10, 13, 20, 30, 32, 46, 71, 80, 104, 110, 124, 126–7, 136, 142, 144; restructuring 8, 14, 17, 19–20, 22, 24–5, 27–8, 63, 66, 118, 121, 133, 135, 140, 144, 150–2

Outsourcing 14, 22, 110–112

Olcott, G. 9, 29, 31–2, 34–6, 58–9, 83, 107–8, 132, 136, 139, 143

Over-announcement 48, 122

Path-dependence 10, 19

Political economy 8, 26

Public announcement 4, 7, 19–20, 25, 27–8, 49, 52–3, 55–6, 69–71, 77, 79, 93, 96, 104–5, 117, 128, 141; claim 4–5, 20, 24, 40–2, 54, 63, 66, 80, 98, 100, 102, 108, 123, 136, 144–5, 153; message 4, 47, 53, 103, 123, 129, 138, 140, 144

Public relations (PR) 3, 8, 42, 48–50, 53, 55–6, 68–9, 83, 88, 93, 101, 111, 113–4, 117–20, 128–31, 134- 8, 141, 145–6, 150

Radical change 14, 17, 37, 47, 126

Redundancy 22

Resistance 127, 140

*Risutora* 3

Seniority based pay system 1, 14, 18, 56, 112, 122–3

Shareholder value 6–8, 11, 19–28, 31, 35, 39–41, 64–6, 70–1, 73–5, 77, 79–80, 85–7, 96, 98–9, 101–4, 135, 137–9,

141- 2, 144, 152; logic 8, 19–21, 24,
    27, 31, 35, 39, 138, 141
Shareholder value added (SVA) 6, 21, 40,
    80, 85–6, 88, 94–5, 98, 102–5, 135
Shinsei Bank 3, 5–6, 9, 28–9, 32–3, 36,
    61, 65, 75, 81–2, 84–108, 133–141,
    144–8
Slow change 14, 16–17, 19–20, 28–30,
    55–6, 102, 129, 136
Smokescreen 5, 9, 56, 71, 73, 98, 104–5,
    109, 123, 128, 133, 139, 147
Stock market capitalism 7, 10, 12, 27–8,
    30, 41, 136, 138, 141
Sub-prime crisis 70, 95, 106
Sweating 97

Takeover 3, 13, 16, 22, 35, 84–5, 89, 96,
    103, 134
Top management 23, 32, 37, 40, 46, 48,
    55, 70, 78, 93, 97, 101–2, 105, 108,
    129, 139, 143
Toyota 3, 4, 9, 12, 16, 28, 34, 38, 42, 44,
    46, 49, 51, 62, 138, 143

US business model 2–3, 7–9, 11, 105,
    134, 146; model 3–4, 8, 11–12, 30–1,
    135, 146

US-style reform 3, 6, 9, 29, 39, 42, 44–5,
    50, 55, 57, 60–1, 63, 66, 77–80, 86, 92,
    98, 110, 133, 135, 139–140;
    restructuring 7–8, 37, 56, 63, 84,
    88–9, 102–3, 118, 128–9, 141, 144–5,
    152–3

Value-Based Management (VBM) 6, 21,
    39–41, 45–7, 50–1, 55–6, 135
Varieties of Capitalism (VoC) 2, 8, 10,
    13, 15, 17, 19–20, 28, 32, 109, 138,
    150
Vogel, S.K. 15, 28–9, 33–4, 36, 59, 83,
    105, 107–8, 122, 136, 143, 151

Welfare capitalism 12
Whitley, R. 9, 28, 33–4

Yokohama city council 3, 5–7, 9, 32–3,
    50, 105, 109–133, 135–8, 140,
    145–8
Yokohama Revival Plan 50, 109–111,
    113–115, 117, 120–1, 123–130

Zaibatsu 3, 7, 12, 16, 38, 58, 61–2, 68–9,
    71, 74, 76, 152

For Product Safety Concerns and Information please contact our EU
representative GPSR@taylorandfrancis.com Taylor & Francis Verlag GmbH,
Kaufingerstraße 24, 80331 München, Germany

Printed and bound by CPI Group (UK) Ltd, Croydon, CR0 4YY
01/05/2025
01858395-0003